The
Suffolk
Village Book

THE VILLAGES OF BRITAIN SERIES

Other counties in this series include

Avon

Bedfordshire

Berkshire

Buckinghamshire

Cambridgeshire

Cheshire

Cleveland

Cornwall

Cumbria

Derbyshire

Devon

Dorset

Essex

Gloucestershire

Hampshire

Herefordshire

Hertfordshire

Kent

Lancashire

Leicestershire
& Rutland

Lincolnshire

Middlesex

Norfolk

Northamptonshire

Nottinghamshire

Oxfordshire

Shropshire

Somerset

Staffordshire

Surrey

East Sussex

West Sussex

Warwickshire

West Midlands

Wiltshire

Worcestershire

East Yorkshire

North Yorkshire

South & West Yorkshire

*Most are published in conjunction with
County Federations of Women's Institutes*

The Suffolk Village Book

Compiled by the Suffolk Federations
of Women's Institutes from notes and illustrations
sent by Institutes in the County

Published jointly by
Countryside Books, Newbury
and
the SEFWI, Ipswich
the SWFWI, Bury St Edmunds

First Published 1991
© Suffolk Federations of Women's Institutes 1991
Reprinted 1996

Countryside Books
3 Catherine Road
Newbury, Berkshire

ISBN 1 85306 134 4

Cover Photograph of Kersey
taken by Bill Meadows

Produced through MRM Associates Ltd., Reading
Typeset by Acorn Bookwork, Salisbury
Printed in England by J. W. Arrowsmith Ltd., Bristol

Foreword

The County of Suffolk is a scenic patchwork, stretching from the rolling heath at Newmarket through breckland, fenland, cornfields and woods to the shingle strand where the land merges into the North Sea. Everywhere one is aware of that broad sky which so inspired John Constable. Great churches, buttressed castles and stately houses remind us of a vital and absorbing history. In 1214 the Barons assembled in Bury St Edmunds and vowed that King John should sign the Great Charter. Three hundred years on and Thomas Wolsey, the son of an Ipswich grazier, was Chancellor of England.

However, the past and present co-exist harmoniously. The ports of Ipswich and Felixstowe are thriving components of the 20th century economic system and agriculture in the region relies heavily on modern technology. The small market towns remain an integral part of the communities they serve and, despite the encroaching developers, the Suffolk villages with their mixture of timber-frame and flint cottages still exude an air of tranquillity.

Patricia Farrow
Chairman Suffolk West Federation
Helen Huish
Chairman Suffolk East Federation

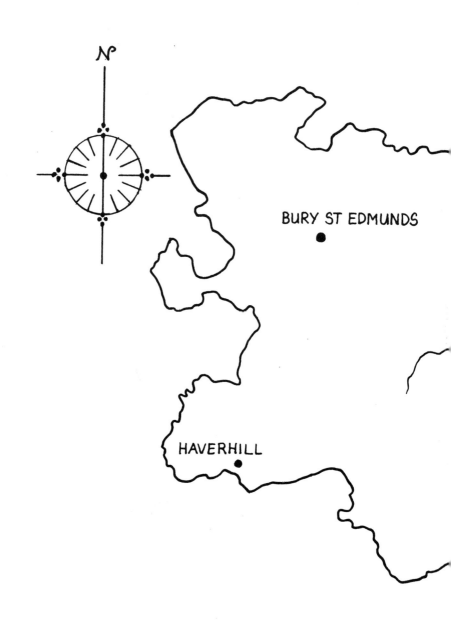

LOWESTOFT

River Dove

River Alde

STOWMARKET

River Orwell

ALDEBURGH

IPSWICH

FELIXSTOWE

County of
SUFFOLK

Acknowledgements

The SWFWI and the SEFWI wish to thank all Institutes whose members have taken part in this book by providing material and illustrations of their villages.
We are grateful for additional contributions from:

Mrs Silke Pinson-Roxborough (Offton)
Mr Noel Edgar (Waldringfield)
Mrs Sylvia Laverton (Freston)
Mr Jack Carter (Stowupland)
Mr George White (Cockfield)
Mr George Thornalley (Worlington)
Mettingham Women's Institute (Affiliated to Norfolk Federation but in Suffolk)
Finally, special thanks are due to the co-ordinators of the project, Elizabeth Quarmby and Ann Holloway, assisted by Joy Shipston.

The Waveney Valley and Homersfield Church

Acton 🦪

A tapestry of Acton's history would far exceed the available space in the parish church of All Saints. One of the first sections would be a Saxon map, headed Aketun, which possibly means 'oak settlement'. Balsdon Hall and the northernmost boundary are exactly the same today; Balsdon Hall has historical connections with the battle of Maldon, Essex. Acton Hall is sited a short distance from the church.

Many centuries later, light from a single candle casts long shadows in the chancel of Acton church. The body of one Charles Drew is being interred, surreptitiously, near the altar. At 25, the young man had been convicted of killing his own father, resident of Long Melford and a wealthy man. Charles Drew Senior had kept his son's allowance at a very low level, because of his wild and reckless ways. The vicar of Acton at that time, 1740, was the murderer's brother-in-law.

The gallows overshadow the picture of young Catherine Foster. She stands outside her thatched cottage, the end one of a terrace of three and adjoining the village pump. Only 17, she poisoned her husband with a dose of arsenic, after three weeks of marriage. It is said that she had no real affection for her husband, who was older than herself. She was hanged publicly at Bury St Edmunds in 1846, the last woman to be so executed. The village pump stood until the 1960s, when the Queensway housing estate was built.

Who has not heard of the Acton Miser, William Jennens? He left a vast fortune, but made no will, and the dispute of the so-called claimants to his wealth lasted for 80 years after his death and suggested the plot of *Bleak House* to Charles Dickens. The narrow leafy lane which was once the drive to the old vicarage has been named after the Jennens family; the lane bisects the estate of Lime Tree Park. The building of this large estate in the 1970s brought new life to the village, which now has a new school, public house and four shops, one incorporating a sub-post office and ladies' hairdresser.

Second World War Acton had many facets, and this part of the tapestry features some of them. Liberator and Flying Fortress bombers symbolise the aerodrome that was built on the Acton and Great Waldingfield border. Four figures are shown grouped together with a background of prefabricated huts. They represent the Air Force Hospital staff, the German prisoners of war, the Ukrainian displaced persons and the 'squatters', who inhabited the pre-fabs and Nissen huts built over the parkland of Acton Place. Jam jars and wasps show the work of the Women's Institute, who trundled hundreds of pounds of jam on a flat cart from their hall, to be stored in a side room at the Crown public house.

The last decades of the 20th century are shown in a three part scene, small factories on a thriving Acton Place industrial estate; the playing field and village hall, built in 1965, nestling behind the Crown; and the new village school with its background of the lime trees of Jennens Way. The village has grown considerably since the beginning of our story, to a present day population approaching 2,000.

Alderton 🐖

In the early 1920s Alderton consisted mainly of The Street, a few detached houses and rows of small terraced cottages, the front door opening into the living room and the stairs hidden behind a door in the kitchen. Every week the front steps were scrubbed to a pristine whiteness and woe betide anyone who inadvertently trod on them. At the junction where the main roads met The Street was a small triangle of grass known as 'The Knoll', much frequented in the evening by the local lads. There was no mains water supply, sewerage or electricity. Water was obtained from wells or pumps and one's personal needs were met by a 'privy' located in an outbuilding often quite a distance from the cottage – on a rainy night you took an umbrella! Lighting was provided by oil lamps and the kitchen range provided both heating and cooking facilities.

In those days Alderton was well served with shops. In addition to the butcher – still located on the same site – there was a pork butcher and general store not many yards away. Pigs were slaughtered on Thursdays and sometimes a frantic animal would make a dash down The Street followed by the butcher and his assistant. On Fridays there were home-made pork sausages, pork cheeses, pig's fry and, children's delight, 'scraps' – crunchy bits of fat at a halfpenny a bag.

Not far away another small shop sold bread, sweets, a few groceries, corn for chickens and bags of coal. The latter was also sold from a horse-drawn cart. At the corner of Beach Lane a small post office was run by two elderly sisters, while at the other end of The Street was a large, double-fronted shop. One half was devoted to the sale of groceries – tea and sugar weighed out on demand and bacon cut to the required thickness – the other to household goods, haberdashery and newspapers. In addition the village also boasted a harnessmaker, a barber and a cobbler, as well as a building firm, undertaker and a doctor.

Facing each other across The Street were two public houses, both well patronised, and a jug of beer could be obtained at the back door for home consumption. Only one, the Swan, now remains, the other having been converted into private residences. The post office has moved to a new site and the old shop is a flourishing general store; the other shops are now private houses.

Lying back from the village was a windmill, then still grinding corn, now alas gone completely. The large church of St Andrew still stands, but the imposing rectory has long since been sold and even its replacement is now a private residence.

Nearly all the men worked on the neighbouring farms, cycling to and from work. Married women stayed at home and younger girls went into domestic service. Today only a handful of men work on the land, others go into town or to the American air bases, and a fair percentage are retired.

Aldham 🌿

Aldham is a large parish geographically but a small one population-wise, comprising some 60 households. Most dwellings are along the quarter mile of Aldham Street and there are clusters of houses in other parts of the parish and a few isolated farms. There is no shop, the pub closed shortly after the First World War, and the village school closed in 1930. There are six listed buildings: the church of St Mary and five timber-framed dwellings.

The oldest part of the Hall probably dates from the 15th century and major additions were made in the 17th century. The Hall first became owner occupied in 1911 when the lord of the manor sold it. Previous owners, who included the Earls of Oxford and Edward Coke, Chief Justice of England, had been too elevated to reside in Aldham and left the property in the hands of tenants or bailiffs.

Some way down the lane from the Hall the verge widens considerably and this was the site of the village pound. One octogenarian was told by his grandfather that it was also the site of the village stocks.

At the bottom of the lane is another listed building. Church Lane Cottage was once the blacksmith's cottage, though no blacksmith has lived in it during the 20th century. The forge, which was situated on the opposite side of Church Lane, was demolished in the mid 1920s.

Yew Tree Farm is also listed. The present occupier found a trapdoor in the floor of a downstairs room, intriguingly bolted on the underside, and when digging out a drainage system found traces of a tunnel. A hint, perhaps, that at some earlier time Aldham shared in that flourishing Hadleigh enterprise – smuggling.

If Aldham has ever known prosperity in its past it would most probably have been at the time when Hadleigh was a leading woollen cloth centre. A glebe terrier of 1686 lists a 'Teasle Yard' at the rectory, and the tithe map (1839) shows a Teasill Field, hinting at a link between the village and the woollen cloth trade. Certainly Robert Clyfford, a resident of Aldham, is shown by his contribution to Henry VIII's Subsidy of 1525 to have been one of the wealthiest men in the Hadleigh area.

It is possible that Dean Field is a corruption of Dane Field, the site of a great battle against the Danish invaders. A letter to the local press, circa 1885, from the then rector of Aldham, Rev Barratt Lennard, tells how his sexton was digging on the north side of the churchyard where it was thought no-one had ever been buried, when he 'came upon five skeletons, huddled together – not lying separately, but across each other, as if the bodies had been thrown into a pit anyhow. These bones were uncommonly large in size'. Could they have been some of the Danes who fell in the great battle, the rector wondered.

Another local tradition holds that there was an earlier village to the west of the church and Hall, said to have been wiped out by the Black Death. The unevenness of the meadow and the presence of a spring in the immediate vicinity lends credence to this.

Alpheton 🐚

The name Alpheton derives from the Anglo-Saxon 'Aelfflaede tun' meaning 'Aelfflaed's farm'. Unlike the great majority of personal place names, it is known who this lady was. Her father was Ealdorman Aelfgar of Essex, her sister was Aethelflaed, who was King Eadmund the Elder's queen, and her husband was Ealdorman Beorhtnoth of Essex, hero of the battle of Maldon on 11th August AD 991, when his local levies could not withstand 93 shiploads of Danes. He was buried in Ely Minster, and Canterbury still holds Monks' Eleigh of his gift.

Alpheton Hall, farm and church stand together, far from the village, in a little dell that must have been charming before its trees were felled, through which runs a stream to the river Chad.

At the end of the 19th century, with a population of 249, the village boasted a church school, a pub, shops and a daily bus service. Today all these have gone. The old mill which served this farming community still stands at Bridge Street, although now it is a private house. The farms remain, but now being mechanised most employment must be sought outside the village. But lest you should think that the village is moribund

Alpheton Village Church

there is an active WI, a vigorous children's club, a busy Youth Hostel and a flourishing community life centred around the beautiful old church of St Peter and St Paul, which dates back further than the 13th century, and the new village hall commemorating the Silver Jubilee of Queen Elizabeth II.

There is a former toll house, now a private house retaining its links with its history through its name 'Tallage', for the A134 follows the old sheep drovers road. In 1887 two oak trees were planted and a village pump installed to commemorate Queen Victoria's Jubilee. The parish minutes record that '... there was the Jubilee service in church at 4pm after which all the children had cake and tea on the Tye. At 7pm the pump handle was unlocked by Miss Gardner and the Rector thanked all the kind donors who had contributed to procure the blessing of pure water in so convenient a spot ...'

True to its name given a thousand years ago, farming is still the predominant feature of the landscape today in this lovely undulating area of Suffolk, the fields vast and prairie-like, gold with corn in summer and rape in spring. Beet is also grown and linseed turns some fields blue, whilst the hedgerows still contain poppies and many wild flowers to enrich the landscape. Stock-keeping has begun to come back and once again we see sheep and cattle and small groups of farmyard animals giving new life to the area.

The village is now divided by the A134, which was constructed to assist in the laying out of the American airfield which was based here during the Second World War and made famous in the film *Twelve O'Clock High* starring Gregory Peck. But the road does not divide the spirit and sense of community of the people.

Ashbocking, Swilland
& Witnesham ༄

A well known building in Ashbocking was the Lord Nelson public house, which was a very popular meeting place, run by a local family. Sadly however, this has now been pulled down and a small group of houses built on the site, aptly named Nelson Close.

Almost opposite the Lord Nelson site used to stand a small group of buildings. When these burnt down many years ago, a garage was built on the site. This is still a working garage today and is called Nelson Garage.

Just behind the Nelson Garage stands a concrete post, of which perhaps few realise the significance. It can in fact be found on an Ordnance Survey map as a trigonometry point. It is believed that this post marks the site on which a survey tower was built when the area was surveyed. It was probably during this time that it was discovered that the doorstep of the Lord Nelson public house was level with the top of Otley church tower, although it is hard to see this when driving or walking around the area.

Just a short way down the road from the crossroads on which the Nelson Garage is situated, lies the village of Swilland. Many years ago in this village stood what was probably one of the best known examples of a wooden windmill, which was owned by Colonel Barron. The mill had a transportation fleet of two trucks which could carry 30 hundredweight a time, and a steam lorry which could carry about eight tons. This steam lorry was a familiar sight travelling through the villages of Ashbocking, Swilland and Witnesham in those days. Sadly however, the mill was pulled down about 35 years ago. It was in a state of poor repair, the owner couldn't afford to have it repaired and the Ministry of Works already had Saxstead Mill which, although a much smaller mill, was of the same type.

Also in Swilland there was an old Victorian mill, which was used for biscuit-making. The round house for this still exists today.

Probably the major focal point in Swilland, however, is the water tower. Seen from miles around, this tower was built in about 1938. Made from concrete, it was painstakingly built by hand. Men would stand on top of the tower, pulling a single bucket of concrete up on a pulley, tipping it in and lowering the empty bucket down again for their colleagues below to replenish. How many builders nowadays would be prepared to undertake such difficult and tedious work?

Th actual lay-out of the three villages of Ashbocking, Swilland and Witnesham has not changed much today, apart from the obvious new buildings springing up, including the development of housing estates such as Weyland Road in Witnesham. All three villages have a good community life with many clubs and functions for people of all ages.

Assington 🦃

The village street is dull in comparison to other local villages, and these brick-built cottages appear to be nothing until looked at closely. Then you will notice that here is some fine brickwork – these bricks and tiles were made in the parish.

It is supposed that the straight road from the direction of Colchester was Roman, and the forge has been discovered to have four tiers of buildings on its site. The last smith to work there left after the Second World War.

By 1316 Roger Corbet owned the four manors which became the village. It was he who turned the small monastic cell attached to the church of St Edmund into Assington Hall. In 1515 a wool merchant, one Coutts, remodelled the building, and later in the century the Gurdons established themselves there, until the estate was sold in 1938. In 1957 the Hall went up in flames.

It was John Gurdon in 1845 who formed the whole village into a co-operative society based on Robert Owen's socialist theories. The whole became self-supporting; it was then the houses were improved and encased in brick. The Society brought a better way of life and kept the villagers in work. It went on until 1918 and then was dissolved. Sometimes metal tokens are dug up in cottage gardens; these were payment for work and could be exchanged for goods at the village shop.

The village still has an inn, the Shoulder of Mutton, and a post office stores, but the school went in 1983, after much concern, with the villagers fighting the decision all the way to the Secretary of State. The Gurdon stable block at the back of the Hall was designed by William Kent – this has now been restored as a residence.

Perhaps the most interesting man-made construction is the secret passage between Assington Hall and Assington House, with a section which came up in a clump of trees in the glebeland, since covered over. It is a bricked passage, built to hide Tudor Catholics from arrest, but no one has explored it for a long time.

Most of today's jobs take the inhabitants away to Colchester or Sudbury, very few work on the land; the women pick fruit in season and prune trees in winter.

Athelington 🦃

The name Athelington has been variably spelt over the centuries with a suggestion that it meant 'the prince's town', but there is a figure of Edgar Atheling with his wife on the chancel beam in the church. Could it have been his enclosure?

It is a very quiet village, completely ignored by tourists, though visitors might find much of interest in the Early English Decorated-style flint church of St Peter, dating between 1300 and 1348, its building inter-rupted by the Black Death. It holds exceptional treasures, among them the 15th century oak bench ends of unique and varying design: perhaps the best in Suffolk and well documented.

Since 1902, the benefice of Athelington has been joined to that of Horham. There has been close co-operation between the two villages over the years. In 1504, John Clubbe of Athelington gave 6s 8d towards Horham steeple. Many fetes held in Horham Hall and Horham rectory gave part profits towards extensive repairs, when needed, to Athelington church, augmenting the fund raising by locals at The Grove. The popula-tion had dropped to 40 by 1950 from 126 in 1831. During that time there was much emigration to Canada and Australia and with the mechanisation of agriculture a lot of movement to the industrial Mid-lands from East Anglia. It has been a real achievement to maintain such a beautiful church and attractive village with so few parishioners.

Other connections are very strong between the villages. In the absence of a public meeting place there is a Horham and Athelington Community Centre where many events are jointly held in Horham. There are several active and respected families in the area who have been farmers, regular worshippers and holders of church offices for generations.

Julie Davy, when aged twelve years, recorded this event – 'In the spring of 1974, a fir tree was blown down in Athelington churchyard, it landed between the two graves of Mr Wm. Davy and his wife. There was only about eight inches to one foot of room for it to fall, yet it fell there without damaging the graves. No woodcutter could ever get it to fall so neatly without damaging any of the stones.' Perhaps a modern miracle?

Bacton 🌿

Bacton comprises 2,204 acres and is situated in mid Suffolk about six miles north of Stowmarket and to the east of the A45. It was originally based round seven greens; Bacton, Canham, Cow, Earls, Ford, Shop and Tailors. These are still green areas today.

From 1236 to 1536 Bacton was ruled by the many Bishops of Nor-wich. From 1501 to 1536 Richard Nykke was Bishop and he built a palace in Bacton (when this was demolished bricks were used to build cottages) and his coat of arms can be seen in the south aisle window of St Mary's church. The present manor house was completed about 1732 and bears the Pretyman coat of arms.

St Mary's church dates from the 14th and 15th centuries and is of the Decorated and Perpendicular styles of architecture. The most noticeable feature of this church is the magnificent double hammerbeam roof to the nave. Over the chancel arch are remains of a Doom painting which is considered an excellent example of medieval art.

A tragedy which took place in Bacton was the murder of Maria Steggles, housekeeper to the rector, Rev Edward Barker, between the hours of ten and one o'clock on the 8th May 1853, while the rector was in church. A reward of £205 was offered for any information. William Flack, an 18 year old Bacton boy, was found guilty of the murder and executed publicly in Ipswich. The rectory where Maria worked is now known as The Grange, and is a rest home for the elderly.

Up until the middle of the 20th century there had been little change in Bacton, other than the coming of the railway in the 1850s. The railway geographically divided the village into two and for 100 years brought alternative employment to the village. Finningham station, which was in the parish of Bacton, was closed on 5th November 1966.

Bacton, until recently, has always been an agricultural village with life revolving around the farming community. In 1929 the village had a thatcher, two blacksmiths, a butcher, a maltster and 15 farmers. Today, the farms are bigger and there are fewer farmers.

In 1958 one of its more prominent farmers, Mr David Black of Red House Farm, was awarded the OBE for his services to agriculture. Amongst many other activities, he initiated the formation of the National Farmer's Union in Suffolk and became its first Chairman in 1919. He was one of many Scottish farmers who came to Suffolk at the turn of the century.

Until the mid 1960s there was little new building in the village, but there has been a building boom and the population of the village has doubled and is currently 1,200. Few of these new inhabitants are employed on the land, but commute to surrounding towns.

During the 20th century, five of the six public houses have been closed, only the Bull remains, along with two village shops, one of which, Bacton Stores, incorporates the post office.

Badingham ✣

Badingham is a scattered village lying off the A1120 between Dennington and Peasenhall.

Its history goes back to the Norman conquest and of its three feudal manors, only Colston and Oakenhill Halls remain. Badingham Hall, occupied until 1946, has been demolished. It is said that Oakenhill Hall is the Crakenhill of H. W. Freeman's novel *Joseph and his Brethren* written in 1928. There are also grounds for believing that Oakenhill is the site of a deserted medieval village.

The parish church of St John the Baptist stands on a pagan holy site. Though it is not known when the church was first built, parts date from Norman times. The single hammerbeam nave roof and the late 15th century Seven Sacraments font are Badingham's greatest treasures. It is a Grade I listed building of special architectural or historic interest.

Many of Badingham's houses are also listed; several date from the 16th century. The Old Rectory, at one time a boys boarding school, is now the East Anglian Academy of Transcendental Meditation. During the course of building alterations to one farmhouse a child's leather boot was found bricked up in the fireplace. According to Ipswich Museum it could be 300 years old. Superstitions connected with shoes are legion and this find was not unusual. They are generally found under window sills, floor boards and staircases, in chimney breasts, walls, thatch or rafters. It is suggested that they were some kind of sacrificial offering to ward off evil spirits.

According to White's Directory of 1844 occupations included a tailor, two shoemakers, two wheelwrights, two bricklayers, two carpenters, a plumber and glazier, five grocers, two publicans, two millers, two black-smiths and 27 farmers. In the early 1850s a brickworks was established and continued in operation until 1928. Apart from farming, the number and diversity of occupations carried on today in a small village, are surprising. There are the village shop and post office, the pub, the garage, agricultural engineers, builders, decorators and carpenters, a vineyard and winery, tree care specialists, a PYO apple orchard, a stud farm, a rapid parcel delivery depot, a professional artist and book illustrator, and a potter who makes porcelain reproductions of Victorian dolls' heads.

1984 saw the first of the village's archaeological digs. With the help of a professional archaeologist, enthusiastic volunteers unearthed remains of Roman pottery, bone fragments and a number of flint tools.

Badwell Ash 🐝

The earliest map on which the site of Badwell's windmill can positively be identified is 1758. Mill House, behind which the mill stood, has been owned by the Fordham family for the last 140 years. The mill was taken down in 1930.

The 13th century church of St Mary stands in the middle of the village. Around the top of the tower is an inscription asking for prayers for John Finch and his wife. At the porch entrance in the stonework are carved blacksmiths' tools and a plough.

Peter Stevens was the village blacksmith and wheelwright at the turn of the 20th century, making waggons and tumbrils. Hams from pigs killed in Badwell were smoked in the chimney of the forge, which stood where the Beehive fish and chip shop is now. One of the waggons made by him is still at Shackerland Hall Farm, where it was used for road work as well as carting corn.

The post office and grocery shop had a storehouse where two new houses are now. In the days of horses and waggons it was needed, as the goods came from Ipswich once a month, having got to Ipswich by boat from London. The other side of the shop was a cottage, which was pulled down after the First World War because the tenant would not pay his rent. He was in bed at the time.

The White Horse pub was a coaching inn in the 14th century. It is said that on New Year's Eve every year a ghostly coach and horses drives along the Badwell to Walsham road and all who see the coach are supposed to fall dead or die soon after.

The village bakery was in the Wurlie, a house opposite the pub. It has a kingpost roof inside. Further up the street, on the way to Badwell Green, was the guildhall, which is now converted into a house.

Badwell Ash Hall, also known as High Hall, a house of ornate chimneys, stands about a mile outside the village. The restoration and refurbishment of the building was mainly due to the Payne family who acquired the house in 1852 and made it again into a 'gentleman's dwelling'. They were great benefactors to the village of Badwell Ash, providing the first school, a reading room, and in addition restoring and re-seating the parish church, supposedly using oak grown in the grounds of the Hall. Very much a Lady Bountiful, Hester Payne organised the distribution of soup and plum pudding each Christmas, the villagers trooping up to the Hall to receive their gifts.

The present external appearance of the house owes much to the care and diligence of the Paynes, although, alas, many of the beautiful oaks and beeches surrounding the property disappeared in the gales of 1987.

Barham

The village is quite widespread, being bordered by the villages of Great Blakenham, Claydon, Coddenham and Henley.

Many years ago there was a workhouse close to the village church school. It was demolished in the 1970s to provide for the construction of the Claydon/Stowmarket bypass. Shortly after the bypass completion the land not needed for road purposes was converted by the Mid Suffolk Council to an attractive picnic site incorporating a natural conservancy area plus an information building. Adjoining land, from where gravel was extracted for road construction purposes, has since been transformed to a lovely series of lakes where many species of birds have made their home, including a host of beautiful Canadian Geese.

Whilst a sizeable village, it has never had more than two shops at any one time, and even today it is reduced to a single general store – quite recently modernised, with a self service style.

The church of St Mary dates back to the 13th century with seating for around 200 people and from September 1975 it has been the joint church for both Barham and Claydon – redesignated 'St Mary and St Peter' it stands on a hill in line with the churches of Akenham, Claydon and Whitton. Following the closure of the church in Claydon many of the artefacts from that building were removed to St Mary and St Peter, including the statue of the Madonna and Child, sculpted by Henry Moore – its transfer being personally supervised by the famous creator himself.

Since the Second World War much housing development has ensued, with several roads being named after previous eminent residents, the first being the council housing estate of 58 dwellings in Kirby Rise in recognition of the late Rev William Kirby. Then when the Ryecorn estate was planned, it included Thornhill Road, so named after the late Sir Anthony Compton Thornhill Bart, who resided at Barham Hall, opposite the church, for many years – the roads Bacon, Phillips, Middleton and Eddowes were all named after former rectors of Barham, as indeed is Woolner Close, a fairly new development.

In the past most houses and cottages had large gardens with the menfolk normally cultivating an allotment in addition, but with changing living standards, social pursuits have changed and one of the largest allotment areas of the past is currently being developed as a private housing estate.

Shrubland Hall, the seat of Lord de Saumarez, stands within the village boundary on a bold eminence overlooking the vale of the river Gipping, in an extensive and well-wooded park covering about 300 acres, including superb terraced gardens of some 40 acres designed by Capability Brown. In the mid 1960s Lord and Lady de Saumarez had the Hall converted into the now famous Health Clinic, which is patronised by many well known celebrities.

Barking 🐝

The outstanding feature of Barking is the Tye, 50 acres of common land. The grazing rights belonged to the farms surrounding it and some rights are still registered. There are nine farms, seven of which are still locally owned. The Tye has been cultivated since the Second World War but is now being put down to grass again. In the meantime, cereal crops have provided funds for the parish council to erect six street lamps and to keep the grass areas maintained. Once, three windmills stood on the Tye but all have long gone. There is an interesting village sign, made locally at the forge which once shoed the heavy horses used on the land but now specialises in iron gates and fireplace furniture.

Barking is noted for its stretch of ancient woodlands, consisting of Bonny, Bells, Priestley and Swingens Woods. Timber from Bonny Wood was used to build Gresham's Royal Exchange in London.

Barking is mentioned in the Domesday Book and some local names can be traced back to it. It was a thriving community when the nearby market town of Needham was just marshland and as late as 1874, Barking was described as a 'pleasant village and township including the hamlets of Darmsden and Needham Market'. It was separated from Needham in 1901 and in 1907 part of Barking was transferred to Needham to rationalise the boundaries.

The church of St Mary is somewhat larger than the usual village church, with seating for 600, and was the mother church to Needham Market. Funerals from Needham were brought along the Causeway or

Corpse Way to Barking churchyard as there was no place for burials in Needham itself. This way still exists.

The Georgian mansion, Barking Hall, was next door to the church. In 1756, John, Earl of Ashburnham held occupancy and it remained in the Ashburnham family until the early 20th century when the earldom became extinct, there being no direct male heirs. The original Hall was then completely demolished apart from the stable block and in 1926, sold for its materials. For many years it was used as riding stables, but in the 1980s the building was extended and refurbished to provide a nursing home.

In the grounds of the old rectory stand two of the original three magnificent cedar trees planted by Robert Uvedale, a local botanist. The third fell victim to the October 1987 storm and from its timbers, local craftsmen carved a cross and two candlesticks which were later presented to the church.

Fairfax House was once the residence of the Rev John Fairfax, a vicar of Barking, who was ejected from the living in 1662 due to his nonconformist views. He spent some time in Bury jail before returning to Fairfax House. He is regarded as the founder of the Congregational church in Needham Market, though there was a congregation there before his arrival.

Like many other parts of Suffolk, Barking shows traces of the Roman occupation, and at the end of the 18th century a fine two ft golden bronze figure was unearthed, buried twelve ft below ground, near Barking Hall. This figure, undoubtedly typifying an imperial personage, was presented to the British Museum by Lord Ashburnham in 1813.

The village has changed little in appearance over the years. There is no shop now and the school has become the village hall. Agriculture is still its mainstay but everyday life is vastly different today; no longer does one draw water from the wells on the Tye or depend on Swain's twice weekly delivery of paraffin oil.

Barnby 🐏

Barnby is, by its name, a village of Danish origin, situated along the busy A146 between Lowestoft and Beccles. To the west lies marshlands leading to the river Waveney, with coverage for a large number of birds, and the privately-owned Barnby Broad.

The church of St John the Baptist dates from around 1200. It contains in the south wall an ancient banner stave locker, used in medieval times, and possessing its original door. The wall paintings, recently restored, date from 1410 and in the tower hangs a solitary bell inscribed 'may the bell of St John resound for many years'.

The Great Eastern Railway built sidings at Barnby in 1883 on the Lowestoft branch line, mainly for carrying sugar beet, coal, cattle and machinery. On Christmas Eve 1891, one train ran into another causing the Barnby train disaster. The efforts of Mr Amos Beamish that night were so outstanding they became something of a legend. He was known as the Giant of Barnby – a man of enormous size and strength. There was a cruel fog, but amidst it all could be seen this massive form moving quantities of debris, cutting away with his axe and releasing sufferers who were embedded in the wreck. 'When he died, my grandfather weighed 28 stone', says Mrs Brenda Bartram, now postmistress in Mill Lane. She remembers the old post office next to the Swan inn and can confirm the ghost story linked with Black Shuck, a retriever dog who can be seen on the roads around Barnby at night. Once, thinking it was a neighbour's dog, she bent to stroke it and it disappeared! They do say it was named after Shukr, Thor's dog – yet another link with Viking days.

The village at one time boasted two inns, the Swan and Blindman's Gate. The Swan is now a pub and restaurant, but the Gate has been pulled down and a garage now stands on the site.

W. E. Wigg & Sons was founded in 1902 as a wheelwright's and later became an agricultural engineers and garage. In those days many local people worked there, as well as on the land, and many others went to sea. 'Time was when Jinker Rouse sat outside his reding house selling red herring', says Mrs Edith Bennett. 'There were several reding houses put up for when the men came home with the fresh herring'. Now people work mainly in Lowestoft or Beccles.

The village shop owned by Miss Gladys Baxter is no longer, but there is Newson's Garden Nursery, Lambert's Riding School, an aquatic centre and even a snail farm!

Barningham 🐚

The village of Barningham lies some 13 miles north-east of Bury St Edmunds, close to the Norfolk border, an ancient settlement of mid Anglo-Saxon times.

With a population of a nominal 1,000, the village now comprises the original settlement, three small estates built over the last 25 years plus outlying farms. The original nucleus of the village clusters around those essentials for a happy, thriving community; the shop, the school, the pub and the church, though not necessarily in that order of importance.

Offering an important lifeline to many members of the community is the local shop and post office. It is of course a meeting point for the villagers and an ideal place for the exchange of local news and gossip, as is the thatched public house. The Royal George, once two dwellings and approximately 400 years old, is named after a fighting ship of the line built in 1746 and sunk off Spithead in 1782.

The 500 year old church of St Andrew is built of flint and enriched with fine woodwork and carvings. The 15th century chancel screen is fitted with early 17th century gates, only two or three other Suffolk churches having this feature.

The famous firm of Fisons grew from small beginnings in Barningham. During the late 18th century James Fison was the owner of two windmills in the village. After the turn of the century the second James Fison, who owned the small maltings, dismantled the windmills and converted the maltings into a steam mill. This was one of the earliest steam mills in existence and the beam engine was in service for nearly a hundred years; it is now in a museum in the USA but the mill building is still in use today supplying animal feed.

The end of the 18th century seems to have been a difficult time for the residents. The manor house fell into decay, there were outbreaks of smallpox, and in 1769 the parsonage house burnt down with other houses and five families were made homeless. The rector went to live in Lakenheath and stayed there until his death nearly 50 years later.

Perhaps resulting from these setbacks, the exceptional occurrence of a woman being appointed as an overseer to the poor was made. This is the only recorded example in England of a woman serving in this situation in this period. The job required a certain level of education and intelligence and Widow Morley was obviously considered capable of carrying out these time-consuming and difficult tasks.

Barsham 🐚

Driving from Beccles to Bungay on the B1062 road you may hardly notice the village of Barsham, but it has many points of interest.

The thatched church of the Holy Trinity, dating back to Saxon times with its round tower and ring of five bells, has a large east window with remarkable lozenge-shaped tracery reaching to the ground. It stands well back from the road behind its holly hedge and fine row of old limes. On 13th September 1979 the roof caught fire and was destroyed without great damage to the rest of the church. The church was repaired and rethatched and returned to regular use in three and a half years.

'Old ladie Ichingham' was buried in the churchyard on 30th July 1584 at the reputed age of 110 years. There is a verbal tradition that part of the burial ground should not be used as it is reserved for plague pits; it may well have been last used at the time of the Black Death.

The former rectory is of equal interest, its graceful facade fronting a house of great character with a priest's hole, a secret cupboard dated 1500, and a ghost who rearranges objects on a dressing table. It was the home of Catharine Suckling, mother of Lord Nelson.

The recorded history of Barsham Hall goes back to 1348, built by the Etchingham family and passing by marriage to the Blennerhassetts, one of whom is said to make a ghostly journey along the old road at midnight on Christmas Eve with a coach and four black horses. The Blennerhasset arms bearing the date 1563 can still be seen on one of the remaining buildings. In the 17th century Sir John Suckling, the poet, kept 100 men-at-arms for the king.

Barsham City is a row of cottages in a lane leading to City Farm, from which it takes its name; it is believed the farm originally belonged to the City of Norwich. The area known as the Ink Factory is of more recent date, consisting of a master's house and four cottages where workers made ink to supply the Beccles printing works.

The village school was closed in 1961 and the building was subsequently sold to a committee of villagers to become the village hall. Though without a pub, Barsham has an important waterworks! The first borehole was sunk in 1949 and its water is now supplied to a wide area.

The village sign, a gilded sun rising from a stout oak trunk, caused much controversy when first erected. Made by Keith Payne as a celebration of the sun and the earth it is now a familiar and well known landmark.

Come to Barsham in the spring and you can be surrounded by apple and pear blossom and later in the year you may 'pick your own' fruit.

Barton Mills 🐚

Barton Mills is a quiet residential village, one mile from Mildenhall and twelve miles from Bury St Edmunds. In Saxon times, Barton Mills was known as Barton Parva (Little Barton). It was during the 18th century, when the new turnpike road from London to Norwich was built to the south-east of the old village, crossing the river Wridewell (now the Lark), that it began to be called Barton Mills. At one time there were two corn mills and a fulling mill in the village.

The famous coaching inn, the Bull, was built for the convenience of those using the turnpike. In recent years the busy A11 has been reconstructed to bypass the village and therefore no longer passes directly in front of the Bull. This ancient coaching inn has had a chequered history and is still a popular place to wine and dine.

Parallel to The Street, the river Lark, now a sleepy backwater, wends its way through the village. Previously this was a busy waterway with a daily passenger service to Bury St Edmunds, where barges used to unload coal for the village and take away stones that had been gathered from Chalk Hill. Children used to swim from the staunch, and apparently there were so many fish in this river one could scoop them out with a bucket!

Moving further along The Street, we come to the reading room, built in 1919 in memory of Percy Burrell, a high-ranking army officer, by his widow. The village is still benefiting from the Burrell Trust (set up from the sale of the reading room) which helps maintain the village hall.

Barton Mills is still fortunate in having a village shop and post office that is a meeting place for young and old. The shop is almost opposite 'The Dhoon' which was the country home of Sir Alexander Fleming from

1921–1955. He is said to have discovered penicillin in a shed in the garden.

In more recent times the village has enlarged considerably. One of the two new housing estates (Church Meadow) is built on the meadow adjacent to the church, which was once a winter playground that used to be deliberately flooded and used for skating. At the turn of the century the winters were very harsh, and Barton Mills people used to skate up the river to Mildenhall rather than go along the road which was often blocked by drifts.

St Mary's church is one of considerable charm. It was begun around 1150 but there is evidence of an even earlier building. A rector, Jacobus de Scabellis, who spent little time in the parish, had the Pope as his Patron. Another rector, James Davis, stayed for 39 years. He must have been a caring man because he left 14 acres of land to the churchwardens and overseers of the poor, from which the income was to be shared out annually. This same income is still shared out each Christmas, though it is very much greater in value now than the 40 shillings it yielded in 1709.

Bawdsey 🐚

Before the sea and river walls were built in the 15th and 16th century, Bawdsey was at every high tide an island, with the boundaries extending to Shingle Street and to the ferry.

In 1886, Sir Cuthbert Quilter built Bawdsey Manor on the cliff, blowing up a Martello tower to make a sunken garden, and shoring up the cliff and planting shrubs on it below the manor.

There had been a ferry at the mouth of the river for many years, but Sir Cuthbert installed a chain ferry which could transport carriages and cars. This was given up in the 1920s and has been replaced by a sequence of motor boats. He owned the main part of the Bawdsey estate, and built the model cottages in the village and the village hall. He established the recreation ground, as well as a flourishing smithy where his fine stud of Suffolk Punches was cared for.

After several generations of Quilters at the Manor, it was sold in 1936 to the Air Ministry, and here Sir William Watson-Watt perfected radar. Vast metal scanners were erected in the north-western area of the grounds, and these disappeared when missiles took their place. Today, the Air Ministry have left and the Manor is up for sale.

The Cavells lived at Bawdsey Hall, whose daughter Nurse Edith Cavell was shot by the Germans in the First World War, for helping prisoners of war to escape.

In medieval times, the village was far larger than it is today. A market was held in the area between the Old Star and the church, and being the first village on this side of the estuary, it must have been of some importance. The first house to the east of the church is recorded as a manor house, and between it and the church the school was built in

Victorian times. The present school is in East Lane. In living memory there were more houses in East Lane, a bakery at the top, a pork butcher's further down opposite the existing farm buildings, and fishermen's and coastguard's cottages near the sea. The concrete fortifications were built in the Second World War.

The church of St Mary has a 14th century tower. In 1842 the whole building was badly damaged by a fire started by boys playing with fireworks, and it was rebuilt on a much reduced scale.

In the Quilters' time the majority of the inhabitants of the village were employed at the Manor or on the estate. After that most worked on the farms owned by James Mann at High House and Norman Simper at Manor Farm. Today with increased mechanisation there are few agricultural workers and they have been replaced by builders and several self-employed trades. There are a number of new houses and holiday homes, and with the closure of the pub in the early 1970s, and the shop in 1990, the village has lost some of its cohesion. But valiant efforts are being made with the annual fête, coffee mornings and a flourishing Women's Group.

Bentley 🐚

Bentley Hall, with the herringbone tithe barn, was once home of Mr Elkington, founder of the *East Anglian Daily Times* and inventor of machinery for the printing press. Dodnash Priory Farm was owned by the Great Eastern Railway. Lord Claud Hamilton, chairman of Great Eastern, and other officials visited the Priory at Easter, Harvest, Christmas and during the shooting season.

At the forge in Grove Road, Mr Death, the village blacksmith with hammer and anvil, shod the horses, and at a cottage in Grove Road, the doctor held his weekly surgery and there he mixed his own medicines for patients to take home.

William Cooper, the village roadman with brush and shovel trimmed the roadside, cleaned out ditches, etc, and kept the village tidy. He was commonly known as 'Tater Cupper' and lived in Case Lane, near the inn – the Case Is Altered. There were two other public houses – the Railway Tavern and the Tankard which was on the Bentley side of the old London Road.

In Church Road stands Bentley school, built in 1853 and still going strong. Further along the road, almost hidden by giant cedar trees, is the little church of St Mary. The fine hammerbeam roof of the nave is 600 years old, and the lovely east window of the Ascension has eleven apostles in green, red and blue cloaks. Unfortunately, in the 1987 gales some of the beautiful old cedar trees were blown over.

In the days gone by, many labourers brewed their own beer (enough to last a year) with malt and hops in big wooden tubs. To get a haircut men would walk to Manningtree – the cost of the cut being two pence. All water was drawn from a well or pump and milk had to be fetched daily from a farm. Saturday afternoons the village lads played quoits and formed a Quoit Club; there was also a football team, nicknamed 'The Bentley Wide-a-Wakes'.

These days are long past and perhaps there is a touch of sadness that we no longer stroll down the shady lanes with gay hedgerows and see the many lovely wild flowers that once bloomed by the wayside; no longer hear the blacksmith's hammer on his anvil or pass the time of day with 'Tater Cupper', or on a dark Sunday night see along the road the twinkling lights from lanterns carried by village folk on their way to evensong!

However in spite of change, Bentley still retains a 'mystery' as yet unsolved. On one of the Dodnash meadows stands a large stone – the ruins of the old Dodnash Priory. Legend has it that there was an underground passage from the priory to the nunnery at East Bergholt, and if anyone could raise the stone, hidden treasure lies beneath! So far no one has been able to raise the stone, so 'treasure', if any, still lies hidden!

Bildeston 🌿

The village of Bildeston lies on the B1115, north of Hadleigh. There are several interesting and ancient cottages and houses, and the lovely church of St Mary stands away from the village centre on a hill.

On the south side of Bildeston churchyard, a raised granite slab marks the grave of Captain Edward Rotheram, one of the heroes of the battle of Trafalgar.

Captain Rotheram was not a Bildeston man and his burial in the village was fortuitous. He happened to die while staying with his friend and fellow-Northumbrian, Richard Wilson, of Bildeston House.

Inside the church, on the south wall, close by the side chapel, there is a memorial tablet with the following inscription:

'To the memory of Capt Edwd. Rotheram, RN who commanded the *Royal Sovereign*, the leading ship at the battle of Trafalgar.

He died suddenly at Bildestone (sic) House and was buried in this churchyard November 6th 1830 aged 77 years. A brother officer erected this tablet.'

Blundeston 🌿

Blundeston, a village community of some 1,200 folk situated close to the coast on the Suffolk/Norfolk border but sufficiently far inland to be safe from the predatory ravages of the North Sea, has been permanently marked by its only real claim to fame: as the 'birthplace' of the fictitious

The Plough Inn, Blundeston

character David Copperfield in Charles Dickens' novel of the same name. So vivid is this character in readers' imaginations that many a villager has been almost at a loss for words to give directions to bewildered visitors from abroad on a pilgrimage to 'David's grave'.

The well-preserved, mainly Norman church of St Mary, with its older, tall, slim Saxon round tower now over 1,000 years old, has a sundial over the south porch which is mentioned in *David Copperfield*.

In the centre of a nearby three-way road junction, on the only plot of land in the village still owned by the lord of the manor, stands a well-kept pound which was used as a depository for straying livestock until the turn of the 20th century. With animal farming in decline, today its usefulness is more frivolous but suggests its rarity value: it is a popular 'destination' for competitors in car treasure hunts and similar events.

Opposite is Blundeston's village sign, showing David Copperfield as a boy looking at the church, presented to the village by Blundeston & Flixton WI in 1965. The Plough inn, an old coaching house built in 1701, is where 'Barkis the Carrier' was alleged to have started his journey to take David Copperfield to nearby Great Yarmouth.

Blundeston once had three large residences. Of these Blundeston Hall, a partly moated country house, and Blundeston House, a recently restored three-storey building designed by Sir John Soane and completed in 1786, still stand today. The third and largest of the residences, Blundeston Lodge, gives the village a further link with literary excellence: it was once the home of Norton Nichols, whose friend the poet Gray is said to have been inspired to write his famous *Elegy* while staying there. But here, fact has consigned fictional charm to history: in the late 1950s, when preserving the country's architectural heritage was still a cause far removed from public concern, Blundeston Lodge was sold to the Home Office, which subsequently demolished it to make room for a grade II security prison. The beautiful grounds are now part of the prison complex, which itself forms an integral element of the village community.

Blundeston school was opened in 1726, 144 years in advance of the 1870 Education Act which made schooling compulsory. A Blundeston schoolmaster who died in 1835 left instructions in his will that three iron spikes were to project from the top of his tombstone to deter the boys of the village from jumping over it – a well-loved and respected person it seems, but certainly an accurate judge of human instinct. One of the spikes, now time-corroded, is still effectively fulfilling its purpose.

Blythburgh 🖋️

Happy indeed, as its name implies, is this little village commanding the head of the estuary of the river Blyth and overlooking the tidal Angel Marshes, part of the Suffolk Heritage Coast and an area of outstanding natural beauty. Whether you come upon the village from Ipswich and the south or by crossing the river on its northern side you see immediately that it bestrides a vital trunk route from London to the coast and its North Sea ports. It is this situation that gave Blythburgh much of its wealth and importance in its Saxon heyday when it was the scene of a battle between Anna, the Christian king of East Anglia and Penda of neighbouring Mercia; it was also a royal 'burgh' housing a mint and according to the Domesday survey of 1086 taxed at a rate of 3,000 herrings.

Whatever your business here you will surely catch your breath in wonder as you glimpse the magnificent 15th century priory church, the 'Cathedral of the Marshes', one of the greatest of the great East Anglian churches whose towers and spires puncture the wide skies of this lovely countryside. This church is a treasure-house of medieval stonework, flying angels, 15th century wood-carving and fascinating legend, as the finger-marks of the Devil, scorched upon the inside of the great north door as he fled northwards after causing devastation and death in the great storm of 1577, bear witness.

Blythburgh has always been a village of farmers and smallholders, as well as fishermen, thatchers and churchmen, and the wealth of its countryside is well demonstrated by the variety of its crops and livestock. In the past, hemp for its shipbuilding and fishing trade was grown on many small plots and in the early 19th century John Brooke of West-wood Lodge, tenant of the biggest of the medieval manors, was commended by the farming enthusiast, Arthur Young, for the excellence of his husbandry and classed among the great improving landlords of the Agricultural Revolution, who did so much to make the light soil farming of East Anglia a lucrative business. Today, along with grain is grown sugar beet, rape and linseed, and instead of the flocks of sheep of the past and the horses grazing on the marshlands, we have a good stock of pigs on the fields round the village.

29

In the 18th century smuggling was at its height, and this led to Blythburgh's most famous ghost. In 1750, on the last Monday in June, a young Walberswick girl was alleged to have been murdered by one Tobias Gill, a negro drummer in Sir Robert Rich's regiment of dragoons, stationed in Blythburgh to control the smuggling. Protesting his innocence, he was taken to Bury St Edmunds, tried and sentenced, and brought back to Blythburgh crossways, where he was hanged in chains. His ghost is said to haunt that quiet lane even now, though it does not seem to have disturbed the many holidaymakers who enjoy the picnic site on 'Toby's Walks'!

On Bulcamp ridge stands the old workhouse, whose building in 1764 caused a riot. In 1818, shortly after the battle of Waterloo, it housed as many as 558 paupers; today it is used as a hospital for the elderly, but is about to be closed.

The village caters for its travellers still at the well-known White Hart inn, and by selling local and imported produce from the Red House Farmshop. It still has its own post office and village shop, and a Blythburgh Pottery where Dorothy Midson, a full member of the Society of Designer Craftsmen, sells her wares.

Botesdale 🐾

Through the ages, Botesdale has been known by an interesting variety of names including Botolph's Dale, derived from a supposed connection with St Botolph, a Benedictine monk who was believed to have visited the area during the 7th century.

Botesdale is a thoroughfare village, its most important buildings lining the road from the point where it leaves Rickinghall. The road was a turnpike from 1769 and tolls for the maintenance and improvement of roads were collected at the Round House at the eastern end.

The road passes to the south of Redgrave Park and village, and it was natural for a market to develop where the coaches, as many as eight a day, as well as carriers' wagons, slowed before labouring up the hill. Some of the large houses and public houses were originally coaching inns and most had a paddock in Fen Lane for the overnight stay of draught animals. Crown Hill House, at the top of the hill, was one such inn, and it is said that its upper storey, which still juts out over the pavement, was a vantage point for watching for the coaches approach and that refreshments would be passed through its windows to the passengers. The cattle that were raised in Scotland and the North of England travelled south on the hoof and diverted to East Anglia to be fattened before the last 80 miles of their trek to London.

The Greyhound is mentioned in Lenard P. Thompson's *Old Inns of Suffolk* in connection with the annual 'Petty Sessions for the Hiring and Retaining of Servants'. These were held every Michaelmas and were originally intended as a means of hiring ploughmen and other agricultural workers for the whole year instead of from day to day. By the middle of the 18th century the custom included servants in general and chiefly involved servants being re-engaged by their present employers.

An open space in the village called the Fairstead, now mostly taken up by recent housing development, was used by certain villagers for grazing their animals, and an annual fair was held there in the late spring until the 1960s. The road from the main road to this is still called the Drift, an old name for a drove road.

Botesdale adjoins Rickinghall, and is only about a mile away from Redgrave, so many of its amenities are gladly shared. Villagers enjoy meat killed locally, fresh bread and cakes and the convenience of a fish and chip shop which sells a wide variety of 'take away' food. There is also a general store which stocks nearly everything, a delicatessen-cum-florist, two hairdressing salons and health centre.

Boxford 🐖

Boxford in the past had a population of about 500; most families having lived there for generations, some still living there today.

Although not a large village, Boxford was very busy with many more shops than today. There was a cobbler and a watchmaker who also sold bicycles and sundries, a radio shop, three butchers, two bakers, a general stores and post office, three confectioners, a haberdashery and clothes shop, a grocer and a dairy. Everyone's needs were there on the doorstep. Cars were few and some villagers can remember bowling a hoop and spinning a top in the main street. Their elders walked up the yard to play bowls on the green behind the Fleece.

Boxford also had a blacksmith, a wheelwright, a brickyard, a carpentry shop and undertakers in Kemball House, where the bench and part of the wood lathe and wheel are still in place today. W. B. Kingsbury and Son, the local building firm, employed some 200 men at one time, with skilled local craftsmen, but sadly they ceased trading in 1984. At one time there was a maltings, a brewery, a watermill and a windmill, all of which are no longer in existence.

A vivid memory is the Wall of Death erected in the White Hart yard. The rider was 'Tornado Smith' who was son of the landlord. He had a lion in a side-car as one of his stunts and, when he rode singly, the lion stalked round on the ground. The lion, named Briton, became a common sight walking round Boxford on a chain. He was eventually buried in the front garden at the White Hart and a stone was erected in his memory.

Of course the grand St Mary's church still dominates the centre of the village and the Congregational chapel in Swan Street is still in regular use, but many old cottages throughout the village have been demolished over the years and the large old police station is now a private house.

The Boxford fire engine was manned by local men and kept in what is now the bus shelter. It was pumped by five men on each side and very smart they looked in their uniforms. Cases of beer had to be supplied for every fire! One day in August 1934 the watermill for grinding corn was burnt down. The doctors' surgery now stands on this site. Behind the watermill there was once a wide river in which children swam, canoed and fished, but after the fire this became the small stream it is today.

In the past 25 years the population has trebled with the building of four new housing developments in different parts of the village, but businesses have declined dramatically. There is now a baker, a butcher, a grocer, a newsagent, a post office, a hairdresser, an art gallery, an antiques shop, two garages, a coach company, a haulage company and only three public houses.

Bradfield St Clare ✤

Bradfield St Clare is the central village of three Bradfields, situated five to six miles south of Bury St Edmunds.

Its chief claim to fame is the possibility that this was the site of King Edmund's martyrdom. Tradition has it that he was killed at 'Haegelis-dun' (now degenerated to Hellesdon) and his body taken first to a chapel at 'Sutton'. There is a field in Bradfield St Clare labelled 'Hellesdon' on the tithe map, an ancient site called 'Sutton Hall' where the boundaries of Bradfield St Clare, Bradfield Combust and Cockfield meet, and in Rougham there is a house and street called 'King's Hall', all within a few miles. This theory is supported by documentary evidence that in the days of Bury abbey the cellarer paid rents for two small pieces of land; the 'Aule de Saint Clarisbradfield' and 'Suttonhal', suggesting that the abbey venerated two sites connected with his martyrdom.

With the Norman Conquest came the St Clare family, who added their name to the village. Their manor occupied the moated site of St Clare Hall, which dates from the 13th century.

North of the church is another small moat which is believed to have been the site of a retreat for the monks of the abbey. Until the 1870s the rectory was situated there, until a large Victorian house was built near the railway bridge.

The original dedication of the church was to All Saints, but at the time of the Reformation the use of dedications lapsed, and when they were resumed the village assumed that it was dedicated to St Clare because of the St Clare family. It is the only dedication to her in England.

The Bradfield woods are very well known to naturalists and are of national importance. They are part of the original woodland and belonged to the abbey. Part of them is still known as 'Monk's Park Wood'. They are noted for their rare flora and fauna, including nightingales. Part of the woods is now owned by the Suffolk Naturalists Trust. They have been continually worked and coppiced in the same way for 700 years. Until very recently, they provided wood for the rake factory at Little Whelnetham for the production of rake handles, scythe handles, broaches for thatching etc.

The village today is sadly no more than a hamlet although it still retains its parish council and an active lively church. There is no school, no pub, no shop and buses on only two days a week. Everyone has to go to Bury St Edmunds to work and therefore must have their own transport or share lifts. There are several farms in the parish which do not employ extra labour, with the exception of the extensive fruit farms which provide welcome part-time work for many women in the parish.

Bramford ✒️

Bramford is a village north-west of Ipswich, separated from the urban sprawl by the new A12–A45 link road. The main London–Norwich railway runs through the village but the station was unfortunately closed in 1955.

There are two attractions for today's visitors, a picnic site by the river Gipping, and a watersports park created from old gravel workings, where enthusiasts learn to canoe or windsurf. The picnic site is very picturesque, with 14th century St Mary's church standing on the opposite side of the river. The church is composed chiefly of Suffolk flint, but traces of Roman fabric can be found. A great feature of the church is the 13th century stone screen of three arches, which marked off the chancel for use by the monks in the early days.

Barges used to ply the river from Ipswich to Fisons factory and on to Stowmarket, stopping at Bramford mill to unload corn. The walls of the old lock are still to be seen. A favourite pastime of children in those days was standing on the old wooden bridge to watch the lowering of the barge funnel, and running across to the other side to watch the funnel rise again. The old wooden bridge was replaced by an iron one in 1904. In the floods of 1939 the iron bridge was washed away. Several residents can recall the day, as school children, they were to be taken across the bridge in an old tumbril, but the horse stopped and refused to go. The next minute the whole bridge disappeared.

The main thoroughfares are Ship Lane and The Street. Ship Lane derives its name from the old Ship inn on the corner of Church Green, a beautiful timbered house dating from 1499. The old flint school was built in 1860. This is now the home of the Bramford uniformed organisations.

On Cock corner is the old Cock public house, with many exposed beams and very low down from the road. Further along the street is the Angel, but years ago Bramford boasted six public houses, and there was a ditty about three of them:

'The Cock that never crew,
The Elm that never grew
The Angel that never flew.'

The other three were the Raven, the Elm and the Ship. When the Ship inn, in domestic use for many years, had its plaster overcoat removed to expose timber framing (for conversion into flats) it revealed a pair of 18th century children's shoes, a larger shoe and a spur.

The Street still has many original houses, and modern shops where most of the daily needs can be obtained. The old village lock-up can still be seen beside the British Legion. Behind the Street is Cherryfields, a modern building with accommodation and housing for the elderly.

Legend has it that the 16th century part of The Gables, standing at the south-eastern gateway to Bramford, is haunted. Both present and previous owners testify to a 'presence' in a north-facing bedroom where a teenage servant girl is said to have been murdered by the squire and her body thrown into the river Gipping. Despite ample central heating, the room is constantly cold and occasionally the sad presence moves through other rooms in the old part of the house, leaving the occupants chilled, though not fearful.

Brandeston ✿

To the newcomer, the village of Brandeston seems spread over a wide area, as there are two main roads leading through the village with the playing fields between, often on winter Sunday mornings echoing to the cries of supporters at village team football matches.

On the lower road is situated the parish church of All Saints, built in the late Middle Ages. It contains a 13th century font. This is important because in the 13th century, supposedly due to colder and wetter weather, there was an outbreak of a virulent form of influenza in East Anglia, from which many skilled, highly trained people perished, among them stone masons and craftsmen.

In the churchyard can be found the grave of Nicholas Revett 1720–1804. He made a distinguished contribution to the history of 18th century landscape gardening. Among his many commissions was the design of West Wycombe Park, Buckinghamshire, for Sir Francis Dashwood.

John Lowes, 1572–1646, the unfortunate vicar of Brandeston, was accused of witchcraft by the Witchfinder-General Matthew Hopkins, and subsequently hanged at Bury St Edmunds.

To the left of the church prolific bird life can be observed over the river, which meanders through the fields. Situated in that direction is the cottage 'Lots Hole', that was once the abode of Margaret Catchpole, where she lived with her uncle. Later when she was in service at Ipswich, she stole a horse so that she could ride back to warn her lover, the smuggler Will Laud, that he was in danger of capture. Soon after she was caught and sentenced to be transported to Tasmania, from where she sent her former mistress at Ipswich a present of a stuffed lyre bird.

On the right of the church, Brandeston Hall was built in 1543 on the site of a Norman manor by Andrew Revett. The family continued in occupation till 1809. The building is now an independent boarding and day school and is a preparatory school for Framlingham College.

In 1813 the Queen's Head inn was opened and is still today a focus for the life of the community. The village hall is constructed from a First World War army hut and is the venue for many village events. The beautifully designed wrought iron entrance gates were made at the village smithy, still in working use today.

The village mill was burned down in 1893, and now only the name survives in Mill Lane. There, can be found the thriving post office and shop. Brandeston is considered a very healthy place to live, the older members of the community leading active happy lives many years after retirement age.

Brandon ಏ⁀

Brandon is 16 miles from Bury St Edmunds and six miles from Thetford in Norfolk, and the population is roughly 8–9,000, with a third of these being senior citizens. There is a mixed complex of housing, bungalows and large council estates as well as two industrial estates. Brandon itself has a variety of shops, banks, estate agents, a post office and a large supermarket with good parking space. There is also a new paved over shopping precinct which is the Market Square and the market is held here every Thursday and Saturday.

Brandon was first used as a gun flint centre during the height of the Napoleonic Wars, when over 200 flint knappers were employed at workshops throughout the town, the skills being handed down in famous knapping families such as the Snares, Fields, Edwards, Carters and Bashams. A skilled knapper could produce 300 gun flints per hour. Unfortunately the trade was not without its pitfalls and hazards to health as knappers could catch a disease caused by inhaling the fine silica dust where workshops were badly ventilated.

The trade went out of fashion in the mid 19th century when the percussion gun was adopted by the army, although they were still shipping orders to the Far East and South America as late as 1930 and more recently the interest has been renewed by historical societies, especially in the USA.

A lot of the old buildings have gone due to replanning and delapidation, but the oldest part of Brandon was originally the site of the Remembrance Playing Fields. This was recently excavated and found to be an Iceni village – they found actual markings of the houses, several items of adornment such as pins for clothing and a part of a very small cross, all of which went to a museum in Ipswich and then eventually to the British Museum. The village itself was ringed by water with a bridge going to it.

Brandon Park was originally built by Edward Bliss in 1826. The estate itself has roughly 2,500 acres; along with all this came the title of lord of the manor of Brandon and Edward Bliss became High Sheriff of Suffolk in 1836. He also had the old mausoleum built so he could be buried within its ground. This was duly carried out on 17th March 1845, and in

1859 his wife was interred there, but unfortunately their remains were removed earlier this century and put in the local churchyard in Brandon. Because of this Edward Bliss is said to return on Christmas Eve and ride up the drive of the old manor house. The next owner of the Park was a Baron Baretto, a rather odd character who collected human skulls.

The present day owners are the Suffolk County Council and Forest Heath Council and it is now a country park. The house has been restored and is privately owned and run as an hotel.

Bredfield 🎐

The village of Bredfield, like Caesar's Gaul, is divided into three parts. At one end of the long Street the houses cluster round the pump which stands at the centre of the crossroads. The pump, a notable feature, is surrounded by a handsome wrought-iron canopy with gilded crown on top which was put up to celebrate the coronation of Queen Elizabeth II in 1953. The canopy was made at Bredfield forge, where since 1919 the Pearce family has created beautiful gates and other wrought-iron articles which have made their name known across the world. At least one elegant shoe-scraper has found its way to a Royal doorstep.

At the other end of the village is the green, once much larger but built over during a period of expansion 200 years ago. Some of the cottages are coloured traditional Suffolk pink. Along the road lies the pond which once supplied water for this end of the village; nowadays Bredfield has main drainage – but no gas, even though a 24 inch pipe carrying North Sea gas runs under the parish.

Not far from the green is an old Quaker burial ground, the earliest known to have been 'given for this purpose' in Suffolk.

Dominating the centre of the village stands St Andrew's church. Its fine flint-faced 15th century tower contains a regularly rung peal of six bells. On the other side of the road is the Castle inn, which has served as the 'local' since the early 19th century. The shop and the school are sadly now closed. However the school, an attractive Victorian building, is being converted into a house, and a new community shop has been opened in a Portakabin at the village hall.

Bredfield is mentioned in the Domesday Book. Flint and Roman articles have been found in local fields, and a fine Bronze Age axe-head is lodged in Ipswich Museum. Remote and lonely at the edge of the parish are traces of a medieval moated house site, known locally as 'Bredfield Castle', and nearby crop markings show the sites of two post mills.

Its best-known 'son' is the poet Edward Fitzgerald, who was born at Bredfield House in 1809. His most famous work is his translation of the *Rubaiyat of Omar Khayyam*, and on his grave, a mile or so from Bredfield, blooms a rose; the original cutting from which it was grown came from the grave of the Persian poet.

The village has changed little since 'Old Fitz's' day though Pump

Close, a group of houses near the crossroads, has been built on the site of a blacksmith's and wheelwright's shop. Near the Castle is a smaller group known as Robletts. On Robletts Meadow nearly 400 parishioners celebrated the defeat of Napoleon in 1815 with a meal of boiled beef and plum pudding, and in the Second World War a searchlight unit was based there. The field's name dates from the 16th century.

Brettenham 🐝

A lane shaded by tall trees leads into and through the village. Formerly an estate village, it was a close-knit farming community, at one time self-sufficient with its own mill, butcher, wheelwright, carpenter, blacksmith, district nurse, parson, school teacher, policeman, dressmaker, sexton and undertaker, and presided over by a paternalistic squire at Brettenham Park manor house.

The Wenyeve family had guided the fortunes of the estate from the early 1700s until 1830, when it entered an unsettled period, coming up for sale several times between then and the end of the century. A brief moment of historic importance occurred when, about 1834 (and in rather mysterious circumstances) Joseph Bonaparte, Napoleon's brother, lived there for a time.

Sir Courtenay Warner, who eventually settled there, gave the estate over 50 years of stability. The estate owned most of the farms for miles around and almost all of the 90 or so houses and cottages in Brettenham. The Second World War brought changes but basically the old village life continued until the mid 1950s when, like a bombshell, the announcement came that Squire Warner (by then Sir Courtenay's grandson) had decided to sell up and move away.

St. Mary's Church, Brettenham

While everyone wondered who would be the new squire, news of the estate's impending sale reached the headmaster of Old Buckenham Hall, a boys preparatory boarding school in Norfolk. He was looking for new premises, his own having been destroyed by fire. He acted quickly and acquired the 'middle 70 acres', including the H-shaped Elizabethan house, before the estate went on the market.

Over the years, amenities acquired by the school have been shared with the village. To those who join the relative clubs, the heated outdoor swimming pool, tennis and squash courts are available. In term time the tiny congregation at the 14th century church of St Mary is swelled by boys from the school, with their choir and organist. Old Buckenham School employs a staff of about 50, many of whom either come from or live in the village.

There is now no primary school, no public house, no shop or post office, all of which is a pity. Brettenham is not on the tourists' itinerary, but those who live there find it a peaceful and pleasant place where they can share in its progress towards a new identity.

Brightwell

Brightwell, meaning bright or clear spring or well, is a small village on the old Woodbridge to Felixstowe road, just to the south of Martlesham. One source suggests that it was one of Suffolk's holy wells, said to have healing powers for ophthalmic problems. Bronze Age barrows in the north are part of a chain built across Foxhall to Waldringfield.

The village is centred around a wooded valley where Mill river flows east, then south-east to Kirton creek and the river Deben. The old vicarage, built about 1830, now known as Brightwell House, looks over the valley from the south with the church opposite on the north hill. The church is dedicated to St John the Baptist and its beauty lies in its simplicity and the furnishings made by local craftsmen. Both the church and the churchyard are well cared for. It dates from about 1300 and was extensively repaired in about 1656 by Thomas Essington, of Brightwell Hall. There are two pathetic but beautiful monuments in the chancel commemorating two of his children – Thomas, who died in 1656 aged five years and Anna, who died in 1660 aged 17 years.

Brightwell Hall was extensively altered and rebuilt in about 1663 by its new owner, Sir Samuel Barnardiston MP, leader of the Suffolk Whigs and a deputy Governor of the East India Company. His family hatchments are in the church today. The Hall was demolished in about 1755. Terraces mark the parterres and garden walks still.

At the bottom of the valley the stream formed a 'splash' or ford, with a pedestrian walkway on one side. The bridge and road were built in the late 1920s, curving past the old smithy. A painting of the church and village by John Constable, painted in 1828 or 1829 but looking much as it does today, was rediscovered in Essex in 1980.

Many tons of sand were removed from the hill behind the village hall in the 1960s for use in building Felixstowe docks. Another link between the village and the port is the choice of the name *Brightwell*, in 1986, for a powerful new tug.

Several folk have heard of a ghost who rides through the valley with his head under his arm . . . but no one admits to having seen him. A more recent reality was the discovery in July 1983 of the body of Mrs Diane Jones of Essex in the north of the parish, an unsolved murder to this day.

Brockley ✤

Brockley is a parish and scattered village seven miles south of Bury St Edmunds. The population in 1981 was 273 and it now seems settled at that level after an increase in building in the 1970s. This was the first increase since the population decline of the mid 1800s; the 1841 census showed a peak of 380.

It has retained its character of a farming area over the centuries, and still has a number of old farmhouses that are listed buildings. The most notable historic building is of course the church of St Andrew, an Anglo-Saxon foundation belonging to the Abbot of St Edmunds. The present building dates from the 13th/14th century and the tower was added in the 16th century. In the churchyard is the base of a Tudor cross. The population centre was then probably at Pound Green near the church and Hall, but later expansion moved to the higher common land now known as Brockley Green.

Close to the village green, the Baptist chapel was built in 1841 on land given by Mr R. Bevan, a local wealthy landowner. Also on the green stood what must have been a landmark for many years, a windmill for grinding corn, first recorded on a map of 1824. Unfortunately it was demolished in 1930. It spent its last years with only two sails, and a stationary steam engine for use in calm weather. Nearby the building that was the Six Bells became an alehouse in the early part of the 19th century. In 1868 it was sold to Edward Greene, brewer, of Bury St Edmunds, and later became part of the Greene King empire. It was closed in 1988, a great loss to the village.

The village has recently lost another asset established by the White family in 1924, the village shop and petrol filling station. A post office still exists and fortunately the village still enjoys the benefit of a well equipped village hall, built by communal effort in 1978/9, and where all the present social events are centred.

Most local industry was formerly connected with farming, with such trades as wheelwright, blacksmith, miller, carpenter, etc. Now there is an agricultural engineer, car repairer, and plant and coach hire. Brockley is a small community able to keep in touch with all its residents and not seeking any great changes in the future. An eagerly awaited event is the delivery every quarter of the village newsletter, the *Brockley Seasons*, produced and issued free to all residents by the Community Council.

Brome & Oakley 🌿

The villages of Brome and Oakley, which have been linked ecclesiastically for 300 years, are spread out along two roads, half a mile south of the river Waveney and four miles east of Diss. They contain a good collection of old cottages and farmhouses, which until 1925 formed part of the estate of Brome Hall. There has been some sporadic modern building, but the villages have so far been spared large developments.

The two churches of St Mary's Brome and St Nicholas' Oakley, have, for over a thousand years, stood on their present sites. There are memorials to the Cornwallis family who were closely involved in part of the history of France and the establishment of the United States of America. St Mary's church is considered to be an outstanding example of restoration work by Thomas Jekyll. It also has one of the largest collections of work by the Suffolk sculptor, James Williams, 1798–1888. The distinguished portrait painter Henry Walton is buried in the churchyard.

Thomas Cornwallis built Brome Hall in 1590. It is still possible to trace the outline of the old Tudor garden. The Cornwallis family continued to live there until 1823, when it was sold to Matthias Kerrison, the father of General Sir Edward Kerrison, of Waterloo fame. The outer wings of this vast house were demolished and the interior altered, giving it an Elizabethan shell with a Victorian interior. It was finally demolished in 1960 and a new house built on the site.

With the closure of the primary school in the early 1970s the opportunity was taken to purchase the building and with much local effort to convert it into a village hall.

Oaksmere is a beautiful house set in spacious grounds, where the famous 'Dancing Ladies' – a yew hedge – encircle the lawn. This was originally the rectory for Brome and is now an attractive hotel with plans for a leisure centre.

Almost opposite is the Old Curacy, again originally a church property now privately owned, a thatched house of great character dating back to 1540.

Next to the village hall are the Cornwallis Cottages founded by the Cornwallis family as almshouses and continuously occupied since Tudor times.

The post office and village shop have gone but the shops in Eye and Diss are only three miles away, without the parking problems of the bigger cities.

Bromeswell 🌿

The village was first mentioned in the 1086 Domesday survey. Its name probably derives from the broom bushes, of which there are many in the area, and also from the large number of wells in the village, several of which are still used today.

The church still retains its 12th century archway to the entrance. St Edmund's has a hammerbeam roof, to which are affixed figures of angels and heraldic shields. The originals were destroyed by Cromwell's men but the angels were restored using plastic replicas in the 1970s. There is a 15th century font, and a rare Flemish bell.

Bromeswell is a rural community and once had three farms, but now there is only one. Other employment is to be found in two garden nurseries, and a business growing and supplying willow for cricket bats, and also rushes for thatching.

There was a village cricket club until 1939. The chief amenities today are the nearby golf club and the village hall. The village has no road lights nor shop but there is a public house. All roads are narrow and there is no public transport, so cars are essential.

The footpaths through and around the village are walked regularly and thus kept open to the public. The common was registered by the parish council, and now also possesses a flourishing nature reserve. There is also an attractive private fishing lake.

Villagers are kind and helpful and it is a friendly place in which to live, also scenically it is most attractive. Each year the WI hosts a Harvest Supper for the residents and this and the annual church fête are the only communal functions in the hamlet.

Bucklesham 🌿

Bucklesham, near Ipswich, lies immediately to the north of the Seven Hills interchange, on the A45 to Felixstowe and the A12 (north) to Woodbridge and Lowestoft. A screen of young trees has recently been planted between the village and the dual carriageway. Mill river and its tributaries flow through the area, on to join the river Deben at Kirton creek. It passes through farmland at Bucklesham Hall and on to the mill. One history records that in 1466 the mill was used for bleaching cloth, which had been woven locally. By 1930 it was no longer used for corn and in 1934 was adapted to become a pumping station supplying water to Felixstowe.

'Bucca's Ham' or settlement retains much of its rural atmosphere in spite of some modern housing developments. The Domesday survey of 1086 records a small wooden church which was replaced with a more substantial building in about 1250, and almost entirely rebuilt in 1878. St Mary's retains some old features: a fine door at least four centuries old, a 14th century octagonal font and the bell, later recast as a peace thanksgiving after the First World War.

On the church wall there is a memorial to 'John Steele, churchwarden 1822' who, like St Paul, was suddenly converted to Christianity. He'd had a very bad reputation and was a frequent visitor to the Shannon public house, where he would batter down the door with his pony's hooves. Before his death he preached and worked to reform those men he had previously led astray.

The Shannon was named after Sir Philip Broke's ship, which won a famous battle fought against the Americans at Boston in 1813. At times the pub has also served as a post office so that the classic excuse 'just off to the post' was accurate. The Shannon is still popular today.

The village post office and shop closed in 1990 and is sadly missed. It is a strange comparison with 150 years ago when the place boasted a shoemaker, shopkeeper, butcher, victualler, blacksmith, corn miller, farmers, wheelwright and undertaker, as well as domestic staff and dressmakers.

There is a resident molecatcher still. One farmhouse is now a riding and livery centre, another a comfortable bed and breakfast establishment. Other people commute to a wide variety of work in Ipswich, Felixstowe and around. The playing field supports two football teams for regular fixtures.

The listed buildings also include The Forge, a timber-framed, weatherboarded thatched cottage from the 17th century. Hill House was built late in the same century around an earlier core, and its barn had been built about 100 years before. There are other interesting houses, from the unique Gothic Cottages and Potash House and Cottage, where perhaps 'pot ashes' were originally burnt for use as an early fertilizer, to the modern residential developments.

Today the people of Bucklesham are concerned about the proposed new village settlement on the Felixstowe peninsula which would encroach upon the village and alter its character, although they appreciate the need for new homes.

Bungay 🐝

Bungay is a small market community situated on the border of Norfolk and Suffolk with a population of approximately 5,000. It is very attractively sited, with a lovely common, around which the river Waveney sweeps in a large loop. Bungay still retains and has done certainly for a thousand years, a Town Reeve and Feoffees, the only such ancient office in England today.

The castle, now a ruin, built by the Earl of Bigod in 1165, stands just behind the shops in the main street. It can be visited, as can the museum which is located in the council offices. The Butter Cross in the Market Place is surmounted by the figure of Justice without blindfold and holding the scales (like that on the dome of the Old Bailey in London). This is a well-loved landmark. Present day Bungay has a market held at the Butter Cross each Thursday.

There are four churches, Holy Trinity, St Edmund's, the United Reformed and St Mary's, the largest, which is now redundant. There are five schools; one of these is the High School which evolved from Bungay grammar school. There is a library, a new fire station, and the Mayfair Cinema is the last privately owned cinema in the Waveney valley.

In August 1577, during the morning service at St Mary's, a terrible thunderstorm occurred. Two men lost their lives in the belfry and many parishioners were injured. In the midst of the storm a large black dog, thought by worshippers to be the Devil and believed to come from Blythburgh, bounded into the church. In 1933 a weathervane was erected on the site of the old town pump to commemorate this happening, the design of which was the result of a competition for local schoolchildren. In 1688 the town was practically destroyed by the Great Fire. Rebuilding during the 18th century created the gracious terraces of houses that can be seen in several streets.

From an early date point-to-point racing was enjoyed by many visitors to the common, the course boasting two grandstands. This amenity ended after the Second World War. The common was also the venue for various air shows from the 1930s.

The wherries used to come up the river from the sea via Beccles to the staithe and many people regret that the river is not now navigable as in previous days. In 1860 the railway was brought to Bungay, connecting Tivetshall and Beccles. Unfortunately this track was taken up exactly a century later. The site of the track now forms the basis of the bypass.

The largest employer is Clays Bookprinters for the World. Nurseys Sheepskins is an old established family firm which has celebrated 200 years of business. There is a small industrial site on the outskirts, but many people travel to work in the surrounding area.

Bures 🦋

The village of Bures nestles in the valley of the river Stour on the edge of Constable Country – a community united yet divided since it lies in two counties with Bures St Mary on the left bank in Suffolk and Bures Hamlet on the right in Essex, roughly half way between Colchester and Sudbury.

Bures St Mary has the church and Baptist chapel, junior school, cemetery, post office, village hall and playing fields, all of which are shared and supported by the Essex side. Bures Hamlet has the station on the single-line railway linking Sudbury to Colchester and the main London line.

A very early settlement, it was probably a lake village built up on sticks on a slight rise about a mile upstream from the present village. Legends abound, and in 1405, it is said, there appeared 'a dragon vast in body with a crested head, teeth like a saw and a tail extending to enormous length' which breathed fire and killed (and cooked) a shepherd and his sheep. Attacked by the men of Bures with arrows which just bounced off it, it swam downstream, disappeared in the reeds and was never seen again.

Bures 'history' begins on Christmas Day AD 855 when, it is generally believed that the Saxon king, Edmund the Martyr, was crowned at the age of 15 in the chapel of St Stephen on the site of the stone building now known as Chapel Barn, standing alone, surrounded by fields. For a time Bures, then known as Burna, was the capital seat of East Anglian kings.

The river, during the 18th century, was improved – locks and tow paths were made up and it became the main means of transport, the last barge going through as late as 1913. After the heyday of river traffic came the railway, opened in 1850. The late 19th and early 20th centuries perhaps saw Bures at its busiest – brickworks, gas works, maltings, mill, tannery, blacksmiths and saddlers, now nothing but memories, while the eight hostelries have dwindled to three.

Bures still has its watermeadows; the river provides a home for ducks and stately swans, the heron and the cormorant. It is sometimes a turbulent mud-filled stream and sometimes a quiet, hardly moving mirror reflecting every tree and every reed which grows along its banks. One can still walk through bluebell woods in spring and find footpaths through the fields which surround the village and each year the cuckoo calls in May. People come and settle and become part of the community. The small shops are family owned and shoppers can enjoy the personal service. Maybe it has almost become a dormitory village, a relatively quiet oasis in a country of throbbing motorways and fast-growing conurbations, but it is very much alive.

Burstall 🐝

Five miles south-west of Ipswich lies the village of Burstall, alongside the peaceful valley of the Belstead brook.

Burstall is mentioned in the Domesday Book but its main claim to fame is a connection with Cardinal Wolsey. In 1528, Henry VIII granted the manor of Harrolds in Burstall to the Cardinal to help finance Wolsey's college in Ipswich, a project which never progressed beyond the gateway which still stands in St Peter's Street, a reminder that ministers of the crown fall out of favour. A persistent tradition hereabouts has it that the coat of arms found over the mantelpiece in Mulberry Hall was placed there by the Cardinal in an effort to show his loyalty: so did he ever live or visit there?

Its houses today cluster around one main street which snakes down the hill to the Half Moon (until 1977 the village pub) rising then into open fields before dipping down to the hamlets of Burstall Hill and Flowton; a surprisingly hilly part of Suffolk, this. Many of these houses have been built in the last hundred years. Older residents remember a village where nearly all the men worked on the land, where you fetched your water from a well (one was where Wellend House now stands and another opposite the Old Schoolhouse), and where you managed without electricity (the clock tower next to the village hall seems to have been built to house the equipment which produced acetylene gas for the hall's lighting). The children attended the village school (closed 1958) and Sunday school in the church, villagers sang in the church choir (and probably in the Half Moon too), played bowls on a crown green behind the hall, joined the youth club, or the men's club, or the WI.

A few small businesses exist here today: a watchmaker, a gas engineer, a property manager, a cattle haulier (a family concern for the last 50 years) and the village post office and shop. Although there is neither gas nor mains drainage, that is a small price to pay for the space and serene countryside surrounding us.

Villagers insist that there is still a community spirit, and this is reflected in the recently erected village sign, standing on a swathe of reclaimed grassland newly planted with shrubs and trees. This bears the coat of arms of Henry VIII and three enamelled pictures: St Mary's church, the Cranfield Memorial Hall and the clock tower. Three significant buildings, but the church is the pulse of the village. Fluted pillars give it a dignity unusual for a small village church and recent restoration work has revealed the medieval beauty of the chapel behind the carved screen of the north aisle.

Butley 🐚

The original village was a settlement on the field north of the church and was destroyed by the Black Death in 1349. The common graves of the victims lie to the north side of the church.

The Gatehouse of Butley Priory (now a beautiful private residence) was founded in 1171 by a Suffolk man, Ranulf de Glanvil, who was chief minister to Henry II. The Reformation saw the destruction of the monastic buildings, but Thomas Cromwell spared the renowned Gatehouse and its great 1320 armorial. During the 19th century and until 1923 the priory was used as the vicarage. St John the Baptist, the beautiful parish church, was built in Norman times. However, an earlier church was mentioned in the Domesday Book. The tower is 14th century but has much earlier foundations.

Butley has one village inn, the Oyster, named no doubt when Butley was famous for its oysters. (In recent years the oyster beds have been restored and are well known in neighbouring Orford.) The inn is older than its Georgian/Victorian facade would have you believe, and can trace part of the building to the Elizabethan period. It is noted for its good beer, food, and country singers.

The original water-mill was recorded in the Domesday Book and stood about one and a half miles from the site of the current one. In 1536 it was removed to the present site and has been in the hands of the Hewitt family for the past six generations. The mill was driven by an under-shot water wheel as are most Suffolk mills. These days it is all run on electricity but is still a working mill. The mill house (separate from the mill) has a remarkable Regency porch which would grace any Brighton villa.

Not all the area is given over to agriculture, and the famous Staverton Thicks with its deer park, and Butley Clumps are part of the landscape. The former is a remarkable oak woodland mentioned in the Domesday Book. The wood still called the Thicks has large areas of ancient pollard oaks and holly trees growing alongside which are as tall as the oaks. The oldest recorded trees now growing in the park date from 1540. Mercifully most of the Thicks survived the hurricane winds of October 1987. A public footpath skirts the Thicks so a walker can see the park without entering.

The clumps were planted in 1790 by the Marquess of Donegal who was then living at the Gatehouse and wanted to beautify the approach to his house. This was an avenue of trees planted in clumps of five, consisting of four beeches in a square with a pine in the middle. The technical term is a quincunx. The idea was to create a woodland without spoiling the view. Winds have brought the ancient beeches down, and though replanted they will take many years to mature.

People seem to live to a great age in this district, the most outstanding being Mr William Cooper Large, a wheelwright, carpenter, builder and undertaker. He lived to be three months off his 100th birthday. He was on the parish council for 57 years and became chairman at the age of 97. He could recall Butley having at the end of the 19th century two working smithies, two bootmaker's shops, a tailor's shop, three carpenter's shops, three timber saw-pits and two general stores. They have all gone; modern Butley, alas, has no shop at all.

Buxhall 🐑

Buxhall is a quiet village four miles west of Stowmarket, sprawling over 2,560 acres of fertile land, with many miles of roads connecting farms, houses and cottages of varying age from Tudor times to the present.

Although the population over the years has remained constant, at about 450, village life has changed considerably. There is no longer a shop, post office or school, but still a pub, the Crown, a disused mill, a Primitive Methodist chapel, and a parish church.

St Mary's is a fine 14th century church, with a font of the same age and fragments of 15th century glass in some of the windows. Its strong, square buttressed tower houses six heavy bells of mellow tone, considered to be among the finest in Suffolk. Groups of numbers on the tower arch are thought to have been scratched by 16th century campanologists.

The Flower Service in June is traditional, with hymns unique to Buxhall, when children bring bunches of flowers for distribution to the elderly. Many years ago, when families were large, huge quantities of flowers were sent by train to London's East End.

Buxhall Mill was once a majestic working tower mill, belonging to the Clover family, but in 1929 a terrible gale destroyed its sails, which were never repaired. For many years afterwards the mill was in use with a hammer-mill driven by diesel, until the owners transferred the business to Stowmarket. However, Buxhall mill, a listed building, still towers on the sky-line as a silent reminder of its former glory.

Buxhall Vale is the home of Charles Freeman and family, whose mother Lady Winefride, of the Fitzalan-Howard family, was born at Arundel Castle and lived at Buxhall Vale until 1987.

The rectory was built in 1710 by Rev Thomas Hill, one of a long succession of rectors and lords of the manor named Copinger, Hill and Copinger-Hill. When the rectory became empty, the late Misses Rhoisia and Bridget Copinger-Hill, twin nieces of Rev Henry Copinger-Hill, who were born at The Whalebone, Buxhall, began a long struggle to prove it belonged to their family. The building is being extensively renovated, renamed Copinger Hall, and will be occupied by members of the Copinger-Hill family.

Yesterday's mixed farms provided the main work for men. Women worked as domestic servants. There were usually three maids, a cook and two gardeners at the rectory. Today, there is a dairy herd, but farms are mostly arable with small amounts of stock. A craft shop also sells delicious refreshments, and a farrier works at the forge where for many generations there has been a village blacksmith.

There is an ancient wood, Pye Hatch, and many footpaths, some of which have been freshly sign-posted. Years ago, the numerous fields and meadows had names. Bloody Meadow was supposed to have been the scene of a vicious fight between two harvesters armed with scythes who, legend has it, cut each other's heads off!

Capel St Mary 🎴

Many villages in Suffolk have changed over the centuries but none so dramatically, during more recent years, as Capel St Mary. Where there used to be sheep grazing in green fields and a few cottages spread out along the village street, there are now large estates of modern houses; where once a wealthy Roman invader built his villa and more recently the stones of a post-mill ground corn, now stands a council estate. Where once stood the Victorian men's reading room-cum-village hall converted from part of a much older rectory barn, now stands a nearly completed new rectory house. Where once the two-lane motor traffic was halted for the Bentley to Hadleigh railway level crossing gates, now a six-lane highway streams with traffic bound north and south on the A12, cutting the village into two until the recent opening of a much needed underpass; and where once 600 souls lived out the trials and tribulations of their rural existence, now over 3,000 inhabitants reside in a thriving, socially active and very caring community.

Care has been taken to integrate old and new residents and many improvements were accepted as the bonus of careful planning. Roads were given old Capel field names to retain links with the past and services like mains water, gas and sewers were the first priorities to be installed ahead of actual building. Gone at last were the septic tanks and privies. Modernity had arrived along with street lights, a new, modern village hall, a complex of essential shops, a large up-to-date surgery, a library – and on the newly acquired playing field, tennis courts, bowling green and sports pavilion. It took several years for the community to re-establish its new identity, but 'Capel Garden Village' as it was then called has lived up to its name.

Many stories of past residents survive; the case of one who died by 'spontaneous combustion' defies belief, whereas the sad event when the Victorian national school was struck by lightning, killing many of its young pupils, is well documented. John Constable sketched cottages here, his father Golding Constable having owned land in the village. Some medieval farmhouses and cottages survive the march of time, evolving with the changing uses demanded of them. The oldest building is, of course, the church which – dedicated to St Mary the Virgin – gives the parish its name, Capel being translated from 'capella', meaning chapel. However, the remaining fragments of machinery from the Domesday water mill at Churchford must be the oldest reminder of the invisible past.

Carlton Colville

The village of Carlton Colville is about three miles west of Lowestoft. Over the last 20 years it has grown to the extent (with a population of 3,000+) that it is virtually a suburb of Lowestoft. It dates back to at least Saxon times. Until after the Second World War the village was predominantly agricultural with numerous farms. Only Bell Farm now exists as an entity.

The church of St Peter has a very long history – as long ago as 1473 one Matthew Belynegham desired 'to be buried in the church of St Peter of Carlton'. It was extensively rebuilt in the late 19th century and the remains of two earlier buildings were incorporated into it. At the present time it is well attended and recently new church rooms were built attached to the church.

In 1884 the church of St Mark (now in Oulton Broad) was built to serve the growing population in the east of the parish, which at that time extended to Mutford Bridge at Oulton Broad and as far east as Kirkley

Run in Lowestoft. The parish of Oulton Broad was created in 1931 and so Carlton Colville reverted to having just one church.

Opposite the church is Carlton Hall, which was built about 1740 on the site of an earlier house destroyed by fire in 1736. The parish registers up to that time were also lost in the same conflagration.

In Chapel Lane, across the fields from the church, is Hedley House – a large mansion in extensive grounds. At the present time it is a well-known hotel and caravan park. Next door to it is the East Anglian Transport Museum, nationally known for its road transport collection.

Nowadays the village has three public houses – the Crown on Beccles Road and the Bell inn and the Old Red House in The Street. Until about the turn of the century there was a fourth – the Ship – also on the Beccles Road. In 1932 the Old Red House was the first building in The Street to have electric light. In bygone days a Billy Harper kept this hostelry and is remembered also as the village chimney sweep, charging one shilling a chimney and the same to whiten the ceiling! A previous owner of the Bell inn ran a pony and trap service taking, among others, fishermen and their bedding rolls to join their ships in Lowestoft. He also had a fish-curing smoke house at the back of the pub.

At its northern part the parish runs to the river Waveney and Oulton Broad. It is recorded that in 1800 the poor of Carlton were allotted marsh land (formerly glebe land) which gave an income of £100 per year. This was distributed to the poor as coal during the winter, a practice which continues even now as help with heating bills for the poorer folk. Nowadays a large part of the marshes is Spratts Water Nature Reserve, managed by the Suffolk Trust for Nature Conservation.

Cavendish ᘒᕰᕲ

Nowadays, if Cavendish is known at all to the outside world, it is through the picture of the church, the green and the almshouses which has appeared on countless jigsaw puzzles and calendars, unfortunately without royalties.

The amphora (earthenware jar) which was dug up here in 1958 is proof that the Romans passed this way, and the long straight stretch of the High Street may be a remnant of one of their roads superimposed on a muddy track on the banks of the Stour. Whether or not they left a settlement behind them, there was certainly one in Saxon times.

One occasion when the village emerged from the mists of history was in 1381, during the Peasants' Revolt, when the leader Wat Tyler, as depicted on the village sign, was killed at Smithfield by John Cavendish, son of Sir John Cavendish, lord of the manor and Lord Chief Justice of England. Sir John was hated by the peasants and when they caught up with him, after a chase, they beheaded him in the marketplace at Bury St Edmunds. Sir John bequeathed £40 to Cavendish church – sufficient in those days to rebuild the chancel, substantially as it is today.

If legend is to be believed, Elizabeth I, even if she did not sleep here, probably passed through, as the brass lectern in the church is said to have been her gift. In the 1650s St Mary's was visited by the fanatical and infamous Puritan, William Dowsing, who smashed the stained glass windows and mutilated the font, in pursuance of his self-appointed mission against 'graven images'.

Besides the church, rebuilt in its present form between 1300 and 1485, there are several notable buildings – the Old Grammar School and the Old Workhouse, both now private houses; Pocky (Smallpox) Hall, once used as an isolation hospital; Nether Hall, surrounded by the vineyard which produces Cavendish Manor wine; the well known almshouses on the green, known as 'Hyde Park Corner Cottages'; and the Sue Ryder Home, headquarters of the Sue Ryder Foundation and home of Lady Ryder of Warsaw and her husband Group-Captain Leonard Cheshire, VC – besides many cottages dating from the 15th and 16th centuries, some with thatched roofs.

Apart from these landmarks and the farms on the outskirts, the appearance of the village has changed considerably in the last hundred years, with the addition of modern housing, a decrease in shops and local industries and a tendency for those of working age to commute to local towns. The school only caters for children up to nine, and the village has lost its local policeman and railway station, but there is still a post office and a doctors' surgery.

There is strong local patriotism, though perhaps not so strong as in the 19th century, when football was played up and down the High Street, with large numbers on either side from Glemsford and Cavendish and no rules, usually ending in a pitched battle.

Charsfield ❧

Listed in the Domesday Book as 'Caresfield', Charsfield is a small village of some 400 people. The village is situated near one of the many tributaries of the river Deben called Potsford brook, known locally as the 'Black Ditch'. The rich and fertile Deben valley attracted settlers from Roman times and earlier and by the time the Norman conquerors arrived it was part of the most densely populated area of Britain.

Farming has always been one of the principal areas of employment for inhabitants, with fruit farming predominating. With modern agricultural methods and mechanisation this has meant that fewer people are required to work on the land. The blackcurrants are mechanically picked but the apples and pears are still hand-gathered and provide a useful source of seasonal employment. Many inhabitants of Charsfield now go much further afield for their employment.

Faced with the threat of closure of the school recently the villagers combined together to mount an energetic and vociferous campaign to save it. Their success was all the sweeter for the fact that the school has gone from strength to strength. The schoolchildren enjoy taking part in village affairs and have given entertainment and pleasure to parents and visitors alike when they present their Nativity play or give a display of country dancing at the annual church fete in the vicarage garden.

Charsfield's best known resident is probably Mrs Peggy Cole. Mrs Cole took the part of the mother in Sir Peter Hall's film *Akenfield* based on the book of the same name written by Ronald Blythe. Mrs Cole was presented with the village sign used in the film which now stands proudly outside her house and welcomes visitors to her garden. This beautiful and interesting garden is open each summer from May to September and up to the beginning of 1990 Mrs Cole had raised over £34,000 for various charities both local and national.

The village has both a Baptist chapel and a Norman church of St Peter. The lives of these two institutions run for the most part side by side, occasionally coming together in friendship and harmony at times such as Rogation when the whole benefice comes together to ride around the local farms on tractor-drawn waggons, afterwards enjoying 'tea and buns' in one of the village halls.

Despite or perhaps because of the naturally occurring changes in the village as people move in and out, life is never dull. Charsfield may be situated near a tributary of the river Deben but it is not and never will be a 'sleepy backwater'.

Chattisham ✣

Chattisham, the sister village to Hintlesham, is smaller and well off the major roads. Its lovely old 14th century church, All Saints and St Margaret's, small and intimate, has recently been tastefully renovated. Its registers date from 1559, and it still has some old brass.

Chattisham has had a strong element of nonconformity in its history. Rev John Meadows was ejected from his living and brought before the Sessions three times for his nonconformist principles. The Wesleyan chapel built in 1817, although still standing, has been converted into two dwellings.

In the 1640s there were witch hunts and Chattisham did not escape the terror. Mary Bacon, a married woman, was hanged and Nathaniel Bacon, her husband, was said to have sealed a covenant with the Devil in the shape of a 'rug dog', and to have received from Mother Skipper two imps which he suckled at his breast.

In 1864, Thomas Haward rebuilt the present Chattisham Hall, which had been fire damaged, for his bride, Anna Lot. The old Chattisham Hall stood on the site of Chattisham Hall Farm, and was at the latest a Tudor building.

Almost opposite the road to Hintlesham is a charming thatched property which, sometime after 1864, caused something of a scandal when a sign was erected over the door – Chattisham Ale Stores.

Corner Farm, now very much altered, had a cherry orchard behind it. The owners had enormous problems with birds eating the fruit. They put jangling bird scarers in the trees and tied lengths of string from them to their toes in bed, so that they did not have to get up with the birds in order to frighten them off.

Another very old house is Charity Farm. During renovations it was discovered that part of it was built in the 14th century. Alterations disclosed ancient oak beams and leather thongs holding the wattle palings. The earliest records found date back to 1581, but in 1699 it was appropriated to the endowment of the lectureship of Dedham grammar school. The lecturer was allowed to let the house according to his discretion and thus help support himself. From this comes the name Charity Farm.

Many of the picturesque old cottages have gone and the village is a mixture of old and new. Although it shares its public house and shop and school with Hintlesham, there is a friendliness and sense of community that people associate with living in a village.

Chediston 🐝

The 2,500 acre parish of Chediston (sometimes shortened to 'Cheston'), is two miles west of Halesworth. The finding of Roman pottery of about AD 60 and traces of buildings provides evidence of early Roman occupation.

Although a church is mentioned in the Domesday Book, the present church of St Mary, probably on the same site, is of Early English origin. The register dates from the year 1630 and the square tower contains six bells but unfortunately these are no longer able to be rung as a new frame is needed. It is hoped that remedial action will be taken. The building is well cared for and has several features of interest: a 14th century oak chest, a Jacobean pulpit, traces of wall painting, a 15th century font, and of particular recent interest a well restored Commandment panel which is believed to date from the 18th century.

Henry Smith, a prosperous London merchant, visited several country villages during his lifetime and in his will of 1627, he directed that the poor and aged of 109 parishes he had visited should receive a yearly gift of food and clothing. Chediston was one of these parishes and until about 1970 its annual share was around £10. This has now risen and yields several hundreds of pounds. A further major source of income (£5,500) was derived from the sale of the Claxton almshouses and invested in the Charity Commission. After the sale, the almshouses were demolished, but a bungalow built on the site retains the original external features and blends in quite well.

There was a village common or green, about half a mile west of the church but this disappeared between 1880 and 1900 (there is no record of its annexation in the parish records). At one time Chediston Hall estate comprised around two thirds of the area of the parish. The old Hall, once the home of the De Lacroix family was damaged by fire in about 1950 and demolished. A new modern building was built in the 1960s and the estate is now owned by the Aldous family.

Chediston Grange is a moated site dating back to the 13th century and has been farmed by the Burroughes family since 1955. The late Harry Burroughes, his Suffolk Punches, and a large collection of horse-drawn implements, were well known locally and he was featured in the writings of George Ewart Evans who published books on horses and oral traditions.

The Gregory family, fruit and vegetable farmers of Ash Farm on the green, employ a number of casual seasonal workers and they offer 'pick your own' facilities which draw many people to the village.

Inevitably over the years the face of the village has changed with the loss of the shop, pub and school and a decline in the number of people employed on the farms. Chediston has however acquired new life, attracting a basket maker, potter, furniture maker, wood carver and sculptress. A prize winning crime writer and many artists live in the village and it is hoped that with the newly restored church room, exhibitions and sales will be held to illustrate the wealth of talent alive and flourishing in Chediston.

Chelmondiston & Pin Mill 🐚

The parish of Chelmondiston, standing on the main Ipswich to Shotley road, includes the hamlet of Pin Mill nestling by the river Orwell. The evidence of stone tools found in the local fields shows that the area has been inhabited for thousands of years.

The village is well provided for, having a post office, newsagent and butcher, all of which sell a wide variety of goods, plus hairdressers, Chinese takeaway and fish and chip shop, boat builders and boat chandlers. A bus service to Ipswich caters for those needs which cannot be supplied by the village. There are also three pubs, three places of worship and a primary school. St Andrew's church and the primary school are both fairly new, a doodlebug having demolished the previous ones in 1944.

Older villagers recall times when the community was even more self-sufficient, having its own flour mill, coal merchant, forge, undertaker, shoe repairers and two carriers whose names were Last and Late! Grain and coal for the steam-powered mill were transported to the village in large steamboats which moored in Butterman's Bay and off-loaded their cargoes into lighters for delivery ashore.

The character of Pin Mill has changed little over the years. It is well known as a beauty spot and for its sailing. It is home to a thriving sailing club, and though there are now fewer working boats, there has been an enormous increase in the popularity of leisure boats and the summer

The Butt & Oyster at Pin Mill

months bring a throng of sailors from all parts of the country and the continent. The best known event of the year is the Annual Barge Match organised by the Pin Mill Sailing Club.

The National Trust owns a stretch of woodland beside the river, known as the Cliff Plantation, and though there was damage to numerous trees in the gales of 1987, there are some beautiful walks giving fine views up and down the Orwell estuary.

Arthur Ransome, the author of *Swallows and Amazons* and other children's adventure stories, spent a lot of time at Alma Cottage, Pin Mill. He had boats built at Harry King's boatyard, and his famous boat the *Nancy Blackett* was kept at Pin Mill. The plot of his story *We Didn't Mean to Go to Sea* begins there and his character, Miss Powell, was a real local resident.

Sailors from all over the world seem to have heard of the Pin Mill pub, the Butt and Oyster. Its first licence was issued in 1553 when licensing started. Here the river water laps against the pub wall at high tide, and a large bay window gives views of the river. It is easy to imagine the smugglers of past centuries planning the landing of their contraband goods. Tales of smuggling abound in the area bordering the estuary. It was these same shores which harboured the rats blamed for the outbreaks of plague earlier this century, believed to have been the last in this country. The last deaths were in 1918 and it is to be hoped that such a disease will never return.

Chelsworth 🐝

Much water has flowed under the little double humped-back bridge at Chelsworth since Julian Tennyson, great grandson of Sir Alfred, Poet Laureate to Queen Victoria, discovered 'a perfect village of my own finding', during a tour of Suffolk in the lazy hazy days preceding the outbreak of the Second World War – the war that would claim him as one of its victims.

Now, more than 50 years later, the village, still nestling cosily in the valley of the Brett, remains much as it was then, with well kept timbered houses and thatched cottages, set mostly on the north side of the half mile of one street. Only the daily round of the inhabitants has changed.

Farm workers no longer gather outside the pub after their midday meal, for five minutes of comradeship and local gossip, before mounting their cycles and dispersing to the four farms. Young men now set off early in the day to the factories, workshops and offices of Sudbury, Hadleigh and Stowmarket, whilst the lone farmer tills the soil of his prairie-like acres, with huge machines which cannot be taken on the road without due warning.

Once a year everyone works overtime to make their little bit of England presentable for Open Gardens Day, an annual event believed to be the forerunner of many similar days in the locality. It helps to bring in the thousands of pounds needed to keep the little Norman church of All Saints in good repair, alas with only one bell now. In 1746 the other three were sold to raise money to repair the steeple. A local wag composed the following limerick:

'The churchwardens and parson of Chelsworth
Said, "What is our fine peal of bells worth?"
When the answer was told,
They at once had them sold,
And we now have but one bell at Chelsworth.'

Though much has changed, much remains as it was, and to many this small village is one of the magical places of Suffolk.

Chevington 🐝

The village of Chevington lies about halfway between Bury St Edmunds and Newmarket on the ancient pathway from the abbey at St Edmundsbury called Chevington Way.

It lies on the edge of the great Ickworth Park estate and for many years the lords of the manor of Chevington have been the Hervey family. The name of the village derives from Cifongas, the name of an early Anglian tribe. The surrounding countryside is pleasantly undulating with plenty of trees, and hedges surrounding small fields. It is traditionally part of

Britain's corn growing belt but the cereal fields are now interspersed with bright yellow fields of oilseed rape. The proximity of Newmarket ensures the influence of the racing fraternity, and thoroughbred horses are much in evidence in beautifully kept paddocks.

In medieval times the parish was under the authority of the Abbot of St Edmundsbury who had a hunting lodge at the manor near the church. Following the Dissolution of the Monasteries the lands passed into secular hands, although from mid Victorian times a family of great influence in the village were the Whites, three of whom were rectors of the parish, covering a span of about 150 years. On the death of the Rev John White III it was written in the *Bury Press*, 'The name White spells Chevington'.

There are a few early buildings in this rather scattered village including a fine 12th century church of All Saints, which has an interesting medieval south porch and which was built on the site of a much earlier church. There are also several thatched cottages dating from the 17th century or earlier, and Chevington Hall which is built on a much older site and has the remnants of the moat still around it. Until recently the round base of the medieval windmill stood on a site near the Greyhound public house, but unfortunately it collapsed during renovation and a modern house now occupies the plot. The miller's thatched house still stands on the adjacent site.

The Victorian village school is now closed and the children have to be transported to a neighbourhood school two miles away. During the 19th century there was a clothing factory which gave employment to several villagers but this closed in the early part of the 20th century and the buildings have been incorporated into one of the local farms. There is no longer a local industry apart from agriculture and horse breeding, and most villagers, and the in-comers who enjoy the rural life, travel to the surrounding towns for employment. Village life today centres around the one remaining shop-cum-post office and the village hall.

Chillesford 🐚

The tidal river of Butley only a mile away across the marshes does not seem to have brought trade to Chillesford, but the fine windmill standing on rising ground acted as a good landmark for small craft coming up the river from Orford. The windmill suffered the fate of many mills and was destroyed by fire. One winter night the villagers heard cries of 'fire' and on looking out beheld the great sails 'turning in the breeze like wheels of fire'. The last windmill (strictly speaking a wind-pump) fell victim to another element when it was washed away by the devastating East Coast floods of 1953.

The ancient brick and tile kiln was working until the First World War. Many of the old houses in the area testify to the strength and good colour of these bricks. Recently the clay pit has been reopened to supply clay to the nearby Aldeburgh brickworks.

The only other village industry was the decoy in the woods behind the Froize Inn. This was run on a commercial basis with a man enticing ducks down a tunnel or pipe from the pond. This tunnel narrowed like an eel trap and, with a dog to discourage escape, the birds were caught and had their necks wrung. These days decoys are only used for ringing; there is one at Nacton near Ipswich.

The church of St Peter stands on a good site, a high knoll just outside the main village. The small church is 12th century but the tower is part of an older building. The bricks in the tower are thought to be Roman.

The village inn has suffered a very checkered history, starting life as an inn in the early 18th century, though part of the building is Tudor. It was called the Froize Inn, an unusual name thought to be after a kind of pancake much favoured by the monks of Butley Priory. It fell into disrepair and became two cottages called Decoy Houses, but the inn was reinstated in 1981 and given its original name.

The principal activity is agriculture, and there is a flourishing riding school. The village wasn't always the peaceful sunny place it is now; it once had a reputation for smugglers (the Butley river being close at hand) and poachers. It still has a small post office and store thanks to a local benefactor.

Clare ﹏

Clare was a medieval wool town on the Suffolk/Essex border. In the great days of the wool trade it was one of the most important towns in Suffolk. Because of this, many great houses and buildings such as Nethergate House were built and can still be seen today. Another fine building is the Ancient House, built in 1473, which has an example of pargetting (local plasterwork) on the exterior. Today the building is a museum, open during the summer months, showing local historic exhibits.

Clare Castle once dominated the landscape and in the 14th century was a grand building with a household of 250 persons. At the end of the 15th century the castle passed to the Crown and was no longer used as a residence. It soon fell into ruin and many of the timbers were used in other local buildings. In 1863 the Great Eastern Railway line was built through the bailey. The station was closed just over 100 years later in Dr Beeching's cuts. When the weighbridge was installed at the station a number of skulls were dug up, along with a cross, which can now be found in the British Museum. Now the castle grounds form a country park.

There were once 13 public houses in Clare; one was in the churchyard, which was very handy for the bellringers once their work was over! Now Clare can only boast five public houses, but it does have its own brewery which makes Nethergate ale. The aroma along High Street sometimes has men diving into the nearest hostelry! The Bell Hotel, once the Green Dragon and then the One Bell, used to make candles at the rear of the premises and tinkers came from all over Norfolk to purchase them to take back to sell.

Clare Common has been dated from the Iron Age. In Roman times it was an important border fortress between the kingdoms of the East Angles and the Saxons. The common is now used as pasture and allotments and is administered by the trustees of Clare Combined Charities.

Clare Priory was formed in 1248 by the Austin friars until its dissolution by Henry VIII in 1538. The building remained in private hands until 1953 when it was handed back to the Augustinians. The building now used as the church was once the infirmary.

Clare has grown over the years with the building of estates at Highfields, Westfield and Clare Heights and now has a population of over 2,000. The community spirit is very evident and with over 50 organisations there is always something for people to do.

Claydon 🐝

The village of Claydon is situated four miles north of the county town of Ipswich on the old Ipswich to Norwich/Bury St Edmunds road. The river Gipping flows through the village and is the boundary with Great Blakenham for a short distance.

Horse-drawn barges used to travel from Ipswich to Stowmarket passing through a series of locks, one of which was in Claydon near a humped-back bridge, so designed to permit horses to draw barges underneath. The bridge was replaced with a less hazardous type after water-borne traffic ceased to operate commercially on the river. The river itself was diverted when the Claydon/Stowmarket bypass was constructed, and yet another bridge was erected for road traffic.

Sadly, St Peter's church, on the hill overlooking the village, was declared redundant from 30th September 1975 and many of the furnishings and valuable items were removed to Barham church and that church renamed 'St Mary and St Peter' on 30th March 1977 – the fine organ was despatched to a third world country. The ensuing years saw a measure of vandalism whilst the authorities were endeavouring to sell the property, but the Redundant Churches Fund took over in the end and have restored the masonry, windows and roof to an acceptable standard.

A village blacksmith's shop was located on the main road near Paper Mill Lane for a considerable number of years, where it was an everyday sight to see horses being led through by farm workers, one man often leading two animals to be shod. Children gathered to watch the skilled farrier make and fix the shoes and even enjoy the aroma from this process, whilst the horsemen took advantage of the wait to catch up with the local gossip. Solid fuel wash-boilers of the day, commonly known as 'coppers', were frequently taken to the blacksmith for him to repair with a metal patch.

Chalk was excavated from a site in Church Lane by the Garnham family for generations and taken by horse and tumbril to their Paper Mill Lane premises for processing. There, chalk blocks were neatly arranged on shelves, lime slacked and sold for mixing with cow hair to produce mortar and whiting, purchased for treating ceilings. Chalk and lime was supplied to farmers from the Church Lane site, by horse-drawn and mechanical transport until recent times, but the premises are no longer in operation.

Two public houses have graced the village throughout the century, the Crown inn which had a thriving bowls club attached to it for many years and the Greyhound inn which boasted an active quoits club for a goodly time.

Cockfield 🐓

'But where is Cockfield?' said the irate motorist, having followed numerous signs all plainly stating the way to Cockfield and all pointing in different directions. Where indeed! Cockfield is in effect a group of eight hamlets each identified by the name of a green although some of the actual greens have almost disappeared. These hamlets are in an area of intense agriculture, the boundaries of which are approximately three miles apart in any direction.

Cockfield is lucky enough to retain its school, its church, the general shop and post office, and a very fine village hall, and perhaps because of this inhabitants feel a loyalty to this elusive 'Cockfield' as well as to their own particular green.

Cockfield began its existence as 'Coccas Field' and was mentioned in the Domesday Book where its biggest claim to fame was the existence of a mill. This mill only functioned in winter – presumably due to lack of water power in summer.

In the 19th century Cockfield was a prosperous agricultural community with a variety of artisans to support the farming life. There were carpenters, blacksmiths, a carrier, a butcher, a grocer and baker, a draper, thatchers and last but not least several publicans.

Great Green is the largest green – big enough for two football pitches, a pavilion, a children's play area and a pond. Adjoining the green a small estate – Dukes Meadow – was built in 1982 whose inhabitants have added greatly to the continued success of Cockfield as a community. On the opposite side of the green to this is a small estate of beautifully kept council houses. The pub is still there and further along on what was 'happy Sam Mortimer's meadow' is the garage.

A few hundred yards down Chapel Road is Birds Lane and at the end of this is Colchester Green. There is not a lot of Colchester Green left – most of it being incorporated into adjoining land.

Further along Chapel Road – originally called Muddling Lane – is Parsonage Green, a small verdant triangle which sports a beautifully carved village sign and a wooden seat won by Cockfield in the Best Kept Village contest of 1985. One of the houses bordering the green was a general store and draper's and on the third side of the triangle is the Old Rectory. Cockfield rector, Dr Babbington, was the uncle of Robert Louis Stephenson who often stayed at the rectory and is said to have written *Treasure Island* while on one of these visits – perhaps being inspired to write about Long John Silver by Peg Leg Brinkley, the local roadman.

Adjacent to Parsonage Green is a thatched house, now called 'Dormers', which was the village workhouse and had the 80 ft deep village well in its garden.

The next green is Cross Green. It has many old houses and some long established families still live there.

Windsor Green is a long, thin green now scarcely more than a wide grass verge. In 1950 there were 17 dwellings, a smallholding, a kennels and two farms. Until 1952 the only water supply was from ponds and a pail and chain well.

Along the road to Lavenham was Smithwood Green. This is still a small community of houses and also a chapel built by voluntary contribution. Unfortunately Smithwood Green has disappeared – probably under a now disused airfield which was built during the Second World War for the USAAF.

Opposite Smithwood Green on the left hand side of the Lavenham Road is the Three Horseshoes public house. This is one of the oldest buildings in Cockfield probably dating from 1470 and a small cluster of houses has built up in this area although it does not have its own green.

Last of all is Buttons Green, down a road also on the left of the Lavenham Road. This is the prettiest green. It has a pond, some thatched houses and small farms.

So there we have it – just a flavour of the Cockfield which the irate motorist found so elusive.

Coddenham 🦢

Coddenham is a relatively unspoilt village, part of which is a conservation area. It is within easy reach of the coast and railway station, and near main roads to London and Norwich, making it a popular place in which to live.

The Romans had a settlement called Combretonium, later to become the Saxon 'Coddenham' which was an important administration and transport centre with a fort near the present hump-backed bridge. The Domesday Book shows 75 houses and nearly 400 inhabitants. There are timbered pink-plastered 15th century houses, one being the present post office. Another is Gryffon House, once said to have been the home of an archer named Wodehouse, knighted by Henry V at Agincourt. There were several inns in the village, one being part of the Old Lodge next door to the post office.

The beautiful old church of St Mary has 13th century flint and stone walls with a 14th century tower with clock and bells, and angels under canopies in the hammerbeam roof of the nave. A richly carved alabaster crucifix is believed to have belonged to a local nunnery 300 years ago.

There is a story of a Father Ignatius who in 1863 paid a visit to Coddenham church which was three miles from where he was in residence at Claydon. He found the doors barred against him and was also refused admission when he went to the rectory. While walking through the village he came upon some men building a house and they asked him to lay a brick. This he did and it is to be seen to this day.

The village school closed some years ago. It was originally built by Lady Gardemaux for poor boys and girls, and a trust was set up which still exists today, and is used for the benefit of the village. The population has decreased since the last century and is now around 600. Many of the old families have disappeared as have most of the small shops. Farming is no longer the main occupation and only a small number of people work locally. Others travel to Ipswich and the surrounding area for employment, and some commute to London each day.

Combs

Combs is a large parish with an area of 2,900 acres and apart from the estate at the Combs Ford end, the parish is very scattered. In 1934 much of Combs was swallowed up by Stowmarket when the civil boundary was moved. Much of the farmland has been sold to developers and there are new housing estates where once was grazing land or cornfields. The latest development is on the church meadows and a cornfield which local people called the 'hundred acre field'.

'One Church at Combs' was mentioned in the Domesday record of 1086. The reason for the church's isolated position was its proximity to Combs Hall which was demolished in 1756. The present building belongs mainly to the 14th century when great families, such as the Thorpes, the Uffords and the Willoughbys were lords of the manor. St Mary's church is as rich as any in the country with its fine medieval stained glass. The glass suffered greatly when much of it was blown out as a result of a gun-cotton works explosion in 1871. Many fragments were replaced with great skill in 1952.

Situated behind the church is Combs Wood, an area of superb beauty recently made a reserve by the Suffolk Wildlife Trust. This was mainly due to a rare British breeding bird, the Hawfinch, taking up residence.

Combs Tannery was started in 1711 by an Irish family called Denny. It was later sold to the Webb family. In the early days the leather was made into harnesses for horses and leather belting was sent to India for machinery. It is interesting to note that in the Crimean War, leather was sent to Russia for boots for both armies and elephant hides called 'gin' leather went to Egypt. A new method using bark for tanning, was introduced here. The Tannery closed in 1990. Cottages in the village that were built for the workers are now privately owned.

The Webb family started the model farm with its own distinctive entrance of wrought iron and bell tower. The farm once had 30 employees, it now has four.

The village primary school was built by the church in the 1800's, and all the pupils lived in the village. Children now attend the Combs primary and middle schools which are built on Combs churchland within the Stowmarket boundary. The former Combs Ford primary school is now a community centre, the venue for many social activities.

At one time there were eleven working farms. Three remain and of these, Fenn Farm, owned by Mr V. Scarffe, has expanded from 42 acres to 375 acres and a freezer and electrical applicances business is connected with the farm.

There are three public houses, the Live and Let Live has closed, the Gardiner's Arms and Punch Bowl remain open.

Joe Rowe, Harry Rowe and Eddie Morphew, a thatcher, are all in their late eighties and have lived in the village all their lives, and another local celebrity is Nurse Fenn, who was a popular district nurse for 26 years.

The village sweet shop, post office and butcher's are part of a bygone age, today's population consists mainly of commuters, who work in the surrounding towns.

Coney Weston ❧

Coney Weston is a small rural village in the north of the county close to the Norfolk border. Its present population is about 330. The land is a mixture, being heavy clay to the south, sandy breckland to the north and fen in the south-east.

The name Coney Weston has nothing to do with rabbits (although there are plenty of them here) but is derived from the Norse 'Konungs' (Kings) and the Saxon 'tun' town and appears in the Domesday Book in 1086 as Cunegstuna (Kings town). The 'West' crept in by a reference in 1326.

The ancient Peddars Way passes through the parish and it is thought that the existing road running north to south between the church and the village is the old main route from Bury St Edmunds to Norwich.

The small church of St Mary is of the Decorated style of the mid 14th century. Its nave roof is thatch on the original scissor truss roof and fortunately, from the maintenance cost angle, the tower fell in 1690 and was not rebuilt. The church stands nearly a mile outside the present village.

The appearance of the village seems to have changed very little from the 17th century when most of the listed houses were built, until the

Second World War when the whole village was engulfed by the USAAF aerodrome known as Knettishall. Most of the village was within the camp boundary and several groups of huts were built in the village.

In 1988 the population of the village was doubled by a boundary change which officially incorporated the Swan end of Barningham into Coney Weston. It was a logical move as that outlying settlement of Barningham was a mile from the main village and was right on the edge of Coney Weston village centre.

Although the shop is gone, there are still six farms, a builder's yard, a pub, a hairdresser, a joinery works, a curtain factory, a sawmill and timber yard, a game farm, an hotel and restaurant, two nurseries and a telephone exchange. These enterprises between them provide employment for about 120 people. For recreation, there is a playing field, a village hall, a bowling green and a fen managed by the Suffolk Wildlife Trust.

The parish council are striving to get the village given conservation area status in the new local plan as the village street looks almost exactly the same as it did in old photographs of 1900. They are anxious not to spoil the look of the village whilst encouraging it to thrive in every other way.

Copdock & Washbrook 🐑

Copdock and Washbrook is perhaps the longest named village in Suffolk, but a name the inhabitants soon get used to saying. They are in fact two separate villages and there is fierce loyalty to the 'side' on which one lives – but an even fiercer loyalty to maintaining the full title – Copbrook or Washdock or, horror of horrors, Copwash simply won't do.

The rural villages of Copdock and Washbrook have almost doubled in size over the last 20 years and in the last ten an area of Washbrook contiguous with the Ipswich boundary has become a vast suburban estate, causing a lot of political problems as urban interests come into conflict with rural ones. The joint parish council has had to try to balance these diverse interests.

The village school survives and flourishes in its 19th century building, the Brook inn does good trade with both the locals and an increasing number of outsiders and the village shop, created from a new council house some five years ago and still supported by grants from the parish council, continues to serve mainly the less mobile of the population. The building of Copdock Mill Tesco (within Washbrook parish boundary!) is an obvious attraction for shoppers with transport.

The two villages each have their own church, both of them a good half mile away from the centre – Copdock St Peter's, the younger of the two, high on the hill and Washbrook St Mary's, most likely founded in the 10th century on a pre-Christian centre of worship, down in the valley. Sadly, the declining church congregation has resulted in the handing of

Washbrook church over for redundancy. Washbrook also has its Baptist chapel, loyally supported by a small but devoted congregation.

The building of the Bentley Wood spur road (the 'new' A12) in 1984, bypassing the London Road, brought peace and quiet to most of the inhabitants, though some on the high ground can now hear the noise from elsewhere. As the Department of Transport was unwilling to pay for an official opening the villagers opened it themselves at six in the morning, with the local dressmaker cutting a till roll with her scissors and a maroon rocket fired off by the chairman of the parish council. We have now got used to hearing again the birdsong and the conversations of neighbours.

Cotton 🐑

Cotton is a parish of 1,921 acres situated in Mid Suffolk between Mendlesham and Bacton, Finningham and Gipping/Old Newton. It is largely agricultural as far as land use is concerned, though few of the 550 inhabitants are employed on the land. It is a scattered community, the church being at the western edge of what was probably a large block of common land stretching eastwards to where the village hall is now built and north to the Stowmarket–Finningham road.

Village life probably continued with less change between Domesday and the second half of the 19th century than in the succeeding years. First came the railway from Stowmarket to Finningham and later on to Diss and Norwich. The railway was axed by Dr Beeching in 1966. The school was opened in 1875 and closed in 1964. At one time there were three public houses, a post office and general stores, a shop attached to the Trowel and Hammer public house and a butcher.

The local planning authority has kept a tight control on building. In the 1920s and 1930s building was only allowed within 60 yards of drinking water unless a private well was sunk. In more recent years building has not been allowed within the village 'envelope'. The late 1980s saw a small building boom which has brought many new people into the village, but has failed to provide housing for local youngsters, a situation compounded by the sale of council houses.

The present Cotton Town Lands Trust, the proceeds of which are divided between the church and the elderly of the village, seems to be a remainder of the sale of the town/village lands or common lands, together with the sale of the land on which houses for the poor had been built, the proceeds of which were invested for future use. Unfortunately the rectory was burnt down in 1932 and many records, including those of the Trust, were lost.

St Andrew's church is Cotton's greatest treasure. It was built in the 14th century in the Decorated style with a clerestory added in the 15th century Perpendicular style. It is large for such a small village, aisled and built of flint. The porch is beautifully decorated, leading to the important and magnificent south door. There is a double hammerbeam roof decorated with carved angels. The pillars, particularly on the north side, lean alarmingly, but are evidently kept in balance.

Cratfield 🦃

Cratfield is a small village situated in the north of Suffolk. The population is under 400; services are basic – mains water, electricity and talk of main sewers in the near future.

St Mary's church is an impressive building of flint, partly Decorated and partly in the Perpendicular style. It has a fine chancel roof. The last full peal of bells was on 14th June 1930, when 5,040 changes were rung. Thereafter ringing gradually ceased because of weakness in the tower. With permission a small group of people provided new ropes and with oil and grease and some minor repairs have got the bells going again. The church has one of the finest rings of six in the county.

South of the church is the Town House, once the guildhall of St Edmund, then used as almshouses and now a weekend house extensively modernised inside. There are about 150 houses, ranging from the 16th century to the present day. Farm buildings are chiefly large and modern but three old wooden barns are still in use.

There are a few areas where wild flowers are conserved, including the bee orchid, ragged robin, campanula, etc. On the whole the farmers are conservation conscious. Trees have been planted along some road verges and an increase in winter crops has made the prospect in winter much greener and the acid yellow of fields of rape brightens the spring. A few embarked on 'prairie' farming but at the top end the owner of Linstead Farm uses modern machinery and technology while conserving and developing the countryside's natural features. Trees and hedges have been retained or replanted, ponds created or restored. There is one small organically farmed market garden. Agriculture is mainly arable, with one fairly large orchard and a nursery. Livestock is chiefly horses, pigs, a dairy herd, chickens and turkeys.

Most houses are owner-occupied, although a few tied cottages remain but not necessarily rented to farm workers. There are ten council houses. The Victorian school, three other pubs and the Town House have all been turned into private dwellings. Planning permission for new houses is very limited.

The village shop has now closed leaving just the public house, the Poacher (to which the shop was attached); the nearest shop is situated in the village of Laxfield, some four miles away.

The Cratfield Town Estate Charity is administered by three ex-officio trustees (the vicar and two churchwardens) and six other representatives elected by the parish council. The monies are divided equally between the church, public purposes and the poor.

Creeting St Mary 🐚

Creeting St Mary is part of the land once settled by Craeta and his people; Creeting St Peter is still a separate parish but Creeting St Mary, Creeting All Saints and Creeting St Olave, three different parishes, are now consolidated under the name of Creeting St Mary. The sites of the other two churches are known but nothing remains of the buildings. Materials from the church of All Saints were used to enlarge St Mary's, which stands on high ground overlooking the Gipping valley.

Other changes in more recent times have been the closure of the village shop and post office and one of the two village public houses. The former rectory has been a private school and is now an office complex. The farms, once the main source of employment, now only employ one or two people. The number of houses has doubled in the last 30 years and the village school still educates the children until they are nine years old. The inhabitants, providing they have a car, are well placed for work in a wide radius, for both the A45 and A140 main roads pass through the village. Luckily very few houses are on the routes of these busy roads.

Some local craft workshops and trades have started in the village in recent years and roadwork contractors have their main office and storage on the site of former sandpits. The village hall provides the centre for a number of groups and a social club.

The most notable of past characters was Sally Wood, who continued to live for the rest of her life in the large brick chimney of her cottage after the rest of it had fallen down. She is remembered by the lane which bears her name but the chimney has disappeared.

Cretingham 🐚

Cretingham is a village on the river Deben, five miles south-west of Framlingham and four and a half miles south-east of Debenham.

The river Deben crosses the parish near the church. The church (once named St Andrew's but now known as St Peter's) has a nave with boxed pews, chancel, south porch, hammerbeam roof, magnificent three-decker pulpit and a lofty tower with five bells. When the vault in the chancel was opened in 1826, the skull of Lady Cornwallis, who was buried in 1603, was found perfect, with long plaited hair.

In 1887 the most appalling tragedy occurred in Cretingham. The vicar, Rev William Meymott Farley, aged 73 years, was murdered at the vicarage by his curate, Rev A. E. Gilbert-Cooper. At midnight on Saturday, 1st October 1887 while he lay in his bed, the curate came into the vicar's bedroom and cut his throat with a razor.

The Inquest was held at the Bell inn, Cretingham on Monday, 3rd October 1887 when a jury, composed of farmers and tradesmen of the district, heard the case, which ended in Rev Gilbert-Cooper being charged with the wilful murder of Rev Farley. The *Suffolk Times and Mercury* reported that the curate's conduct was at times very eccentric, he frequently suffered symptoms of the effect of a sunstroke sustained while a lad in India. During the inquest he appeared bewildered and kept repeating that Rev Farley was not dead! At his trial he was found guilty but of unsound mind and it is understood that he was sent to Broadmoor for 40 years where he subsequently died.

In October 1967 a Tudor building, believed to have been a manor house, became the New Bell inn. The name was changed recently to the Cretingham Bell.

The Cretingham village sign is unusual in that it is a mosaic of traditionally cut tesserae set in a wrought iron frame mounted on a twelve ft long oak post, cut at Shrubland Park saw mill. The panel was designed and made by Jessica Costello of Kelsale and the wrought iron work by Hector Moore of Brandeston. The sign depicts on one side a typical Anglo-Saxon agricultural scene, with a family at work with primitive tools. Almost certainly the Vikings (Danes) landed and eventually settled in the area. The other side of the sign shows them sailing up the river Deben with the existing dwellers fleeing in terror.

Cretingham in 1881 had 303 inhabitants – in 1981 there were 175. It still has its church, an inn and a post office/shop, as well as several newcomers; nevertheless, there are some original inhabitants remaining in the village.

Crowfield

Crowfield is a very scattered village, like so many in Suffolk. It lies for the most part along Stone Street and Debenham Road, which as Stone Street's name suggests, form part of a Roman road running from Coddenham to Peasenhall.

Until about 20 years ago the old timber-framed houses were still in the majority, now there is a pleasant mixture of ancient and modern, the new blending in with and not, so far, swamping the old. Particularly pleasing is a small development for the older people, red brick bungalows, mostly off the road and set round a traffic free space.

The church of All Saints is nearly a mile from the main street at the end of Church Road, hidden among trees, with open fields around. But it is well worth the effort of looking for it, as it is an extremely pretty church with a unique timber-framed chancel and a small Victorian bell turret with open work sides, and a 'witches hat' top. There are rough arched braces and a curved beam across the church at the junction of the nave and chancel, which are the twin of those in at least one house and barn in the village.

Although the church is isolated except for one nearby house, which has fortunately been rescued and rebuilt from its former neglected state, it was not always so alone. There is a moated site next to the churchyard which must once have been occupied by a building of some importance; and to the north of Church Road there is an area marked on the map as Crowfield Green. In the middle of the 19th century it consisted of several cottages and allotments.

The village has one public house, the Rose, situated not very handily on the northern edge of the village, but none the less flourishing. Old maps show a Rose inn there 150 years ago so the name is older than the present building. There was another pub – the Bell, but this has long been a private house.

In the days before mains water arrived people collected rain water or got their supply from wells or more likely ponds. There was a pump where the village hall now stands and some ponds had a pump and a filter to help to purify the water. The pond at the corner of Ipswich Road and Stone Street, apparently known as the Jubilee pond, was another widely used source of supply. Legend has it that a horse fell into it and drowned. It probably didn't make much difference to the quality of the water. As Crowfield is built on clay and the land is flat it takes a lot of draining and there are plenty of ponds and ditches, mostly fairly stagnant. It is not really surprising that there flourished an illness known as pond-pox!

Tollgate Cottage housed the collector of tolls on the turnpike road to Ipswich. A small smock mill, still standing not far from the village hall, used to be a pumping mill used to drain the marshes Yarmouth way and was brought from there about 1920 to replace an earlier mill which was burnt down. The sails are long gone, having blown off, narrowly missing the pony sheds, soon after it came here, but a few years ago it was given a smart new smock and cap by its owners.

The name of Clay Cottage (at the Coddenham end of the village) is now the only reminder that nearby was the clay bed where the men of Crowfield once played quoits.

Culford 🌿

The five villages of Culford, Ingham, Timworth, West Stow and Wordwell, approximately five miles north of Bury St Edmunds, form an entity because they comprised the Culford estate which existed for nearly 400 years.

All the villages are mentioned in the Domesday Book (1086), and the known history of two of the five – Ingham and West Stow – goes back well beyond Domesday to pre-Roman times. The Icknield way, an ancient British road, marks the northern boundary between the villages of West Stow and neighbouring Icklingham. There is still a distinct track marking this well-documented route which ran from Norfolk to Dorset. Two Romano–British cemeteries were found at Ingham during the 19th century.

The Anglo-Saxons also left their mark on West Stow – an early farming settlement thrived there between AD 420 and 650. The site was excavated in 1965–72 under the guidance of Dr Stanley West, the Suffolk County Archaeologist. The first house was reconstructed in 1973, there are now seven buildings on the site and the work is continuing. The village, approached through a splendid new visitors centre, is open to the public. The site of the village forms part of West Stow Country Park which was opened as a public amenity by St Edmundsbury Borough Council in 1979 (it had previously been used as the corporation rubbish dump).

Culford has two churches; that in the village proper and another in the hamlet of Culford Heath about three miles to its north. The church of St Mary, Culford in the grounds of Culford Hall was wholly rebuilt with the exception of the tower, in 1857 by Rev E. R. Benyon, the squarson (squire and parson) of the estate. The second church, St Peter's, Culford Heath, was built by Rev Benyon in 1863. It was a chapel of ease for 'distant parishioners' living there. The population of this hamlet has declined and the church is now, sadly, in a ruinous state.

The church of St Bartholomew at Ingham was heavily restored in 1861. Much of the original materials were used in the tower and nave, but the chancel appears to have been rebuilt. The church of St Andrew, Timworth was restored in 1868. The south porch, which is part of the tower, is of 14th century origin. St Mary's church, West Stow was also extensively restored but shows evidence of Norman craftsmanship. The church of All Saints, Wordwell, now in the care of the Redundant Churches Fund, is the smallest of the six churches (it is about 30 ft long) but of great historic interest. It has two early Norman doorways with intriguing carvings in the arches (tympana) above them.

Culford Hall was the seat of the owners of the Culford estate, which in 1873 covered 9,500 acres and comprised the whole of the villages of Culford, Ingham, Timworth, West Stow and Wordwell. The original Hall was built in 1591 by Sir Nicholas Bacon, and it passed in 1660, through marriage, to the Cornwallis family, who remained at Culford for over 150 years.

The estate eventually passed to the Cadogan family in 1889. The fifth Earl of Cadogan greatly altered the Hall which became the stone faced edifice of today – it formerly had 20 bedrooms but latterly had 50. The Cadogan lifestyle, including royal shooting parties, lasted for just over 40 years until the death of the sixth Earl in 1933. Because of death duties and size of the house the estate was sold in 1935.

Over 5,000 acres were sold to the Forestry Commission and named the King's Forest in commemoration of King George V's Jubilee in 1935. The house and park were bought by the Methodist Education Committee, and their school continues to flourish as a co-educational boarding and day school for 700 pupils.

The other important secular building is West Stow Hall, which was a manor (ie a farming community) owned by the abbey at Bury St Edmunds. It was bought by Sir John Croftes in 1519 shortly before the

Dissolution of the Monasteries. He was Master of the Horse to Mary Tudor. It is said that Mary Tudor actually stayed at the Hall. The building has a splendid brick turreted gatehouse built by Croftes which originally crossed a moat. In the room above the gateway are naive Elizabethan wallpaintings depicting the four ages of man, represented by a young man out hunting 'Thus do I all the day', a man embracing a woman 'Thus do I while I may', a middle-aged man looking on 'Thus do I when I might' and a bent old man leaning on a stick 'Good Lord, will this world last ever'. The Hall is still in private occupation and although the main building has been greatly altered the gatehouse remains much in its original state.

The river Lark which runs through West Stow was canalised in the early 18th century and barges went through a series of locks, the remnants of which still remain, en route to its terminus at buildings on the Mildenhall Road, Bury St Edmunds of which the Gateway supermarket now forms part. The advent of the railways tolled the death knell for the canal. The village of Ingham had a railway station built in 1873 on the Bury St Edmunds/Thetford line, this was axed at the time of Beeching in the 1950s.

The main occupations of the tenantry were agricultural for the men and domestic for the women (a large number of servants – mainly women – would be needed to run Culford Hall). The estate did, however, include a brickworks which was near the northern boundary of Culford Park close to West Stow. Bricks were being produced in 1825 when the estate was sold to Benyon de Beauvoir, and their production continued until 1947. The drying sheds for the bricks still survive as does the brickmaker's house, Kiln Cottage. Present day occupations, with the exception of Culford School, are agriculturally orientated. They include forestry, farming and gravel extraction, a saw-mill, racehorse stables, a racing stud, an agricultural seed merchants and a fish farm.

The Forestry Commission continues to own the King's Forest and is increasingly making its woodlands a public amenity. There are three major farmers and gravel extraction continues apace along the Lark valley and at a new site at Timworth.

Ingham has the only public house, the Cadogan Arms, formerly named 'The Griffin' but renamed by the Earl. There are also two licensed clubs in Culford and West Stow. These were built by the Cadogans as unlicensed reading rooms for the tenantry, the two former public houses in those villages having been closed.

There still remain in the villages elderly people who remember life on the estate. Although it was a secure and well ordered existence, no one seems to mourn its passing.

Dalham 🦌

Dalham is a delightful conservation village consisting mainly of flint and thatched cottages, with some large barns well converted into individual homes. The river Kennett passes through the village with several foot-bridges spanning its stream and then runs into the Lark, which joins the Ouse to flow out into the Wash.

Above Dalham, on one of the highest points in Suffolk, stand St Mary's church and Dalham Hall with its surrounding stables and ken-nels. The church is 14th century and, after its spire toppled down in a storm, Sir Martin Stuteville had the spire replaced with a tower, built in 1627. This cost £400, as recorded on a large inscription high above the back of the church, of which the people of Dalham contributed £124 1s 4d 'assisted by the religious bounty of divers barronetts, knights, ladyes, gentlemen and gentlewoemen'. The outside inscriptions on the tower are in Latin facing the Hall and in English, eg 'Keep my Sabbaths' for the villagers! Also on the outside walls of the church are monuments to faithful servants of the Affleck family including a 'punctual poultry-woman'. Near to the altar is a memorial to Sir Martin Stuteville, who lived in Dalham in the 17th century and who 'saw the new world with Francis Drake'.

Dalham Hall was built in 1704 for Bishop Symon Patrick of Ely with orders from the Bishop to build upwards until Ely Cathedral could be seen across the fens on a fine day. This view was enjoyed until 1957 when someone working on the top floor caused a fire and since then the repaired Hall has had only two storeys. The Hall has had a varied history. Wellington lived there for a time and later it was bought by Cecil Rhodes who sadly died before he could reach Dalham. His horse was brought here by his brother, who erected the village hall to Rhodes' memory.

Dallinghoo 🦌

Dallinghoo is a small village situated some six miles from Woodbridge. It forms part of the same benefice as Charsfield and lies approximately one mile south-east of that village.

The original church of St Mary at Dallinghoo was built around 1066 and was served by the monks of nearby Letheringham Abbey. In its original design the tower was situated in the centre of the church but after being struck by lightning in the 17th century and thus losing the chancel, the tower ended up where it can be seen today – at the east end. At the entrance to the churchyard stands a fine lychgate which was erected to commemorate the Golden Jubilee of Queen Victoria in 1887. Exactly 100 years later it was severely damaged in the October gales but has now been lovingly restored to its former glory.

Some of the houses and buildings in Dallinghoo have had a change of use and ownership over the years. The lovely old rectory which stands next to the church is now a private house, as is its more modern replacement a few hundred yards up the road. Moat Farm stands on a hill to the south-east of the village and is a splendid example of Tudor architecture which has been lovingly restored over the past few years.

Dallinghoo school stands some way out of the village and although it is now occupied as two private houses the form of the old school can clearly be seen. It was built between 1845 and 1847 for £600, raised by public subscription, and owes its unusual situation to the fact that it served Charsfield as well. It finally closed in 1941.

Not every village can boast that it contains what was once the smallest parish in England. Dallinghoo Wield is approximately 34 acres in size and forms a border with the neighbouring village of Bredfield to the south-west. At the end of the Wield nearest to its boundary with Bredfield there is the site of a moated medieval manor (immortalised in the name of the public house in Bredfield, the Castle). During the 1981 boundary changes the Wield was merged with the village of Dallinghoo despite local and national protests.

Darsham ✒

The village of Darsham is much larger and more widely scattered than most people driving along the A12, over the level-crossing by the station, realise. For the long ribbon development of houses and a garage form only the outskirts of the triangular-shaped village that stretches eastwards towards Dunwich and Westleton.

Darsham is surrounded by farms and farmland. Today, there are few livestock and the farms are mainly arable, cared for by the farmers and their families with occasional seasonal help. A shop and post office, a working pottery, two inns, a garage and a garden centre, plus the railway station, mean that they are not isolated.

Darsham was an 'estate village', in fact it was a closed village. Everyone worked for, either inside or outside, the two big estates and their owners. The oldest estate was Darsham Old Hall, belonging to the Bedingfield family. It was burned down and rebuilt in 1600. This family became Nonconformist and if you worked at Darsham Hall you had to worship at the Primitive Methodist chapel.

Darsham House was built in 1796 by the Purves family and their workers had to worship at the church. This family and succeeding owners of Darsham House have been great benefactors to All Saints' church, parts of which date from Norman times.

When the 17th century Garden Cottage near Darsham House was purchased by a man who was very tall, the floor had to be lowered as the ceiling could not be raised. Under the hearth, they discovered a Bellarmine jar containing, among other things, human nail parings and an iron nail; these were said to guard against witches.

Not far from this cottage one may meet a ghost – a Grey Lady who glides from the vicarage and by the gates of Darsham House into the churchyard opposite. People who have not previously heard of her have spoken about a glimpse and a feeling of a presence. That part of the Low Road is always cold, quiet, very still. She is not sinister, but one feels a silence and does not linger.

It is said that contraband from the beach at Dunwich was hidden behind the church altar and that the smugglers employed a Jack O'Lantern in Devil's Lane to scare people and keep them indoors.

Today in Darsham the past mingles with the present. There are still young children descended from those who lived in the estate or closed village. The two estates no longer divide the village, and there is a closeness in the community. Houses and cottages are now nearly all modernised and no longer do the men have to draw the water from the ponds and wells for their wives to do the washing while they had a 'pint' at the local. The ponds now provide homes for the ducks and the 'Grey Lady' will continue to give this lovely village a slight air of mystery as it remains hidden from the mad passage of traffic tearing along the A12.

Debenham

Debenham lies near the source of the river Deben amid quietly beautiful valleys, where wild primroses, violets and cowslips grow in profusion and orchids can still be found. The alkaline, heavy, moisture-retaining clay soils give some of the largest yields of barley and wheat in the world. It was here, about 1820, that a farm labourer noticed an exceptionally large ear of barley sticking to his shoe. He planted seed from it in his garden and the following year showed the resultant plants to his landlord, Dr Chevallier. The doctor arranged for the strain to be marketed and emigrants took it to America and Canada. The Chevallier strains of barley have only recently been supplanted by genetically engineered varieties.

Debenham has so many picturesque timber-framed buildings dating from the 14th to the 17th centuries that it was the East Anglian village chosen for Architectural Heritage Year, 1975. It was only then realised how ancient and unspoilt the buildings were and ever since a team has been studying their history. The base of St Mary's church tower has been described as the finest piece of Saxon work in Suffolk.

In 1650 Timothy Abbott moved to Debenham and set up business as a cordwainer. In 1707 his descendants purchased a local grocery store and to this day the same family own and run the shop, now as a small department store. Another resident of the village left and founded a chain of High Street stores which he named 'Debenhams' after the place where he grew up.

In 1824, £110 3s was raised towards buying a fire engine, and a fire station, manned on a part-time basis by men living in or around the village, has existed ever since. The present police station is modern but the original station, built in 1849, still exists and is the earliest purpose-built police station in East Anglia still surviving and possibly the earliest in the whole country.

In the Domesday Book of 1086, mention is made of the fair here. The book refers to more people in the Debenham area than in any other part of Suffolk and Debenham appears to have been one of the most heavily populated parts of the area.

The traditions of Debenham are particularly interesting. Here the East Anglian kings are reported to have held occasional court and Blood Field is so named from accounts of a great battle against the Danes. Excavations on Priory Field have disclosed ancient foundations and a cemetery and from this site have come a great number of Roman and early English coins.

Denham ꧁

Denham (meaning wooded hamlet) is a sprawling village of just under 200 inhabitants. It consists now of mostly arable land with scattered farms and small groups of cottages and houses. It is quite flat, the sky is wide and open, and incredibly beautiful sunrises and sunsets can be seen in all their full glory; in the past this was not possible due to the high hedgerows lining the roads and fields and more wooded areas.

The boundary line between Denham and Hoxne at one point goes down the centre of the main road, at other places off at a tangent; this was demonstrated by a family whose cottage stood in Hoxne and who were then obliged to visit Denham in order to use their lavatory at the end of the garden.

The church of Denham St John is mostly 14th century and was once much larger, including a Bedingfield chapel. The Bedingfield family owned much of the land hereabouts.

At the beginning of the 20th century there were twelve farmers, a blacksmith, a wheelwright, a school, a general shop and a public house, the Green Man. There are now only four farmers and two chicken units, the blacksmith and wheelwright have been replaced by vehicle repair and light industrial works, the Green Man is now a private house, as is the school, and only the shop remains.

The Second World War brought a vast change to the village as part of neighbouring Horham airfield was in fact in Denham, including the base hospital. The previously quiet roads were filled with American Air Force jeeps dashing up and down, the air was filled with the thunderous roar of aircraft. The Green Man would be filled to overflowing on the days following a delivery of beer, whilst it lasted.

Several of the buildings still remain, the old wireless station is a private house and another which was bought by a local farmer and given to the village was finally refurbished by the villagers in the 1980s and is the current village hall.

Dennington 🐝

The first written evidence about Dennington occurs in the Domesday Book compiled in 1086, where we learn that at this time the parish had over 300 acres of parkland, which was rare. Dennington is a pleasant village two and a half miles north of Framlingham.

The Square is the centre of the village, having on it an oak tree planted in 1935 to celebrate the Silver Jubilee of George V and Queen Mary. To the south of the Square stands the magnificent church. It is almost certain that there was a church here in Norman times, although the present building was not begun until the early 14th century. Rector's names are recorded since 1470, including John Colet who founded St Paul's School in 1512. Within the church are many treasures, including the tomb of Lord Bardolph who fought at Agincourt.

Dennington Consolidated Charities, governed by a body of trustees, have over the years been left property and money to be used for the benefit of the village and to help individual people in many ways. To the east of the square is the village pub, the Queen's Head, vested to the Trustees in 1694 but now in private ownership.

The school and the Methodist chapel were opened in 1875 and are both still in use today.

Basket making, a blacksmith, grocer's and butcher's shops, and shoemakers are now part of Dennington's past, but the village is presently served by mobile butchers, greengrocer, fishmongers and grocer. Dennington post office is noteworthy as being one of the oldest official post offices in the country. There has been a post office in the same building since 1830.

A new village green has been created and on it a village sign designed and made by a local craftsman, Mr Harry Moore. The well-cared for sports field caters for football, cricket and bowls, and the village is fortunate in having a new village hall opened in May 1988. It is well used during the week by various societies.

Drinkstone 🐝

Peaceful, unpretentious Drinkstone is a place of scattered farmsteads, a 14th century church built on the site of a much older place of worship, two windmills and several historic houses. A relatively unspoilt village in the ancient heart of Mid Suffolk, lying between Woolpit and Rattlesden, with a population of around 400 souls, almost exactly the same number as it was a hundred years ago.

There are seven roads in Drinkstone but the locals have their own names for most of them – which makes it confusing for an outsider. The Queech, Sandfrost Hill, Dooley Dock, these are not places to be found on any map, but in Drinkstone many still talk 'Suffolk' and the oral tradition endures. Several of the names on the current electoral roll are the same as those on the parish records over the past 200 years. The parishioners' place of work has changed, there were eleven working farms in the village at the end of the Second World War. Today there are only four, and most residents of working age now commute to the nearby towns of Bury, Ipswich and Stowmarket.

There is some evidence that the Romans settled in Drinkstone and certainly there was a thriving Anglo-Saxon community. Later the village was on an important stagecoach way from Colchester to Bury St Edmunds, but ploughed fields now cover part of the route. There was a stable for changing the stagecoach horses at Marsh Green, where one old resident can remember watercress was once grown in the stream there, a tributary of the river Blackbourne, which meanders through Drinkstone eventually linking up with the Little Ouse.

In the 19th century the estate of Drinkstone Park was inherited by Joshua Grigby III who loved the place and asked to be buried in a corner of his garden. This piece of land was duly hallowed and on his death in 1829 he was buried there beneath a mulberry tree, which exists to this day and still bears fruit. Legend in Drinkstone has it that Joshua Grigby had had a mistress to whom he had said 'You shall not have a penny of my money until I am under the ground'. And so his widow, to spite the mistress, interred Joshua sitting up, above ground, and the tomb was built around him.

The house at Drinkstone Park was demolished just after the Second World War, having fallen prey to death watch beetle. Only the ice house remains. Four families live in the converted stable block and some recently built houses. Joshua Grigby III's tomb is in the garden of one of them.

In the horticultural world Drinkstone was famous for the Barcocks Nursery, sadly now closed following the death of the owner. Frederick Barcock was a true plantsman and there are several 'Drinkstone' varieties of shrubs and herbaceous plants he bred known to gardeners worldwide. Having such a fine nursery in the village for so many years has meant that many of the residents' gardens have a fine stock of rare and mature shrubs. Every two years Drinkstone hosts a garden walkabout in aid of church funds.

Dunwich 🦢

Standing on the sandy cliffs at Dunwich and gazing out to sea you overlook the site of a lost town, in its heyday the largest borough in Suffolk and an important medieval trading port. It exported wool and grain to Europe and beyond, imported wine, cloth, furs and timber, had a thriving fishing and shipbuilding industry and in 1241 provided 80 ships for the King. There were eight parish churches, several religious houses and the chapel of St James serving the leper hospital in the outskirts of the town.

As the movement of shingle and sand created the sheltered port, so by the end of the 13th century it caused the silting up of the harbour, heralding the decline of Dunwich. After a series of violent storms, erosion so reduced the town that the inhabitants could no longer afford to defend its vulnerable coastline. It still goes on. WI members recollect how in 1953 children were accommodated in the WI hut when the school was inundated and in December 1990 were vividly reminded of the power of the sea when John Easey's tombstone in All Saints' churchyard fell over the cliff. Blocks of concrete had been strewn about like paper and the beach was an awesome sight. It was not difficult to understand how a whole town had been swept away by repeated onslaughts from the sea.

A new church was built in 1830 by the Barne family (All Saints was a ruin) and a small country house near the ruins of Greyfriars. Dunwich became a village with an architectural unity of tall chimneys, latticed windows and handmade brick. The small house was enlarged and craftsmen plied their trades between Sotterley and Dunwich.

After the devastation of two world wars, Lt Col Michael St John Barne sold the estate in 1947. When it was subsequently broken up, and sold at auction there was a sense of shock throughout Dunwich. In the event most of the tenants were able to buy their homes, at very reasonable prices, and a trust was formed to run the reading room and museum. Miss Semmence, headmistress of the school since 1931, remained until its closure in 1964. The Barne Arms, the village pub, reverted to its original name – the Ship.

Today Dunwich is a small village with a modest Victorian church, lacking the splendour of Suffolk medieval churches but well worth a visit; it has no school, no post office, no general store, no obvious centre and, as yet, no sewerage system. The parish is bounded to the west by Dunwich Forest, planted by the Forestry Commission; it extends north to Dingle marsh and south to Dunwich Heath, a National Trust property where the Coastguard Cottages (now housing the warden, tea rooms and shop) overlook the RSPB Nature Reserve at Minsmere. The eastern boundary is four miles of coastline in a constant state of flux where once you could cycle or push a pram from Dingle to Minsmere on a sandy highway.

The population of Dunwich is around 130. Local employment is related to sea, heath, forest and farm and to tourist, service and cottage industries. The designation of Dunwich as a part of a Rural Development area and good wages at the Sizewell construction site have helped local people to become self-employed. There are more longshoremen working from Dunwich beach than for many years.

The community is staunchly independent. When the Union Work-house was built at Bulcamp in 1764 to provide for the parishes in the Blything Hundred, Dunwich was exempt. It had a corporation until 1886 and after the Corporation Act the Dunwich Town Trust was formed to administer the town lands and charities and to be the guardians of the regalia and the Town Chest (now housed in the museum).

Earl Soham 🦅

The most attractive approach to Earl Soham is along the Roman road from Framsden; one is aware of the valley in which the village nestles, of the curves of the village street, the varied roofs, and of Windwhistle Farm and Earl Soham Lodge standing proudly on the high ground.

Passing Cobbolds Row, a terrace of almshouses named after a local brewer, you come to the first of three village greens, overlooked by the Victoria. The largest of the greens is in the centre of the village and here stands the village sign, a carved wooden statue of a falconer, falconry being a local sport, given by the Women's Institute to commemorate the coronation of Queen Elizabeth II in 1953. Behind the village stores is found the third green, known as Little Green. It is a pleasant spot surrounded by ancient cottages, among them the 'Black Chapel', the original Baptist chapel.

Situated just off the main village green is the 15th century Street Farm House, one of the oldest dwellings in Earl Soham. William Goodwin, a surgeon and farmer, lived at this house in the 1780s and he left an interesting diary now in the Ipswich branch of the Suffolk Record Office. He mentioned nights when smuggler's bands passed through the village en route from Sizewell and Dunwich laden with contraband spirits, sometimes to be stored beneath the pulpits in surrounding village churches. The number of horses on the beach at Sizewell for carrying away smuggled goods was sometimes from 100 to 300 and waggons and carts from 40 to 100, the diary says.

The church of St Mary, of more than usual interest, dates from the 13th century. Some 50 years ago a few pre-Reformation pew ends discovered in the rectory stable loft were used as a basis for completely re-pewing the church; so well was the work done that visitors often think that all the pews are original.

In the whole length of the Street most dwellings have their origins in the 16th and 17th centuries with only the butcher's shop and the adjacent house being less than 160 years old. Earl Soham Lodge and moat stands on the site of a Roman villa and the Ordnance Survey map indicates the route of the Roman road passing between The Lodge and the present village street. Aerial photographs have disclosed the sites of pre-Saxon dwellings in the field behind Church Farm.

The mere was drained in about 1970 and was situated behind the present day Baptist chapel. The name Soham indicated a marsh. 'Earl' Soham was the property of the Bigods, later Earls of Norfolk, just as Monk Soham, a nearby village, was ecclesiastical property.

Earl Stonham

Even people who know Suffolk well are inclined to look slightly confused when Earl Stonham is mentioned. For a start it is often confused with Earl Soham, particularly by the local press, causing much frustration and indignation. Then there are our neighbours, Stonham Aspal, on the other side of the A140 and Stonham Parva, also known as Little Stonham, which is between the two. To add to the confusion the village is very scattered and the houses are largely grouped round three ancient greens, Forward Green, Middlewood Green and Broad Green, and these are frequently used in postal addresses.

However, in the midst of all this is a living village, a mixture of families whose homes have been here for many generations and more recent newcomers. The school has closed and the post office and shop are sadly gone too, yet there is still life in the community.

Traditionally it has been a farming area and this is still so, although modern methods mean fewer people actually working on the land. Farm buildings have been converted for use by various small businesses. One large one, British and Brazilian, or B & B, employing many people involved with packing fruit and vegetables, is based at Church Farm.

The founder president of the WI was Mrs Portway, who, under her professional name of Hebe Cox, had her embroidery designs exhibited at the Victoria and Albert museum. However, perhaps closest to the heart of the village is the memory of Mr Bob Haggar, village blacksmith for 80 years until his death in 1988. He broke records for being in the same job for so many years but did not enjoy the publicity which went with his claim to fame. Pictures of him at work have pride of place in the Shepherd and Dog at Forward Green.

The pub is, of course, a centre of village life, particularly since the revival of Earl Stonham Cricket Club. The cricket pitch, conveniently within walking distance of the Shepherd and Dog and beside the village hall, had been used by Stowmarket Cricket Club. Then in 1989 when Stowmarket gained their own pitch the village formed a new club. This is village cricket at its best. The bowls club is situated close by and is also well supported and much enjoyed.

The church of St Mary is another focal point. The splendid 13th century building with its magnificent carved roof, medieval wall paintings and unique hour glasses is well worth a visit. Happily it is used by a thriving congregation which also enjoys sharing work and celebrations with Stonham Parva Baptist chapel and Earl Stonham chapel.

East Bergholt ⚜

East Bergholt is in Constable Country, the name given to describe the area where John Constable RA was born and spent his childhood and youth.

His father owned Flatford Mill, as well as a house of considerable size in the centre of the village. The house is no longer there, although some of the outbuildings remain and his studio is still here. He eventually married Maria Bicknell, after much opposition and later consent from her grandfather, Rev Dr Rhudde, DD, who was rector of East Bergholt and Chaplain in Ordinary to the King.

Long before John Constable, however, the village has known less gentle people. Camulodunum (Colchester) being not far distant, the Romans were here. Indeed the Roman road from London to Norwich crossed the river Stour at Stratford St Mary, just across the meadows. Did Boudicca lead the Iceni through here on her way to attack the Romans at Camulodunum, riding her chariot along the road which became the A12?

By the end of the 15th century, when more wool was being worked in Suffolk than in any other county, there were many wealthy clothiers, of whom East Bergholt had its share. Some of their houses still survive, as also do some of the names of the many Flemish clothworkers who came to East Anglia – Aldous, Folkard and Gildersleeves.

It was during this period of great prosperity that many fine churches were built in Suffolk, including St Mary's. It was intended that it should have a tower as high as Dedham, but that never materialised. There are local legends as to the reason why, one being that Cardinal Wolsey had promised money for the purpose, but having fallen from grace the promise remained unfulfilled, so the bells intended for the tower were placed in the unique 16th century bellcage outside the church, where they remain to this day; a curiosity for visitors from all over the world, and a venue for parishioners to sing carols at Christmas.

Another possible reason for the tower not being built, was that money became more scarce when the cloth industry failed at the end of the 16th century. It affected East Bergholt very badly, although there was, and still is, agriculture.

There were benefactors; notable amongst these was a lawyer named Edward Lambe. He founded Lambe School in 1594. At about the same time, Mrs Lettice Dykes, a widow, assigned lands and property in this area to a body of trustees, with the purpose of educating poor children. This charity continues to the present, but is now used where deemed necessary for material assistance to schoolchildren and students.

The fair is no longer held on what was the village green, although each Bank Holiday a market is held on Church Plain in aid of the church, and young men who normally commute to Ipswich, Colchester and London, dress in fancy costume and race through the village.

The Congregational church holds an annual fete, and throughout the summer several gardens are open in aid of charity, with stalls piled high with home-made produce.

Edwardstone

Discoveries of pottery and coins indicate that the Romans had a small settlement nearly two miles above the ford on the river Box. But the most telling evidence is the presence of Roman bricks worked into the oldest wall of the church nave. Some still have the distinctive speckled Roman mortar stuck to them. Clearly there must have been a Roman building nearby.

King William I gave the manor to the great Norman lord Robert Malet. Robert installed Hubert de Montchensey at 'Eduardestuna' as it was called in the Domesday Book. Hubert had a 'winter mill'. Evidently the headwaters of the river Box were too sluggish in the summer to turn the mill wheel. In 1114 Hubert gave the church with its free land to the monastery at Abingdon and founded a priory cell at Edwardstone. Abingdon sent two monks to attend it. The building of what is now the church vestry, by far the oldest part of St Mary's, may well date back to this time.

John Brand, a wealthy clothier, bought the manor of Edwardstone in 1598. Four hundred years later his charity and those of his descendants continue to benefit the village. The parish trustees administer a number of ancient charities. The first was endowed by John Brand in 1640, the second by Isaac Brand in 1709. Other benefactions followed.

In 1662 Susanna Brand married a wealthy London merchant called John Morden. There is a fine romantic, though unsubstantiated, story of John's earlier days. His ships failed to return and – ruined – he was reduced to working as a butcher's boy. But the ships were not lost, only very greatly delayed. When they finally docked John's fortunes were immediately restored. From that day he never looked back and later he was knighted by James II, not long before the king was deposed. Sadly Sir John and Lady Susanna had no children. Sir John endowed a fine home for 'decayed merchants' which was built at Blackheath to a design by Sir Christopher Wren. Lady Susanna founded a charity with her estate, and over the last 25 years or so very generous donations have been made towards the upkeep and repair of the church fabric.

Morden College still flourishes and residents visit Edwardstone each year for the Harvest Festival and villagers pay return visits. Inside the church is a Brand tomb with some fine brasses. They are a monument to Benjamin and Elizabeth Brand who, after 35 years of marriage, died within twelve days of each other. They left six sons and six daughters and the brasses splendidly record that they were 'all nursed with her unborrowed milk'. A marvellous example of sturdy independence.

Ellough

Ellough is a scattered, sparsely populated parish covering 1,097 acres, and is situated some three miles south-east of Beccles. Ellough Moor is an area of high ground lying within the parish boundaries to the north-west. Although the village is now known as Ellough, and has been for over 400 years, it was once called Willingham All Saints.

At the top of the hill, and surrounded by a flint and brick wall, stands the 14th century church of All Saints. The church, which became redundant in January 1974 because of depopulation, is now looked after by the Redundant Churches Fund. The building is of flint construction with a square tower, which once housed three bells. Inside the church are several brasses, the most notable being an effigy of Margaret Chewt who died in 1607 aged 85 years. She is depicted wearing a head-dress almost half as big as herself.

Beyond the church the road descends steeply towards a narrow bridge and the Hundred river – this forming the southern boundary of the parish.

Across the road, opposite the church, stands the Georgian rectory. It is a very large, imposing house, with a commanding view over the surrounding countryside. The Grange, as it is now called, was for many years a private residence, but in the autumn of 1990 it opened as an independent school to cater for children with learning difficulties.

Two notable houses are Playter's Old Farm and Ellough Hall. The Playter family held the lordship for over 200 years, until it was sold in 1787 to Robert Sparrow of Worlingham Hall.

With the outbreak of the Second World War an airfield was constructed, one of the last to be completed. Its location made it the most easterly air strip in the UK. The B1127 from Beccles to Wrentham runs right across the airfield. Since the end of the war, the airfield and its buildings have been in constant use as a busy industrial complex. One notable war-time structure still in use is an original hangar, situated at the eastern end of the airfield. Today it forms part of British International Helicopters, and houses the helicopters which fly personnel and supplies out to the oil and gas platforms in the North Sea.

Also using some of the existing buildings on the airfield is Mr Card. Reggie and his horse, Mark, are to be seen almost daily making their way to the Beccles waste tip with their totter's cart piled high with an assortment of unwanted goods, and even on the odd occasion with a rusting car chassis perched precariously on top.

Although a considerable acreage of the parish is still agricultural, only a small number of people are employed in farming today. Virtually no new houses have been built in Ellough, so the resident population remains very small. However the total number of people in the village on any one day must run into hundreds, when taking into account all the employees working on the industrial site. Few villages can have witnessed such great changes during the last 50 years, and yet remain so rural.

Elmsett

Elmsett, 'Elmseta' in the Domesday Book, is a compact village in the heart of rolling countryside four miles from Hadleigh and eight miles from the county town of Ipswich. St Peter's church overlooks a scene which has changed little since Thomas Gainsborough painted it in 1750.

John Ladbrook purchased the fine old timber windmill, astride a brick roundhouse, in 1848 and this was to form the nucleus of a business still in operation today. Gradually new buildings were added, power was derived from steam, then gas, a crude-oil engine and finally electric power. The milling and malting have given way to the provender side, animal feeds for farmers and pet-food produced using modern machinery.

Some of old Elmsett remains, including a number of listed buildings. In the moated rectory, now a private residence, once lived John Bois who eventually became one of the translators of the King James Bible. Red House Farm is a fine old house and the Blacksmith's Cottages on the green 'under the spreading chestnut tree' are a pleasant sight. Most of the woodland has gone over the years, but Park Wood, an ancient deer park, remains as a site of special scientific interest.

Elmsett Green as it was in the early twentieth century

The Tithe Memorial, opposite the church, commemorates Elmsett's stand against what had, in the 1930s, become an unjust tax. Queen Anne's Bounty impounded and attempted to take corn and household goods from Elmsett Hall to pay their tithe. When it was known that lorries were coming to fetch the goods, several large elms were felled which completely blocked the farm entrance. This, together with the large crowd gathered, persuaded the lorry drivers to turn back. The goods were never taken away.

St Peter's church – a Norman, mainly 13th century building – has a quiet dignity and simple beauty. There is a new Methodist church, built to replace an older one, on Stock's Meadow; the old site of the village stocks. Near this church is pump corner, where the village pump once stood and provided water for the village.

Elmsett fortunately still has a thriving primary school, a Victorian red-brick building built in the 1870s. The village has two shops, one also a post office, a public house, the Rose and Crown, a garage, and nine farms. Ladbrook's Mill is the biggest employer.

Ten people were killed by a German bomb, jettisoned by a plane caught in a searchlight beam, in the small hours of a beautiful May morning in 1941. A row of eight cottages of different ages and styles but all connected, received a direct hit and in a few moments became a blazing inferno. In spite of the tragic deaths, there were some almost miraculous escapes. Some small children were picked unhurt from among the blazing thatch. The loss of the old cottages and their fertile gardens quite altered the appearance of the village.

Romans probably walked in Elmsett, as a Roman coin was found in a garden in Hadleigh Road. Gold, in the form of a wedding ring, was found with an onion growing through it in a garden in The Street.

Elmswell ॐ

At the eastern edge of West Suffolk lies Elmswell. If you travel by the A45 you cannot miss seeing the church of St John the Baptist, guarding the entrance to the village, its massive flint tower looking across to its neighbour, Woolpit, on the other side of the valley.

Elmswell has a 'lived in' look, functional and homely – Elmswellians can live, work, shop and play in their village for here you find all sizes and styles of dwellings, industry in the small factories (and larger bacon factory), mixed farms and agricultural enterprises and a really good selection of retail outlets from the small friendly nursery to the smart new Co-op. Leisure activities are varied and many. The three churches work together and offer villagers Sunday schools and services.

The village had its first major housing development in the early 1960s, when the population was 2,000, and since then it has spread gently in most directions to reach its present population of well over 3,000.

For the future a million pound project is planned for a new village hall/

leisure complex, as sadly the much loved village hall (built in memory of the Elmswell lads who gave their lives in the Second World War) is no longer adequate for the needs of the village.

Elveden

Elveden is situated on the edge of Suffolk bordering Norfolk, 16 miles east of Newmarket and three miles south-west of Thetford, among fine trees and lush parkland, bisected by the notorious A11 road. It is part of the Elveden estate with Eriswell and Icklingham. Where the three parishes meet a well known landmark is the war memorial, an imposing Corinthian colunm topped by a Grecian urn, the whole 127 ft high.

The Maharajah Duleep Singh lived in Elveden Hall from 1863 to 1888, known locally as 'The Black Prince'. He was heir to the Punjab throne. The Prince was a fine shot and set several records in his day. However, Elveden Hall really came into its heyday when it was bought by Baron Iveagh (later the first Earl of Iveagh), the Chairman of Arthur Guinness and Son of Dublin, in July 1894. He set about building a country seat fit to entertain royalty.

When the second Earl inherited the estate in 1927 his priorities were different. He was scientifically minded and determined to make the estate a farming one. To this end he proceeded to stock the land with cattle to provide humus and fertilizer to stabilise the sandy soil and erected miles of rabbit proof fencing. By 1938 some 5,000 acres were farmed and by 1950 another 4,000 had been reclaimed, making it the largest lowland arable farm in Britain, and the whole was very productive. The present owner, the third Earl, has carried on with the farming but the dairy and beef herds have all gone, the only livestock at Elveden now are pigs.

The present village dates mostly from the first Earl's time when the red brick houses and buildings were erected from 1895, the bricks having been made in the village brickworks. There is still evidence of cottages of earlier times, a row of flint and brick at the crossroads. Semi-detached flint and brick cottages at The Gap, Sketchfar and Albemarle and buildings at the Game Larder are attributable to Duleep Singh. The oldest house in the village is at Chalk Hall Farm and has walls plastered with mud and straw and flint-faced.

The church of St Andrew and St Patrick is probably unique for a village church. The medieval part dates from the 12th century when it was thatched, until Duleep Singh reroofed it in slate and carried out various improvements in 1869. The major restoration came about in 1904–1906, when a new nave, chancel, organ chamber and vestry were added, doubling the size.

The latest innovation is Elveden Forest Village built when part of Warren Wood was acquired by Center Parcs. A holiday village has been built on the site incorporating a great many of the trees from the wood. Its centrepiece is an enormous glass dome housing swimming and other recreational facilities with a constant sub-tropical temperature. Already thousands of holidaymakers have made their way there, though little is seen of them in the village proper.

Eriswell 🐚

Eriswell is situated in the north-west corner of Suffolk on the B1112 road. The parish consists of Eriswell village with 13th century St Laurence's church to the south, and Little Eriswell with the remains of St Peter's church to the north, and there is also an Anglo-American housing estate for personnel who are attached to nearby United States Air Force bases.

The main livelihood of the area has always been farming. The soil to the west was fenland, and to the east the sandy breckland.

During the Napoleonic Wars, Eriswell Warren supplied up to 25,000 rabbits a year, a very important and much needed source of food at that time. The warreners lived in a low fortified tower to protect them from armed poachers, and stones from this building can be seen at Eriswell High Lodge. Fish, eels and waterfowl were also in plentiful supply.

In 1963, a new water channel was cut from the river Lark to the river Ouse, to help control flooding in the fens. As a result the fen and marshland in the parish were drained, so all are now arable fields with the exception of one or two small meadows.

The New England Company bought the manor of Eriswell in 1649 and retained it for over 200 years. The policy of this company was to bring the Christian faith to natives of North America. It is said that Eriswell was the first village they acquired to provide income for them to be able to send their missionaries overseas. They built the old school (now used as the village hall) and also other houses. The initials NEC, are clearly to be seen on these. In 1818, in an apprenticeship scheme, they sent James Paul, a North American Indian aged 14 years, to Eriswell to be educated and apprenticed to Thomas Houghton, the village carpenter and builder. Whether due to homesickness or the climate, he only survived here for two years, and his memorial can be seen in the churchyard.

In Little Eriswell, near the old Hall, stands the 'Dove House'. This is all that remains of the old church of St Peter; two walls and an 18th century window. An early 18th century sketch shows a tower (with beacon) and an already roofless nave. In the will of a wealthy lady, Margaret Bedingfeld who died in 1476, she leaves provision for a chantry priest to say prayers for her soul. Today can still be seen a very ancient oak tree known as the Chantry Oak.

In 1863 the India Office purchased the Elveden Estate for Maharajah Duleep Singh. They also purchased for him from the New England Company, the village and lands of Eriswell. The first Earl of Iveagh bought the estate from the India Office in 1894, mainly as a shooting estate.

A sports field with changing rooms, tennis courts etc, is well used. Amenities are provided by the post office and stores, a range of shops, the Chequers public house, and public transport.

Exning 🦢

Exning, or Esselinga as it is called in the Domesday Book, is an ancient village and before the Norman Conquest Anglo-Saxons had settled here. There is an inhumation cemetery at the top of Windmill Hill. The Devils Dyke was constructed about the end of the Roman period.

The written history of Exning begins in the 12th century when King Henry II granted the manor to Matthew, Count of Boulogne who divided it between four of his knights. They remained separated until they were amalgamated under the Cotton family who lived in Landwade in the 17th century. There are many references to them in the little church. A service is held in the church on the last Sunday in each month.

In 1986 St Martin's church in Exning celebrated the 1,350th anniversary of Exning as a Christian site. It is known that in AD 636 St Felix came to the village and he may have founded the church. He baptised Etheldreda and two of her sisters, Wendred and Sexburgha, of the Saxon royal family of King Anna. The well where the baptisms may have taken place was named after Wendred and is still known by her name. The present vicar uses water from the well for parish baptisms.

One would expect thatched houses in an ancient village but apparently there were many fires at the beginning of the 19th century. Fourteen were reported during the years 1808–1821, when over 20 dwellings, barns and stables including the White Swan and vicarage were destroyed. Only help from Newmarket and their fire engines saved the whole village from destruction.

Well over 3,000 people live in the village now and work in a variety of occupations, some locally on farms, many employed by trainers and on stud farms and some in the village shops. There is a general store, baker's shop, newsagent, butcher, post office, fish and chip shop, hairdresser, four pubs, two garages, a very good hotel and a primary school. There are many clubs and organisations.

The village was a quiet place but now there is more traffic to and from the A45. There are still some peaceful walks and the children like to go and feed the ducks on the stream in Ducks Lane.

Eye 🦢

Although Eye is not strictly a village, its essentially rural character and population of less than 2,000 retains a village atmosphere.

The name Eye comes from the Saxon word for island, being originally surrounded by water or marshland. Even now, after prolonged heavy rain or snow, the river Dove overflows its banks, flooding low level land and roads around Eye.

The Three Horseshoes is one of only three remaining pubs in Eye where years ago more than 20 existed. The White Lion Hotel, in the town centre, once a thriving establishment serving the business and farming community, has sadly closed and has been converted to residential accommodation.

Eye had the distinction of being the smallest borough in the United Kingdom until reorganisation in 1974, when it assumed parish status, although retaining its mayor.

The church of St Peter and St Paul is one of the finest in the county, its magnificent 100 ft tower dominating the landscape. The well preserved timber-framed Guildhall, dating back to 1470, stands between the church and the primary school – originally the grammar school, which closed in 1965 in spite of much local opposition.

A good place from which to view the town and surrounding countryside is the top of the castle mound, recently made accessible by Mid Suffolk District Council. Little remains of the castle building although recent excavations have uncovered the medieval foundations of a tower and walls of the inner bailey at the foot of the mound. Old pictures of Eye show a windmill on the castle mound, which was later demolished and replaced by a residence built within the castle walls.

Prior to the First World War there was a large workhouse on the castle bailey, later converted to council houses. These were demolished in 1979 and replaced by an award-winning council housing scheme, the buildings following the perimeter of the inner bailey and designed with steeply sloping roofs to echo the castle walls and mound.

In the mid 1800s Eye was a thriving market town of considerable importance with a population of more than 2,500. There were many trades and crafts practised including lace making, corsetry, hand made boots and shoes, a foundry, flaxworks and breweries – hence the number of pubs. From the middle of the 19th century Eye's importance began to decline, especially after the main railway line station went to Diss.

Recent years have seen a revival with many new families moving into the town, which has a wide range of shops and amenities including a modern health centre, geriatric hospital and maternity unit. Ideally situated between Norwich and Ipswich, but off the main road, Eye has managed to retain its peaceful and historical character.

Eyke

Eyke is no picture postcard village. Along The Street, on either side of which most of the people live, passes a more or less continuous procession of traffic of all kinds, travelling to and from Bentwaters air base. This is, however, a lively village. The Post Office Stores and the inn on one side of The Street and primary school on the other provide meeting places for various members of the community.

From earliest times the people of Eyke have depended on the land for their livelihood. At the beginning of the 20th century there were several small mixed farms, and various men worked independently at crafts connected with agriculture, making the village partially self supporting. Agriculture is still the chief industry, though the land is now in the hands of three farmers who require only a small workforce to tend their cattle and pigs and to grow barley and sugar beet. Hence people have to seek employment elsewhere. A few new houses have been built within the last 30 years, but the population remains static at considerably less than 400.

All Saints' church is situated on the south side of The Street, but it is not very conspicuous as it has no tower. It is however well worth a visit; built in 1150 it once had a central tower supported by four large Norman arches. Two of the arches which still remain are beautifully carved with the chevron pattern. On the walls of the chancel are two brasses. One commemorates John Staverton and his wife; he was lord of the manor. In 1399 he was appointed Baron of the Exchequer and is shown wearing his judicial robes. The other is of Henry Mason, vicar of Snape and probably curate of Eyke: on his death in 1619 he bequeathed land and money to the poor of Eyke. At the same time Sir Michael Stanhope of Orford Castle made a similar bequest. Each year at Christmas gifts of money are still distributed.

One of the features of the church is its oak carving, nearly all of which was designed between the wars by the rector, Archdeacon J. G. R. Darling. He formed a class of local people to carry out the work. Many of the designs incorporate animals and birds which were of special interest to him. A unique key hangs on the north wall of the nave, dated not later than the 15th century. The head of the key has letters which spell IKE, one of the early versions of Eyke.

Since their arrival at the end of the Second World War, the Americans on the Bentwaters air base have influenced the life of the village. They provide a variety of employment for several people and apart from the problem of the traffic and the noise of the low flying aircraft, the village has lived on friendly terms with its somewhat overwhelming neighbour.

Felsham

In many ways Felsham is a typical rural English village, the majority of the houses being grouped around two village greens with the church, public house, post office and shop, and village hall (formerly the school) all centrally positioned. The surrounding countryside is gently undulating, retaining many of its hedges and it is situated near Bradfield Woods, one of the oldest coppiced woods in England.

However, a village, even with all these constituent parts, is nothing without a thriving community and a sense of history. One of the clearest examples of this living link with the past is the fact that Felsham had families named Cocksedge living there in the 14th century and to this very day members of that family live within the village.

The church of St Peter, built of flint with stone dressings, was established in the first half of the 14th century. The west tower has six bells, all except the treble being made by Miles Graye in 1638–9; the treble was added at a later date as it was made in 1668. These bells give their name to the public house directly opposite, the Six Bells. This is now the only pub in the village; there was another on Upper Green – the Live and Let Live – until relatively recently.

Next to the church is Mausoleum House which owes its name to a long-lasting disagreement between the rector and a former owner, who was determined that the church should not profit from his funeral expenses and so built a mausoleum in the grounds of his house. The feud was later resolved by the family having the bodies moved to the churchyard. Today just a few courses of bricks remain of the mausoleum, the rest having been taken over the years by the villagers for their own use.

There is a range of architectural styles in Felsham. The public house is partly flint and there are some excellent examples of 15th century timbered farmhouses and cottages; Felsham Grange is a fine Georgian house. One of the most striking buildings is Moore's Farm where the previous owner, Mr Steadman, decorated the barn with his own paintings of places far and wide, some of which he had visited; he also built wooden replicas of farmyard animals, Postman Pat, Dusty Bin and a crocodile which are displayed in the front garden. The farm has attracted many visitors and is a firm favourite with local children.

In true village tradition Felsham holds two major annual events which involve the majority of the inhabitants. The Flower Show was until 1987 held in a large marquee on the playing field and attracts many entries from young and old alike. The Street Fair has recently been revived as a village event with stalls and live entertainment, including Morris Dancers; it owes its origins to the granting of a charter to the village in 1618 to William Risby and his heirs which gave permission for a Sheep Fair to be held on the common land.

Fornham All Saints

Situated two miles north-west of Bury St Edmunds, there has from early times been a settlement by the river Lark. It is the site of great Bronze Age earthworks, a medieval stronghold and has been the scene of at least two very well recorded epic battles. Today Fornham All Saints is a most attractive and sought after residential village with houses varying from pink-washed thatched cottages right through the styles to a few modern properties, all dominated by the flint-faced church at the end of the village green. The village is served by a church, Baptist chapel, village hall, community centre, recreation ground, public house, shop with post office, village green and the parish area is about 1,600 acres. In addition there are two golf courses.

The village sign depicts a medieval helmet over two crossed swords. The first noted battle involved King Edward, son of King Alfred, who victoriously fought off claims by his cousin Aethelwald about AD 902. The second battle was in October 1173, when Henry II's Justiciar Richard de Lucy defeated the rebellious Earl of Leicester and his Flemish mercenaries in the marshes at Fornham. Many skeletons have been discovered, several of the skulls showing marks of violence as if pierced by arrows or swords, also old buckles, fragments of metal and rusted remains of weapons.

Air photography has revealed a vast complex of prehistoric ritual sites and later settlements, recognised as one of the most important in East Anglia. It is protected by a Department of the Environment preservation order. These include three ploughed-out Bronze Age barrows, circular 130–140 ft in diameter. On this site a 2nd century coin and pottery have been found, so a Roman settlement must have been nearby.

The present church of All Saints was built in the latter part of the 12th century. From 1750 until recently the right to appoint a rector belonged to the Master, Fellows and Scholars of Clare Hall Cambridge.

There used to be five lime pits up on Tut Hill. On 23rd December 1910 four men collecting chalk were suddenly engulfed by 50 tons of chalk. One man pulled himself free to raise the alarm, to no avail. The funeral procession was described as a 'sad and impressive spectacle' and many mourners were unable to get into the church. The village started the Fornham All Saints Chalk Pit Disaster Fund and raised £310 16s 7½d.

Fornham St Martin 🌿

Fornham St Martin is one of a trio of Fornhams situated about two miles to the north-west of Bury St Edmunds. Fornham St Genevieve, which once boasted a stately hall and church, has now reverted mostly to parkland. Sheepwash Bridge spans the ten ft wide river Lark, and links the parishes. Until the churches joined in a united benefice in 1984, this bridge was, perhaps, the sole link.

Neighbouring Timworth was once a thriving village which has twice died out as the result of medieval plagues and changing economic husbandry. Consequently, St Andrew's stands isolated in fields at least a quarter mile from any habitation. For some reason, shrouded in time, residents still express a very strong request not to be buried on the north side of the church.

The village itself is in three, almost four, distinct parts. The nucleus is centred round St Martin's church, in whose large south porch, ancient wills were formerly proved. The guildhall of the medieval Candlemakers Guild has been converted into three cottages and gives its name to Old Hall Lane. Adjoining the church is the old Priest's House and the

Woolpack inn whose sign recalls the former importance of the once flourishing wool trade. In this old part of the village once lived the 'pie ladies', who in the heyday of St Edmund's Abbey, made the two mile journey on foot, to provide food for the table of the worthy abbot and his resident monks.

Almost a mile to the north-west of the central area is a pleasant, post Second World War council development, and the post office and general shop. A second large modern residential development is situated on Barton Hill, about a mile south-east from the church, and therefore nearer to the Bury St Edmunds' boundary than to the village proper.

Over the last few years Fornham St Martin has seen its largest influx of new blood – young families attracted by modern houses in close proximity to a golf and leisure centre extending along the now placid banks of the river Lark. Golfing enthusiasts would feel much at home here, where each road takes its name from a well known golf course.

Until the fens were drained in the 17th century, the river Lark was tidal as far as Mildenhall, some ten miles distant, and even in the early 1900s the banks were busy with barges bringing sea coal to the residents of nearby Bury St Edmunds, and the water meadows provided water skating for local enthusiasts.

Foxearth, Pentlow, Borley & Liston ✤

The villages of Foxearth, Pentlow, Borley and Liston are situated on the B1064, on the west bank of the river Stour in the county of Essex. Whilst the inhabitants look to Braintree District Council to provide services, they consider themselves Suffolk folk by inclination.

Foxearth was well known for its brewing of beer from the late 19th century. The brewery of Ward & Son was built about 1886. However, the three storey brewhouse was demolished in 1959 and the site developed as a brewery depot. The site is now being developed for housing. The brewery, in its time, was a main source of employment for the area and some houses in the village were built specially for brewery workers.

The church dates from the 13th century and has undergone considerable restoration. The church spire was blown away in a great gale early in the 19th century. Another notable building in the village is a moated farmhouse dating from the 16th century. This is Foxearth Hall, until recently a working farm. It is now merely a residence and the fields are owned by others.

The small hamlet of Pentlow developed on a hill overlooking the Stour valley when the area was in the grip of the Black Death. The church remains on its own in the valley and dates from the 12th century, its round tower originating from the 14th century. Rev Bull was incumbent for Pentlow for 50 years and in 1868 he built a tower in the grounds of the then Pentlow rectory in memory of his parents. The tower still stands, 90 ft high and on a clear day 48 churches can be seen from the top.

Pentlow boasts a pub with a most unusual name, the Pinknan Arms. The name appears to refer to the Pinknan sisters but their relationship to the pub is something of a mystery, as is their origin.

Borley has gained an unwanted notoriety as having one of the most haunted sites in England, the site of the Borley rectory. Inhabitants actually discourage midnight visitors in the form of ghost hunters but this quiet village continues to be disturbed far more by these activities than any hauntings! Media hype in the 1920s reported some ghostly happenings and subsequent authors have fuelled the interest. There are stories of an eloping nun and a groom, a nun walled up for misbehaving, a French maid seduced by a member of the Waldegrave family and subsequently murdered. Certainly human remains were found on the site and Borley rectory was mysteriously burnt to the ground in 1940. It is said to be the site of the Waldegrave manor house, a family whose influence was considerable from the 15th century for 300 years.

Borley church itself is delightful with fine views across the Stour valley. It possesses the grand tomb of Sir Edward Waldegrave who was buried with his wife Frances. Their effigies lie side by side, he in armour and she in a tight fitting bodice and skirt, wearing a flat cap and a ruffle round her neck. Their six children are represented on the side of the tomb.

Liston is a small hamlet comprising around 24 houses in all and nearly all the land is farmed by one farmer. It now has a population of 53.

The original Liston Hall was built in 1710 as a large mansion with four wings in Queen Anne style and had 160 acres with it. In 1870 it was burnt down and rebuilt in a less magnificent style. The house and farm were let until 1940 when it was commissioned by the army and was pulled down in 1952. However two of the wings remain and are lived in. The church is thought to have been built in pre-Norman times and was originally made of wood. Over the centuries it has been rebuilt in flint and brick.

The original factory of Bush Boake Allen was started in 1833 in Finsbury, London as a company for the milling of drugs, spices and distillation of essential oils. The site at Liston was purchased in 1899, 250 acres of land were bought but are on the other side of the river in Suffolk as the river acts as the county boundary. The factory moved down to make use of the land for growing medicinal and aromatic plants. It became uneconomic to grow the plants due to labour costs and climatic conditions and the farm is now contracted out. The plants now used are mainly evening primrose, borage etc and are imported.

Foxhall 🐾

Foxhall is a scattered village immediately to the east of Ipswich. The church, All Saints, fell into such disrepair that it was pulled down in 1530. Minor remains of walls are said to be seen in farm outbuildings at Foxhall Hall. Human bones were found in 1946 in the old churchyard, although there had been no interments since 1533.

To the north is Foxhall Heath, the site of four Bronze Age barrows, part of a chain extending through Brightwell to Waldringfield. Part of the Heath was used for exercises by the Artillery, stationed at Ipswich Barracks, in the middle of the 19th century. Half hidden in the trees is the smallpox hospital, built in 1915 and last used for its named purpose in 1928. The sanatorium was built in 1912 with money from the King Edward VII Fund and it closed in 1947. It has since been used at times to accommodate refugees. Foxhall Stadium is concealed in birch woods at the west end of the Heath, where speedway and stock-car racing have taken place for the past 40 years.

Woodland stretches south from the Heath, much of it planted in the 19th century but extensively damaged in the storms of October 1987.

A local industry was the digging of coprolite, the fossilized remains of huge prehistoric animals and their dung. In the middle 1700s it was spread on the soil as a fertilizer. By 1840 there were 'mills' or factories in Suffolk where it was processed into superphosphates of lime for commercial use. Farm workers were recruited as diggers, with better pay. Foxhall held the record for the deepest pit, 100 ft, in East Suffolk.

South of Mill river is Monument Farm. In the woods close by there is an obelisk, inscribed to the memory of Rev George Routh MA Rector of Holbrook and St Clement's with St Helen's, Ipswich. He died in 1821 and his wife placed the memorial where he frequently walked.

The White House, built in the 17th century, is a listed building. The old alehouse, the 'Waddling Duck' was replaced by a modern home of the same name in 1969. Further south the Shepherd and Dog was rebuilt in around 1963–4 when the road between Ipswich and Felixstowe was widened. Across the road was a small shop run by a Mrs Horton, who also sold cups of tea, even on Sundays . . . but she always had her Bible open on the counter. The permanent site for the Suffolk Show is on the south-west edge of the village.

Framlingham 🐾

Framlingham is a delightful place situated in the centre of East Suffolk. History abounds in Framlingham, with its castle, church, college and many fine buildings. Of particular interest are its two Victorian post boxes.

Names found in places and streets in Framlingham reflect its history.

Roger de Bigod, for instance, was given the manor of Framlingham by Henry I and it was Roger's son Hugh who built the castle. Sir Robert Hitcham died in 1636, and left his estate to Pembroke College, Cambridge. His will ordered that the materials from the interior of the castle should be used to build almshouses and a school for poor children. Both of these still bear his name.

Thomas Mills came to Framlingham in 1640 as an apprentice wheelwright. He eventually acquired the business. He died in 1703 leaving instructions in his will that almshouses should be built and if any money was left over it should be used to provide education for 20 children. His tomb can be seen in the garden of the house where he lived in Station Road. The Mills Grammar School, funded partly from his Trust, has recently been demolished, leaving only the bell tower. A residential home for the elderly, called Mills Meadows, has been built on the site.

The house at the corner of Queen's Head Alley was once an inn. Built in the late 1400s it was originally called the Blue Boar. The inn's name was changed to the Queen's Head before 1800, so it is thought that the Queen referred to was Queen Mary who came to Framlingham twice, once taking refuge in 1550 and again after being crowned. The rear of the inn was used by bear leaders who slept in the dosshouse after they had entertained in the area, while the bears slept in the alley. In the 19th century vagrants used to shelter there.

The pump alongside Riverside is unusual in that it has two outlets. The top one filled the local watercart which was used to settle the dust on the roads.

The railway opened in 1859 and gave the opportunity for travel to London and back within the day. This was closed to passengers in 1952, but continued carrying goods until 1965 when it was dismantled.

The castle overlooks what the locals call the meres. This much photographed setting is now a bird sanctuary managed by the Suffolk Wildlife Trust. In a severe winter the meres make a skating rink and people come from miles around to enjoy the ice. At night they skate by the headlights of their cars.

There are many signposted footpath walks, the longest one completely circling the parish. This is called the Brownsord Way after Miss Ella Brownsord, who for nearly 30 years was a member of the parish council. It was due to her work that there are so many footpaths open for the public to walk today.

Fressingfield 🐝

Fressingfield is one of the largest villages in the Upper Waveney, with approximately 1,000 inhabitants. Situated in the village today are three shops, one of which is a post office, a doctor's surgery, a primary school and nursery, coal merchant, petrol station and a car repair garage.

Fressingfield does not seem to have ever had a resident squire; there were seven, later reduced to five, manors in the parish, but a number of these families did not live in their manor houses.

Although a large proportion of the working population now 'commute' it was not always so, with most people working in the village or surrounding farms. Services in the village included about six shops, two of which sold drapery goods, two butchers and an abattoir, a baker, a carpenter who was also the undertaker, a harness maker, three blacksmiths, a stonemason, a doctor, a policeman and its own fire engine. There were also three windmills which ground corn, mostly for animal feed. The village was well endowed with public houses, having five, the Fox and Goose, the Angel, the Swan, the Bunbury Arms and the Jolly Farmer, of which only the Swan remains as a pub with the Fox and Goose a restaurant.

Other notable buildings include the stable at Church Farm, which is a well preserved 14th century building and is under constant renovation, as well as Ufford Hall, where the Sancroft family lived. One of this family became Fressingfield's most famous son. He went on to become the Archbishop of Canterbury and led the revolt of Bishops against James II, for which he was imprisoned in the Tower of London. When William IV ascended the throne he was released and then sacked for not taking the oath of allegiance. He returned to Fressingfield, and his tomb is by the south porch of the church.

The village sign is of a pilgrim and his donkey, as pilgrims passed through Fressingfield on their travels from Dunwich to Bury St Edmunds.

The Baptist chapel was built by Mr Spratt in 1836, and is one of only two chapels in the country to be built in the shape of a coffin, this is to remind people 'that in the midst of life there is death'.

The Anglican church of St Peter and St Paul was built in the 14th century on the site of an earlier church. The south porch was added in c1420 by Catherine De La Pole to commemorate the battle of Agincourt. The present day rector looks after five parishes, whereas before Fressingfield had a vicar of its own.

Although life in the village has changed a lot over the years, it is still an active place with a number of social activities and societies.

Freston 🐚

Freston is an agricultural parish on the south bank of the river Orwell. Three independent farms and part of the Paul estate occupied 590 hectares at the 1981 census (fewer now since Holbrook took a slice under recent boundary changes).

The road from Ipswich winds along the Strand close to the water, providing superb views of the big ships that use Ipswich Port and – in summer – hundreds of sailing craft. Continuing up Freston Hill the road passes half the village houses. More lie hidden in or near Freston Street beyond the isolated church of St Peter. Three new houses have been built since 1960; the rest are mostly Victorian. Seventeenth century houses include the Boot inn and the Old Forge at the hill top.

Bond Hall, lying empty and neglected at the Street's end, is a former 16th century manor house. A second ancient manor house – Freston Hall in the Park – lost its manorial status long ago, becoming in turn a farmhouse, a base for inoculating patients against smallpox and eventually farm cottages. These were recently converted into three private houses. Freston Lodge, near the church, was an 18th century shooting lodge. Its fine landscaped gardens are open regularly for charity. Its neighbour, Freston House, was once the rectory. A later Victorian rectory is also now in private hands – the parson moved to Holbrook to manage three parishes.

Freston has three remarkable buildings. Monkey Lodge at the foot of Freston Hill was built in 1861 as a gate house at the exit of a scenic drive from John Berners' mansion, Woolverstone Hall. Why Monkey? The legend tells of a pet ape alerting the Berners family to a fire so that all escaped. There were stone monkeys on the gate posts to commemorate the event. Now they are in Berkshire but a carved stone shield on the house wall explains 'del fuego el avola' – he snatched her from the fire.

Latimer Cottages in the Holbrook road have a sinister history. In September 1910 four people died there, victims of one of the last outbreaks of the plague in England. These cottages occupy the site of an old brickworks once owned by a Freston rector. They also lie within the bounds of Freston's 4,000 year old archaeological site – a causewayed camp – revealed as crop marks by aerial photographs. Nothing is visible on the surface.

The Latimers, once lords of Freston manor, have also been associated with Freston's most famous building – the six-storey Tudor Tower in the Park near the old Hall. Some say a Latimer built it but the dates don't fit. Many believe Richard Cobbold's romantic tale of a lord de Freston and his clever daughter Ellen who studied a different subject each weekday on separate floors. Alas, this too has no foundation in fact. Thomas Gooding, a wealthy Elizabethan merchant, probably had it erected in about 1560 so that he could keep an eye on shipping in the river when he lived in Freston Hall. It is privately owned and not open to the public.

Both Tower and manor house stand by the river on a curiously artificial-looking platform similar to ancient sites in the Frisian Islands. Freston's name means 'farm of the Frisians' who settled here as immigrants in the 8th century.

Friston 🐚

'Never a poor person in Friston' has been said since beyond living memory. No-one knows why, but Friston is even now so small and friendly that none need ever be in want of a friend.

The original farm-town was named Bohton until the Frisians came in the 6th century, then it became Freeston or Friston. The village now lies about three miles from the coast in two triangles, the apex of each meeting at the Saxmundham–Aldeburgh road.

The northern triangle is dominated by St Mary's church dating from the 11th century, as was recently proven by the discovery of the 'lost' north door with its beautiful plain, slender arch. More recently, during repairs to the church roof, in the thickness of the south wall, steps were uncovered which had once led to the top of the reredos. Richard de Bedynfeld from Snape Priory was the incumbent in 1305. St Mary's remained in the possession of Snape until the 16th century. Today most of the property belongs to a family related to the now extinct Earldom of Strafford, the Vernon-Wentworths. The mansion is now at Blackheath.

The windmill dominates the southern triangle, rising to 55 ft which makes it the highest in Europe. Built possibly by John Collins of Ipswich in 1811, it is a typical Suffolk post mill and worked until 1972 when it was sold. Now it has lost its sails and fallen into disrepair. The last miller is still living locally. Close to the mill is the Baptist chapel built in 1831 by a Mr Spratt. It is unusually hexagonal in shape.

At the crossroads is the Chequers, an old hostelry much changed by recent owners but now brought back to some semblance of its former appearance, as a restaurant with a 'snug' bar.

The estate was paternal in Friston, keeping a firm hand and kindly eye

Friston Mill

98

on tenant farmers and villagers. In so small a community there were always characters and one such was 'Steddy Will', a local carrier who would convey goods around the countryside. He regularly carried cottagers' chickens and small livestock to market. There are still lively memories of small boys skipping out of school to join Steddy's cart. His old pony, of course, knew its own way home from Saxmundham! Memories too of little fields hedged about and full of wild flowers, each with its own small pond, woods filled with bird-song, and the ghost of Spintoe Wood, 'White Hannah'. Some say she was connected with the old well, long since filled in.

Most of the estate and farm work has gone, being replaced by car maintenance, agricultural engineering, employment in local towns and even in London. Building and thatching is still done, dairy farming, market gardening and bee-keeping. There are no shops although vans call regularly but there is a post office and a reasonable bus service.

Gazeley 🦚

The present church of All Saints at Gazeley dates back to the 14th century. Yearly, on 5th November, the bells were 'fired' (rung) to celebrate the failure of the Gunpowder Plot. The 'gleaning' bell was rung at harvest time, to signify that gleaners could enter the fields, and the 'passing' bell when someone died. The bells, still in fair condition, are not now hung, so sadly they no longer ring out over the countryside.

In 1831, the population of Gazeley was 426. Today, it is about 750. At the beginning of the 20th century, most local people earned a living from the land or associated industries; blacksmith, wheelwright, horseman and with the near proximity of Newmarket, stud farms.

In 1924, civil war broke out in Gazeley. On 15th August, a local farmer in dispute with his men over pay for getting in the harvest, imported 14 men from Isleham. The infuriated Gazeley men attacked the 'furriners', and battle raged through the village. The farmer, on horseback midst the flaying pitchforks, was unable to restore order. The disruption continued through the weekend with ugly threats to fire the farmhouse. Extra police were drafted in, sympathizers from neighbouring villages swelled the angry voices, as meetings took place on the green and in front of the farmhouse. Finally, on Sunday 19th August, Mrs Rhodes from Dalham Hall addressed the disgruntled workers, and by 10 pm peace was restored.

For amusement in those day, boys made peashooters, popguns and whistles from elder stalks, pushing out the pith with an old corset stay. They would make catapults, useful for providing a young rabbit for the pot, or the contents of a rook pie. Their elders would gather at the local hostelry for a game of skittles or quoits. Folk saved the year round, to 'hev a good toime' at Gazeley Spring Fair. Bandsmen walked the twelve miles from Great Bradley to provide music for the occasion. When the first notes of the approaching band were carried on the breeze, excited villagers would flock to meet them, for festivities did not begin until the band arrived.

The old elm tree which stood near the allotment gate has gone. The allotments are now covered by a modern housing estate, yet Gazeley still boasts a smithy, farms and a stud farm. Happily, newcomers and those with roots deep in the soil of Gazeley, live in harmony.

Gazeley's last link with the old culture, Herbert Kidd, died in 1984, approaching the age of 101. A true son of Gazeley, his memory held a wealth of tales of bygone days. One such was the horseman's secret, as follows . . . bury a toad in an anthill. Later, go at midnight to collect the bones. Throw these in a stream. One bone will go against the flow. Keep this one, and while you carry it you will control even the most fractious horse.

There remains one thatched dwelling in Gazeley. Formerly two 15th century cottages, The Hutch is now converted into one residence. The Hutch can tell its own story of links with the past. When the roof was rethatched in recent years, the thighbone of an ox was discovered, evidently an amulet placed there to ward off evil spirits, in accordance with the beliefs of the time.

Gedding 🐝

The quiet hamlet of Gedding has two claims to fame, its Red Poll dairy herd, the traditional Suffolk breed, founded by Captain and Mrs Walmsley of Grange Farm, and its lord of the manor, Rolling Stone rock star Bill Wyman who lives at Gedding Hall.

Gedding Hall, a red-brick moated manor house with a picturesque gatehouse dating from the time of Henry VIII, was originally built in 1273 and rebuilt in the 15th century. The original owners and builders of the hall were the Geddying family who lived there until 1357. There is no longer any evidence of the first manor house, at least at a superficial level. The house was extensively altered in 1897 when the brick tower and the kitchen range at the rear were added.

Early settlements at Gedding are suggested by fragments of Iron Age and Roman pottery found in fields adjacent to the church, which dates back to Norman times. In 1986, a Flower Festival was held to celebrate 900 years since the first mention of the church in the Domesday Book. St Mary's continues its struggle to maintain an active part in this small community rather than to become yet another redundant historical building.

The present structure of Gedding is shaped by Gedding Hall and the church together with four farms, set in arable farming land which has successfully managed to retain meadowland and areas of woodland. The majority of housing making up the body of Gedding consists of council built houses with a few agricultural workers' cottages. In 1841 the population of Gedding was 173 living in 28 houses whereas today there are 130 living in 50 homes.

One of the most dramatic additions to Gedding occurred in 1867 when a post mill adjoining Mill Cottage on the Cockfield Road near Upper Green, Felsham, was moved by a team of 18 horses to the top of Pikes Hill in Gedding. Although the mill has since been demolished, the great-grandson of the original miller now works as a blacksmith on the site, carrying out some agricultural repairs but in the main concentrating on industrial fabrication and domestic ornamental ironwork.

Although Gedding joins Felsham in church, village and recreational activities it still maintains its own independence as a parish with its own parish meeting, the smallest of all levels of English local government.

Gislingham 🐝

Gislingham is a pleasant village situated five miles from Eye. It has a church, village store and post office, a garage, a public house, village hall and an hotel.

The church of St Mary, erected in the 15th century, is a structure of flint in the Perpendicular style consisting of chancel, nave, north porch and an embattled western tower of brick, built in the reign of Charles I and containing six bells. The font is ancient and embellished with carved figures. Only part of the church is now used as it is in need of repair and the community are trying to raise funds to carry out repairs.

The Old Guildhall in Mill Street is a very pretty thatched building dating back to the 15th century, now an hotel which attracts many visitors. The village also has a silver band which has been in existence for over 50 years and which plays at many events in and around Gislingham. There is an assortment of old, quite a few thatched, and modern houses in the village, which has a population of approximately 800.

The footpaths of today were well used by villagers in the past to walk to the surrounding villages. The 1930s brought council houses to High Street and the 1960s and 1970s saw the developments in Westview Gardens and Broadfields. The village scene has changed a great deal since the mid 19th century when there were two blacksmiths and a wheelwright's shop. Gislingham was the only village of three, the other two being Thornham Magna and Thornham Parva, which had a school with an employed schoolmaster. This was situated in Mill Street, much further up the Street than the present school which is now in a more central position. The money for the school came from a charity set up in the 17th century by John Darby.

The scene changed around Gislingham and Thornham around 1850 with the age of the railway. In July 1845 an Act of Parliament gave sanction for the Ipswich–Bury St Edmunds and Haughley–Norwich lines. Trains also ran to Finningham and Burston. The more senior personnel and engineers working on the line took up temporary accommodation with the Gislingham villagers. The nearest stations to Gislingham were at Finningham and Mellis, with a halt for Thornhall Hall some quarter of a mile north of the Thornham Road, the trains stopping by prior arrangement or by the waving of a flag!

Glemsford ✒️

The most impressive approach to Glemsford is from the north on the B1066 from Boxted, along the valley of the meandering river Glem where Glemsford's ancient church of St Mary appears on the right, perched on the edge of the hill. The scene disproves the belief, held by people who don't really know, that Suffolk is a flat county. The hill is said to be unique in England; 275 ft of boulder clay with another 300 ft below sea level.

Domesday Book records the manor of Guthelnesford (Glemsford) belonging in 1086 to Adeliza, the wife of Bishop Odo who was William the Conqueror's half-brother and the man who commissioned the Bayeux Tapestry. Could needlewomen in Glemsford have been involved in stitching parts of the tapestry? Some believe they could, and certainly throughout history textiles have been recorded as one of the principal occupations of the village. On the site of one of the water mills recorded in the Domesday Book stands the present day silk mill which has processed silk thread since 1824. Thread from this factory was woven in Sudbury for Queen Elizabeth II's coronation dress and the Prince of Wales' investiture robes, as well as the wedding dresses of the Princesses Royal and Diana.

More mundanely, during the 19th century there were no fewer than ten factories in Glemsford which wove coconut fibres into matting and in 1906 Glemsford produced the largest carpet in the world, 63,000 sq ft to cover the floor of Olympia in London. The present day firm of E. W. Downs which makes potato handling equipment that is exported worldwide, originated from a company started by the blacksmith Ernest Downs in 1887 to make machinery for the weaving of coconut matting. During the Victorian era, Glemsford had many factories which processed horse hair, but today only that of Arnold & Gould – originally Messrs Kolle Ltd and established sometime around 1848 – remains and is now unique in Britain. It processes and curls the horse hair for making judges' wigs and also prepares it for use in military sporrans and the regimental cockades on busbys and bearskins.

Although Glemsford is not a photogenic village on tourist routes, it has its share of large picturesque, timbered buildings. These include Peverels on Tye Green, built about 1490 for George Cavendish who wrote *The Life of Cardinal Wolsey* in 1554, and the present day Angel public house, reputed to be the home of John Golding, a rich clothier who, when he died in 1496, left £40 for a chapel to be built in Glemsford church –

known to this day as the Golding Chapel. Over the past few years the addition of several hundred new houses has brought the population of the village to around 3,000.

Great Ashfield 🐝

Great Ashfield is a small village consisting of just over 100 homes, a church, a Methodist chapel and two public houses. One, the Hovell Arms, was used by American servicemen stationed nearby during the Second World War.

The now disused airfield was in the front line as Home Defence Air Station from September 1917 to November 1918, and the headquarters to the 385th Bombardment Group, United States Air Force from June 1943 to August 1945. Memory of the American visitors is kept alive, for in the churchyard stands a memorial to their sacrifice, and inside the church is a memorial altar, and a parchment roll recording the names of those who failed to return from their bombing missions.

The earliest known record of a church in the village is in the Domesday Book (1086), but All Saints today dates back to the 13th century. Legend has it that in the year AD 903, the body of King Edmund, who was killed by the Danes, was hidden in the church when it was carried back from Hoxne on the way to be buried at Beodricksworth, now Bury St Edmunds. To commemorate the occasion, a Saxon cross was erected in the churchyard. The cross, shaped from Barnac stone, remained there until the Reformation when it was knocked down, and later used as a footbridge over the stream at the east end of the church. The cross was raised in the 19th century by Lord Thurlow, and now stands in the garden of Ashfield House, where it has recently been restored.

There are three moated plots in the village, one of which stands southwest of the church. Known as Castle Hill, because a castle once stood here, although there are no baileys here to prove this, a man called Robert-le-Blund lived here. His family reigned in Ashfield for over 200 years. Sir William, the last member, was killed in the battle of Lewes in 1264. The mound and moat can still be seen. A farmhouse on the site has been restored in the last few years.

This friendly, unspoilt village offers little employment to local people. One family firm, Miles Agricultural Contractors, still remains, offering jobs to a few village men, but most people commute to larger towns such as Bury St Edmunds and Ipswich, or even to London, travelling by British Rail from nearby Stowmarket. Although not many original families now live in the village, Great Ashfield is a pleasant village to live in.

Great Barton ❧

Great Barton, just two and a half miles from its large neighbour Bury St Edmunds, is a scattered village of some 2,000 residents, who occupy a larger area than that of Bury itself!

Great Barton started its life as a Saxon settlement and by the 13th century had become the 'granary' for the abbey of Bury St Edmunds. Icepits Woods have to this day huge excavations which testify to it being the ice store for the abbey, and the village sign is 'Bertuna, the Gleaner'. Even now Great Barton is in the forefront of agricultural development, and also in bloodstock breeding at Barton Stud.

The village's love affair with horses started in the 18th century when Sir Charles Bunbury lived at Barton Hall. When Sir Charles, in 1780, tossed a coin with Lord Derby in a London club to decide the name of a new horse race, he unfortunately lost the toss, but had the pleasure of owning the first two winners of the 'Derby Stakes'. A village ghost story which concerns the first winner, *Diomed*, states that on the eve of Derby Day a spectral horse can be seen and heard in Hall Park! Hall Park, itself, is part of the grounds of the old Barton Hall which was destroyed by fire in 1914 and, in contrast with some old houses of other parts of the village, contains the most modern of new dwellings.

The Bunbury family has left a permanent reminder of its presence by building almshouses and a school in the village, and a public house some two miles outside the village so that it was not necessary to pass it on the way to church.

The church of the Holy Innocents itself is a 'Plague Church', the original houses which once surrounded it having been destroyed. The Civil War left its mark on the church. Only one of the angels in the old hammerbeam roof still has a head – village legend says that the responsible Cromwellian soldier, having decapitated all the other angels, lost his footing when attacking the last angel and fell on the flagstones to his death. To this day the story is recounted with satisfaction!

Great Barton still has a clear sense of its own identity, has no wish to be absorbed by its huge neighbour and enjoys the advantages of three churches, the pub, two shops and post office, a garage and bus services and a vital primary school. Social life can only be limited by lack of stamina in Great Barton as friendly organisations abound. Do come and visit us!

Great & Little Bealings ❧

In Saxon times there were two settlements in which Beda's people lived, Belinges Magna and its offshoot Belinges Parva, and it wasn't until 1674 that the name Bealings with today's spelling was recorded.

At that time Little Bealings was looked upon as the poor relation, but in the late 1850s it was noted that 'The proportion of well dressed in the congregation at Little Bealings church was unusually large' which leads one to believe that a prosperous village had grown up over the years. The villages are situated between Ipswich and Woodbridge and are surrounded by green fields and wooded slopes which form a beautifully unspoilt valley.

For many years the villages were self-sufficient, most of the men worked on the farms and in the large gardens, and the women helped in the big houses. Milk was collected from the farms each morning, and each village had a shop. Great Bealings had an off licence as well as the Boot, and the Admiral's Head was in Little Bealings. Today life is very different, the milk is delivered from Ipswich, Great Bealings has lost both its pubs, Little Bealings has no shop and most people work in Ipswich, Woodbridge or London. The Admiral's Head is still in Little Bealings, and Great Bealings has the wonderful shop-cum-post office. It is really the centre of village life, where you are sure of a warm welcome, a good chat, and best of all what no supermarket can provide, personal service.

The two churches are totally different – St Mary's Great Bealings stands in green meadows and contains some beautiful wood carvings, while the simple flint and stone building of All Saints Little Bealings stands on a hill. Both churches are enriched with colourful tapestry kneelers representing hours of dedicated work by the many people who embroidered them.

On the boundary between Woodbridge and Great Bealings stands Seckford Hall. This Elizabethan mansion was the residence of Sir Thomas Seckford and his family. He founded the Woodbridge school and the almshouses, and after his death the porch at St Mary's Great Bealings, was built in his memory. Today, the magnificent mansion is a flourishing hotel.

Bealings House, also in Great Bealings, was built in the 1770s. It stands in extensive parkland in which an early British mound was discovered. This was found to contain pottery and implements. There was a time when the house was thought to be haunted, as the bells in the servants' hall would be heard ringing at odd times, day or night. Some said it was the ghost of a maid long dead, some said the wiring was faulty! Nobody ever found the answer and no bells ring today.

Great Bradley 🦌

Great Bradley is a small village situated mid-way between Haverhill and Newmarket on the B1061, although most of the dwellings lie beyond the boundaries of the main road.

The river Stour rises just outside the village and divides it into two parts. It is thought that East Green, which lies across the river to the main village as we know it today, could have been the original village.

The population of Great Bradley has fluctuated greatly over the years.

The peak years seem to have been in the 1830–40s when there were over 500 recorded residents. This number slumped to under 200 in the 1930s. Then in the 1970s, with the building of the new Clarendale estate the electoral roll recorded 300 electors.

St Mary's parish church is an interesting building. It has a well preserved Norman archway at the main door, this has been protected by the porch which was added at a later date. There are three bells in the tower and some lovely stained glass in the east window. This shows a young soldier in the trenches and is dedicated to Rex Wilder, who was killed in the First World War.

The village once had three public houses – the Crown inn, the Three Tuns and the Fox but, alas, now it has none. The Fox was the last to close and is now a private residence. One previous landlord of the Fox is remembered today because although he was blind he confidently served his customers their drinks and always gave the correct change.

Bradley mill stood opposite Mill House at the top of Bradley Hill. It occupied an unrivalled position, providing a fine panorama of the surrounding countryside. It was a well known landmark, particularly for the RAF during the Second World War.

The mill is said to have been built in 1839. The miller provided bread for the whole village and his service would have been invaluable in the days when Great Bradley was an isolated community. In 1908, Jo Nice, the miller at that time, decided to have extensive renovations carried out on the mill. The renovations had almost been completed when a flash of lightning struck the sails during a thunderstorm, causing a tremendous amount of damage. The poor miller had spent all his savings on the repairs and a few days later he hanged himself. The mill was never used again and all that remains now is a mound of earth.

Great Finborough 🦢

Great Finborough, located three miles west of Stowmarket, is a small village of just over 200 houses. It was originally all part of the Finborough Hall estate, part of which was mentioned in the Domesday Book. The estate was finally broken up in 1935, sold off to pay death duties.

The Hall, rebuilt in 1795 after a fire destroyed the earlier Jacobean building, is now a boarding school and has changed much in the past few years, the parkland having lost many fine trees in the gales of October 1987. One intriguing feature of Finborough Hall is the underground brick tunnel which starts just by the kitchen door and comes out beyond the formal gardens at the kitchen garden. One of the squires of the 19th century did not like to see the domestic staff crossing the lawns to reach the kitchen garden and so had the tunnel excavated, effectively banishing them from his sight.

The parish church of St Andrew, a fine example of Victorian architecture with its spire visible for many miles, was rebuilt in 1875 at the instigation of the squire who thought the existing building too small. The medieval porch at the main entrance is all that is left of the old church.

The main village has grown up around the Hall and church, with the pub and shop located in this centre. To the south a hamlet known as High Street Green has several farmhouses of interest. The 500 year old tithe barn at West End Farm remains in use.

In 1880 a local builder with very individual ideas rebuilt some of the estate cottages. In Church Road he built a terrace of three with very tall chimneys. The other terrace of three, on the main road, was built on the site of the original pub, known as the White Horse, and incorporated the old cellar. This group, still known as White Horse Cottages, was more ornate, as befitted its main road location, again with tall Elizabethan-style chimneys and the date worked in coloured bricks.

The next development was in the 1930s when several local authority bungalows were built on the High Road, at some distance from the Hall at the squire's request. Since the early 1970s new estate development has taken place to the south and east of the village centre, including sheltered accommodation for the elderly. The well-stocked village shop and post office can provide for most of the everyday needs of the village. As the parish boundary passes through the middle of the shop the owner works in Finborough but sleeps in Buxhall.

The only custom still surviving in the village is the annual Race of the Bogman held on Easter Monday, together with egg races for the children. The Race of the Bogman was revived some years ago. It is based on a story that two teams of labourers, one from Finborough and one from Haughley, had by accident both been given the job of drilling the fields at Boyton Hall, a large farm on the edge of the parish. Neither side would give way so it was decided to hold a race, starting at Boyton Hall with the first team to reach the local pub, the Chestnut Horse, being awarded the contract. No holds were barred in the race and mayhem ensued. Finborough, of course, won the contract. Today the race is run for fun – but it is still no holds barred as the winners get free beer at the end of the race.

Great Glemham 🐝

There are four ways into Great Glemham – at each of the compass points. The village is three miles off the A12 at Marlesford (south entrance), three miles off the A12 at Stratford St Andrew (east entrance), three miles off the B1119 Saxmundham to Framlingham road near Sweffling (north entrance) and three miles off the same road at the Cransford crossroads (west entrance). All very central.

The south entrance brings you up New Road with the wall of the Earl and Countess of Cranbrook's estate running up on the right, with a lovely view of All Saints' church on the rise to the left. This much loved building has recently undergone the 'new tower' problem of vast costs and a lot of fund-raising. New Road ends in a T-junction with Stone

Cottage directly in front. In its past this house was home of the 'favourite' of the then lord of the manor, who had a special gate built between his land and the road so as to have direct access. The key to this gate still hangs in Stone Cottage. As the lady's power grew so did her cottage until it took on the charming proportions of a Georgian flint-fronted house. Turn right and you join the south entrance to the village and see the local free house, the Crown, on your left.

To the left, at a rather sharp left hand bend round the inn, you will see the old entrance to the manor house which stood for 100 years in the meadow behind the wall, but in 1814 burned down and is now rebuilt on top of a hill directly above the meadow. The old stables and woodworking buildings have been made into accommodation.

Next to the village hall is a new house built by the present occupiers. The owner is by trade a plasterer and all the pargetting on the house and garage wall was done free-hand and designed by himself; the whole village wondered with interest what the next picture would be. If you have sharp eyesight the two hunting scenes on the wall to the right of the garage are especially good with a crafty fox standing on the frame of the picture looking very pleased with himself!

Between the Old School House and the Crown inn are five new houses designed by local architects Mullins & Dowse of Woodbridge. The building of these houses has caused much concern to the villagers but it brought new families and interest into the village, which cannot be a bad thing.

The south entrance to the village brings you across the old USAAF airfield of Parham where the control tower is now a memorial to the wartime activities of the area and is well worth a visit. It is usually open Sundays and Bank Holidays.

Great & Little Thurlow 🦚

The name Thurlow means 'famous tumulus' or the 'assembly hill'. Evidence of Saxon habitation has been found. Being a conservation area the shape of Thurlow has changed little in living memory.

Sir Stephen Soame (1544–1619) was Lord Mayor of London in 1598. He built Little Thurlow Hall, and although his house burned down the present Hall is on almost the same site. It was completed in 1849. He founded the original school in 1614 and the almshouses, both now private homes. Legend has it that Charles II played bowls at Little Thurlow Hall. In Little Thurlow church are all the Soame memorials, including a very grand one of Sir Stephen, his wife and children.

The Honourable W. F. D. Smith, MP, was lord of the manor at Great Thurlow at the beginning of the 20th century and built some of the cottages which bear his crest.

Now there is Edmund Vestey at Little Thurlow Hall and his son,

George Vestey at Great Thurlow, who own the Thurlow estate. They have provided the village with its recreation ground.

Thurlow comes alive on Boxing Day for the traditional Meet. The pack of hounds is now back in the village after a few years absence. Another big event is the Thurlow Fayre held in September which has recently been revived. This sees the village at its best with everyone working together.

The most famous past event must be the pageant produced by Mrs C. F. Ryder in 1938 when the whole village took part. Sir Malcolm Campbell had his famous *Bluebird* on show; this was combined with a produce show. A fete on the grand scale.

The Houghton Charity still exists, which used to provide a loaf of bread at Christmas time for each inhabitant. Now the older people benefit.

There are several 17th century cottages in Little Thurlow, and a mill at Great Thurlow which has been restored. A school is now the Thurlow estate office at Great Thurlow, while Little Thurlow school is now two private houses. The chapel which stands between the two is now a dwelling with a graveyard as a front garden, and of course there are two churches and a village hall. Before the Second World War Thurlow had more than a dozen small tenant farmers, a butcher's shop, two grocers, four public houses, harness makers, post office, two wheelwrights, two blacksmiths' shops, bakers, two vicars and its own policeman. These have all gone except one public house, the Cock, the shop which now houses the post office, and there is a garage which is in the grounds of the old Queen's Head. There is a new primary school in Little Thurlow for five to nine year olds which caters for the surrounding villages as well.

At present Great Thurlow is almost solely owned by the Thurlow estate and people are employed in farming, forestry and building maintenance, living in the farm cottages. Little Thurlow has mostly owner-occupied houses and some council housing. Most people work out of the village in a mixture of professional and factory work.

Great Waldingfield 🐝

Great Waldingfield lies about three miles north-east of the town of Sudbury.

When the Domesday Book was compiled in 1086, the Saxons had three manors in Waldingfield. Earl Giselbert was appointed tenant-in-chief for the parish, with two freemen, one under Robert, son of Wimarc. It is interesting to note that, after 900 years, the name of Whymark still exists in the village.

Until 1800, Great Waldingfield was open heath, known as Babergh Heath. Tracks and footpaths crossed it. Annual fairs were held there with stalls and tents erected around the White Horse.

In August 1648, it is thought that Cromwell's Ironsides were billeted in what is now known as Garrison Lane. In this lane is reputed to be the oldest house in Waldingfield – Malting Barn, once an inn named 'The Bottles'.

In the 14th century, the Flemish weavers arrived. Lying between Lavenham and Sudbury, Great Waldingfield had a fair share of the work, and as a reminder of that period there is a row of delightful cottages of Flemish design in the village today.

The church is dedicated to St Lawrence, and dates back to the 14th century. Changes have been made, but the greatest was in 1869 after the rector, Rev W. D. Bailey, and his sisters, visited the Holy Land. In the chancel there is a mosaic of marble fragments from Rome, and granite from Mount Sinai. The alabaster from which the cross is made, came from a small temple near the Sphinx.

John Hopkins lies buried here. He was rector in the 16th century, and linked his name with Thomas Sternhold. Between them they produced the first metrical version of the Psalms, set to modern music. In four centuries, this treasure has run into 600 editions.

The old village school, now a private dwelling, stands next to the church. A new school was opened in 1970. The population has grown due to new housing. There is light industry, two shops, a post office, a village hall, and an indoor bowling rink.

Groton 🐟

The parish of Groton is pleasantly situated on a plateau 200 ft above sea level, overlooking the valley of the river Box, roughly mid-way between Bury St Edmunds, Ipswich and Colchester. It has a bracing but comparatively dry climate. There is no centre to the village as the parish comprises a number of small hamlets – Groton Street, Goslings Green, Horners Green, Daisy Green, Castlings Heath, Parliament Heath and Park Corner.

The population has remained at an average of 250/300 over the past 60 years. There is a village inn, the Fox and Hounds, but no shop or school – the latter was a church school closed in the early 1930s. The schoolteacher's house (used as the church organist's house for many years) was sold in 1987 realising £37,000 and from this an educational charity was established, 'The Groton Educational Foundation'.

Groton Wood is now owned by the Suffolk Wildlife Trust. Since prehistoric times this site has been wooded and contains the largest stand of small-leaved lime in Suffolk, plus the rare herb paris and the early purple orchid, as well as being home for species of interesting birds – if you are lucky the nightingale may be heard in early summer.

St Bartholomew's church is an imposing edifice. Most of the building dates back to the 15th century, although the lower part of the tower is about 200 years older and the first rector of whom written records exist, was Hugh de Grotene in 1218. There are many memorials to the

Winthrop family. John Winthrop led the great Puritan emigration to New England in 1630 and, eventually, founded the city of Boston and was the first Governor of Massachusetts. Groton church still has connections with the Winthrop family; the present John Winthrop visits the village often with his family who have recently established a trust in memory of a cousin – Groton church receives annual interest from this.

Groton is a large scattered village occupying 1,545 acres which is still devoted to agriculture, mostly occupied by farmers whose livelihood is wholly from the land.

Grundisburgh, Burgh & Culpho

Though Burgh was the most important in ancient times – with Grundisburgh as a dependent area in the low-lying ground – the latter has become the dominant village. All three villages have a church, St Botolph's at Culpho, a small one from Saxon times, Burgh's built over a chapel where St Botolph's bones were temporarily sheltered from the marauding Vikings, hence its name, and St Mary's at Grundisburgh, a 14th century foundation built over an older one. Its flint tower collapsed in the 16th century, and after 200 years Robert Thinge left money in his will for the present red brick tower to be built – though not to everyone's taste. The belfry housed ten bells which were becoming unsafe. The wooden supports have been renewed or strengthened and two new bells were added in January 1991.

At Grundisburgh the old Victorian school and the church provide a focal point across the green which is criss-crossed by paths and divided by the river Lark, which joins the river Finn outside the village. Old houses and shops stand on its other sides, and the A12 runs along it – an old highway linking Ipswich and Woodbridge. When the old school was in use mums gathered on the green waiting for their children, but it is much quieter now the modern school has been built off Meeting Lane. Centuries ago there were weekly markets and annual fairs on the green, but fund-raising stalls and the 'Sheep Roast' are their modern counterpart. A metallic sign swings on the green with the arms of the Cranworths – three golden leopards' heads on a black ground. Grundisburgh Hall and its surrounding lands were bought by the Gurdons from the Blois estate in 1770. Robert Thornhaugh Gurdon, Esq, MP, was elevated to the peerage in 1899 and chose the name of Cranworth from a Norfolk village near where they formerly lived. His silken banner was brought from the Garter stall in Windsor Chapel and now hangs in the church.

The nearby parish room, which began life as a 'Village Club and Reading Room' and had an upper room built on for the church's use, has now become one of the centres of community life. It houses a doctor's surgery, with an office on the first floor, is used by the church two days a week, and all sorts of classes and meetings are held there.

There used to be four pubs in the old days, the Barley Mow, the Sun, the Half Moon and the Dog. Unfortunately only the Dog is left, but behind this is an excellent bowling green.

At the top of Meeting Lane there is a link with Culpho, as a farmer at Culpho Hall who was converted to the Baptist cause erected a meeting house in 1798, all red brick and sash windows. It cost him £400. Twelve years later a small extension for a schoolroom or vestry cost £600. It became a centre of influence extending to many villages, but its congregation now is small.

Thomas A'Wall, a rich member of the Salters' Company, not only extended his father's home, Basts, in the 15th century, but paid for a Lady chapel to be built at St Mary's. His merchant's mark, and the badges of the City of London and the Salters' Company, are carved on its crenellations. The church is floodlit every night. To the villagers, whether churchgoers or not, it is a symbol of ancient values and of the village community.

Hadleigh 🐑

Hadleigh is an ancient place and was important even before the Norman Conquest, the name meaning 'head-place'. The Danish chieftain Guthrum, who ruled East Anglia, lived here for twelve years. He was buried in the wooden church which was replaced in the 13th century. At the height of the wool prosperity, in the 15th century, it was again rebuilt and refurbished.

Early in the 12th century Flemish weavers brought their skills to East Anglia and Hadleigh became a centre for the wool and cloth business. The name of one of the older streets, Long Bessels, was a term used by the weavers for the ends of their products.

One of our most famous citizens was Dr Rowland Taylor who, as rector, was burnt at the stake on Aldham Common for refusing to allow Mass to be celebrated in the church during the reign of Queen Mary. The exact spot is marked by a large stone, an inscription and the date 1555. William Pykenham, another well-known name, built the remarkable Deanery Tower, close by the church and provided almshouses. He is commemorated by a street named Pykenham Way.

The corn exchange, funded by voluntary subscription, was built in 1813 and after various uses is now restored and occupied by the Social Services. The guildhall and town hall complex is in the process of complete restoration to provide extensive community facilities. Close by is the market place which in the early days saw regular cattle and livestock sales on Mondays. Agriculture and cloth then formed the basis of Hadleigh's success. Two industrial estates have brought modern industries whose products include flavours, fragrances, ceiling boards, furniture and electrical goods.

Smuggling was rife in the 18th century and one of the most ruthless and highly organised groups was the 'Hadleigh Gang' who were involved in running tea and dry goods from Sizewell Gap.

Schools were established as early as the 1830s and education is still well served by two primary schools, a high school and a wide ranging syllabus for further education.

For all the modern developments in Hadleigh, the old charm is still there. Timber framed houses and decorative plasterwork are well featured particularly in the broad sweep of the main street with ancient and modern combining wonderfully well.

Hargrave 🐾

Visitors to Bridge Green on a fine summer's day might agree with Arthur Mee's comment in his book of Suffolk that it is 'a charming corner of England'. The pretty lane to Bridge Green is a cul-de-sac leading only to the Norman church, the Old Rectory, the old deserted Hall and a newer house. The green is a peaceful spot where cowslips grow in the spring and blackberries can be picked in autumn and on two Sundays a month a tiny congregation park their cars before walking up the grassy path to the church, which is tucked away and quite out of sight of the village. Hargrave has three more greens, Great Knowles and Little Knowles Green and Hargrave Green.

It might be true to say that Hargrave's only claim to newsworthiness was in the Second World War when the church porch suffered a direct hit when the first German bombs were dropped on East Anglia. The Norman porch was completely demolished and has never been replaced. The church has a Tudor brick tower, a 15th century font and carved screen with carvings of a fox, unicorn, dragon, fish and eagles. These carvings are all on the altar side and it is possible that in one of the many restorations, the screen was replaced the wrong way round.

Once there were three public houses, a post office and shop, and a school. Now only the Bull remains. The post office and shop closed in 1986. The school, which is a flint structure, was built in 1840 for 40 children. It closed in 1947 when Miss Todd retired having taught at the school since 1900. The building is now a small curtain factory.

The Methodist chapel in the centre of the village was built in 1926 and services are held there every Sunday. It is also the Headquarters of the 8th Mid-Suffolk Company of the Boy's Brigade.

The Cock's Head at Little Knowles Green is now a private residence. It was probably a 16th century timber-framed farmhouse; once an alehouse, it was used by drovers going to market, the cattle grazing on the green whilst the drovers imbibed. In earlier times it may have been a hospice for pilgrims making their way to the great abbey in Bury St Edmunds.

The village once had a smock mill which was not pulled down until the

20th century. Mill House dates from the 1400s and is probably the oldest surviving domestic building in the village.

In spite of the hardships suffered by the villagers in the past, they were able to enjoy a pint of homebrewed ale at the Kicking Dicky at Bird's End and maybe listen to the stories of the Horse Men of Hargrave, the men who looked after and had a way with those magnificent Suffolk Punches, shire horses that once worked the stiff and unkind clay soil. Illicit visits would have been made to the cockfighting pit behind Grove Farm and perhaps villagers watching the 'sport' might have been forced to use the secret passage to the cellar to escape the law. In the 1920s and 1930s, a game of quoits was played, described by Mr Frank Jolly who used to live at The Willows, in a cottage now demolished, opposite Grove Farm. The quoit bed was made with clay from the pond, then rammed and pummelled with a weight on a broomstick. The bed was a yard square with logs on three sides; there was an iron pin in the middle, marked with a white feather over which wrought iron quoits were thrown. The quoits were sold in pairs and weighed seven lbs or seven and a half lbs a pair. The Bull also had a quoit bed and there was many a contest between the Hargrave Willows and the Bull.

Harkstead 🌿

Harkstead is a village with no great claims to fame, no known famous inhabitants or great past events. Many books on Suffolk pass it by without mention. But in its quiet, unassuming way it has existed for a thousand years or more and King Harold is recorded in the Domesday Book as having held Harkstead in the Samford Hundred as an 'outlier in the lands of Brightlingsea in Essex' before the year 1066.

The great glory of Harkstead lies in its situation on high land perched above cornfields, sloping gently to the shore of the broad Holbrook Bay, at the widest part of the Stour estuary. At high tide a vast expanse of water stretches across westwards to Wrabness and Manningtree on the more wooded Essex shore and eastwards (but round the corner out of sight) towards the bustling and brilliantly-lit world of dockland at Harwich and Felixstowe. Because of these dock lights the night sky at Harkstead is never absolutely dark. Low tide exposes the shifting mudbanks and flats across which comes the haunting sound of waders and shorebirds, and a sense of remoteness envelops the atmosphere. The oldest inhabitants can recall times when the shore was also a working place, the spritsail barges from London coming in with manure and returning with hay for those same horses who had helped to fertilise the crops.

It is likely that the shore contributed to the building of the church of St Mary (much of it dating from the 14th century), the chief materials of which are flint and septaria, with the battlements renewed in brick. An abundant supply of septaria, characterized by veins filled with a mineral deposit radiating from the centre of the block, may still be found below the cliffs towards Erwarton. The church stands almost alone on high ground, probably originally near the site of the early village. It is a fine typical Suffolk church, of great importance in the landscape. It also makes a grand setting for church and family functions.

Half a mile or so away, separated by open country, is The Street, in and around which is clustered a medley of old restored cottages and comparatively new bungalows mainly occupied by incomers to the village. There is also a well laid out road of twelve good red-brick houses originally built by the council and twelve old people's bungalows. Amongst these dwellings stands the Bakers Arms, now the only public house in the village and a most important asset.

Hartest

Hartest has existed as a village for more than a thousand years and in the summer of 1990 celebrated its millennium with the erection of a village sign showing a hart (or stag) against the background of Hartest Stone. Earlier spellings indicate that the original name meant Harts' Wood.

The centre of the village is the green, and All Saints' church, on the south side, was certainly on its present site in 1086, being mentioned in the Domesday Book. In 1650 the church tower collapsed and fell into the nave and aisles. Because of the 'extreme poverty' of the villagers they were unable to afford the cost of repairs and a petition for money to be collected 'for so charitable a worke' was made to Parliament. Seventeenth century records bring the village to life – a Royalist rector, a Parliamentarian churchwarden, a witch who was charged at Bury Assizes not only with causing two deaths but of turning beer sour and cattle lame – the latter a serious charge in a largely farming community. Like the rest of England the village had its share of plague victims in 1666.

On one corner of the green stands a large glacial stone. It is said to have been found in a farmer's field in the neighbouring village of Somerton and was dragged to its present site on a sledge drawn by 45 horses; patriotic villagers chose this way to celebrate the signing of the Treaty of Utrecht at the end of the war of the Spanish Succession in 1713 – doubtless some of them had served with the Suffolk Regiment under the command of the Duke of Marlborough. For over 150 years the green was also the scene of the St George's Day Fair, another patriotic celebration of thanksgiving in 1789 for the recovery of King George III from one of his bouts of madness.

There has always been a strong tradition of education in Hartest – there is mention of a school in 1567 and there were several schools in the 18th and 19th centuries, including a small boarding school. Records reveal that Hartest parents conscientiously sent their children to school before education became compulsory and wealthy landowners and benefactors provided money for clothing and books. Today Hartest children and those from neighbouring villages attend the Church of England primary school which moved from a small Victorian building in 1966 to the modern school with its grassy playground and swimming pool.

Medieval buildings, often covered with the facade of a later century, are found everywhere. Shops, alehouses and bakehouses which once supplied the wants of a small area are now homes. There was a time when the village was self-supporting with its own carrier to Bury. Times have changed. There are still farmers, of course, and in spite of the commuters and retired folk who comprise a large number of the population, there are still a few (too few) shops and craftsmen whose plastering, wall-building and furniture skills are admired.

Hasketon 🦢

When one talks of a country village, one is apt to see it as a cluster of pretty thatched cottages, nestling neatly around a carefully manicured village green which in turn is next to a limpid pond with ducks swimming on it. Hasketon is not like that at all. It could be described, as was the British Empire, as far flung. It covers a large area, being divided in the early days into three manors, Hasketon Hall, Thorpe Hall and The Old Rectory, which has a moat and is a private house.

The nucleus of the village is around, or adjacent to, the church,

St. Andrew's Church, Hasketon

comprising a number of council houses and privately owned properties. St Andrew's itself is very old and the tower impressive. The bottom half of the tower is round with very thick walls, while the upper part is octagonal in shape and quite uncommon. It is possible that it was built as early as the 14th century by Richard de Brewse for the installation of the bells. The long narrow windows could have been arrow slits.

There is only one inn now, the Turks Head, which is very popular. It is several hundred years old and has a very pleasant garden where meals can be served. There is also an excellent village hall which started life as an army hut in the First World War. The annual fete is popular and strongly supported. Although it is a scattered village people are kind and friendly. They always line the church path to see a pretty bride come in through the lychgate to her wedding and there they wait until the bells peal and out she comes on the arm of her groom. When tragedy strikes they all feel the sadness, wondering how they can help.

As a village Hasketon has had its share of characters: Grandad Tye who lived to be over 100 years old and still did his garden, and could be seen dragging home small branches for his kindling, and Dennis Brown, who was tragically killed in an accident and in whose memory his relatives erected a lovely wooden bench next to the bus shelter.

Altogether, although the school closed years ago and the village has lost a good shop and post office, it is still 'alive', a friendly and nice place to be, especially in the summer when the fields are ablaze with colour, golden rape and scarlet poppies.

Haughley 🦢

Haughley probably typifies an English village, certainly in the eyes of overseas visitors, with its village moat complete with ducks, church, pub and resident lord of the manor.

It is also a lovely Suffolk village with pretty rendered and painted old houses, some thatched, ribboning through its main street. Stand anywhere in the centre of Haughley and close your eyes and forget the parked cars and telephone poles (but thankfully no yellow road markings) and the village has not changed in a couple of centuries.

Happily though, Haughley has not stayed in the past. Just behind aptly named Old Street lies a carefully integrated modern housing development and a little further behind that an exceedingly well planned British Legion development. Haughley Crawfords primary school caters for the needs of the younger families so ensuring that Haughley does not join the ranks of declining villages.

In the Middle Ages Haughley was an important market town before the emergence of Stowmarket (which took over when Haughley suffered a disastrous fire) and well before the A45 cut its path through the countryside. A walk through Haughley's Old Street amply bears evidence of the village's historic importance, with its wide grass verges which housed the market areas. The village duck pond was once part of the moat surrounding the motte and bailey wooden castle which, in its time, was one of the most important castles in East Anglia. Unhappily the timber castle has long since disappeared but evidence of its moat can be clearly seen by walking through the churchyard.

In the days prior to the First World War, Haughley was virtually self sufficient with four pubs (although Haughley New Street still has the White Horse and the Railway Tavern adjoins the old station), numerous shops, a harness maker, a rake maker, an abbatoir, and a coffin maker to name but a few. It still boasts its own bakery, butcher's, hairdresser's, newsagent's, general store and fresh fruit and vegetable store, not to mention the post office which is one of the earliest recorded post offices in the United Kingdom.

Close to the old rake-maker's shop it is said that a ghostly grey lady passes through the wall, lifting her skirts as she goes, as if the threshold was unusually high. The threshold is no longer there but in olden times it was and one villager recalls regularly falling over it as a small child. More recently a villager out with his dog one foggy November night, saw quite clearly in the dirty broken window of a then empty house, a ghostly hand raising an old fashioned yellowing lantern. Needless to say, the villager, together with dog, made a very hasty retreat to his own home.

Hawkedon 🐚

Hawkedon is mentioned in White's 19th century Directory of Suffolk as 'A scattered village on a pleasant acclivity, near a rivulet. Six miles north-north-east of Clare, and nine miles north-west of Bury St Edmunds. In its parish 359 souls and 1,461 acres of land. It is in two manors, viz Hawkedon Hall and Thurston Hall.'

Things have changed little since then. The small river Glem still scurries below the bottom meadow behind the Hall. The acreage is the same but the population has dwindled to retired people, week-enders and a few working families. There are still the same 20 or so houses built on land rising from the green, but several council houses have been tucked away at the top of the hill down a small lane. The shop closed some years ago. The shopkeeper was in his late eighties when he retired. He was the last of a local family that had provided wheelwrights, blacksmiths and builders for about 150 years. Hawkedon is designated a place of outstanding beauty, and no further building is allowed. The pub survives – just.

The village and church is mentioned in the Domesday Book. St Mary's stands in the middle of the village green, accessible only by mown paths. The church door is now locked after vases and candlesticks were stolen recently.

Farming has been the backbone of the village, with sons working on the land, and the daughters in the farmhouses around. Some of these maids experienced a bed of their own for the first time on going into service. Some of the cottages (now made into two) had only two rooms down and two up, and families were often seven or more children. The farms are now run with little village help.

The hamlet of Thurston End is a mile south of the village, and was at one time an important place. Swans Hall there is a delightful house, which still retains much of the atmosphere and spirit of a more picturesque period than our own. It is now owned and farmed by a remarkable lady, Mrs Edith Plumb, who in her eighties still supervises her land. Thurston Hall was created in Henry IV's reign, and like all old houses passed through many hands. The present owner and farmer is Mr Tim Orbell, an old Hawkedon name.

One of the tales told to newcomers concerns three particular farms, each a mile from Hawkedon, north, east and south: Gallowgate Farm – where the gallows were, Hungriffe Hall – graves of the hanged, and Scolesgate Farm – where the skulls were exhibited. One wonders how much truth there is in that!

Hemingstone

Hemingstone, referred to in the Domesday Book as Hamingestuna, is thought to have been settled by a Danish sea king in the vicinity of Stonewall Farm, the timbered farmhouse near the crossroads first seen as you come over the hill from the direction of Henley village. The oldest property in Hemingstone, it is of a rare distinctive type in East Anglia known as 'Wealden' from their origin in the Weald of Kent. Stone Hall, as it was then called, was the home of the Cantrells, a Catholic family, who later settled in America. The small vestry in the parish church is known as 'Ralph's hole'. It contains a squint into the nave with no view of the altar, and was constructed by Ralph Cantrell, who refused to attend the reformed church and to avoid the penalties of disobedience, used the room as his chapel.

The thatched cottage next to Stonewall was once the village post office and the business was still carried out from a tin box in the living room until it was closed in the 1960s. Across the road was the blacksmith's forge. Outwardly Hemingstone has changed little from the days when on a Tuesday, butter and eggs were taken by horse and cart to the market in Ipswich.

Look along the valley to catch your first glimpse of Hemingstone Hall, perfectly positioned with the land rising steeply behind and facing south over meadowland. Built in 1621 by William Style, though there is evidence of an earlier timber-framed house, it is finished in Tudor red brick, has Dutch style gables and a Jacobean porch. The old walled kitchen garden now has lawns and flower beds, and climbing plants are abundant over wall and old apple trees alike.

St Gregory's church should not be missed. Look for the Cantrell tomb and the memorial stones to the man who died twice! The door to the tower is 14th century, iron-bound, and the octagonal font is described in Cautley's book of *Suffolk Churches* as 'one of two of the most beautiful in the county'.

Hemingstone is still a thriving village in spite of being small with about 120 inhabitants. Agricultural implements are made in the village, there is a fruit shop attached to the orchards, a haulage business, and at Old Hall on the main road, the lady of the house sells her surplus vegetables, fruit and plants . . . it is well worth a visit to see yet another lovely old house which still has many of its original features. Opposite is Old Hall Cottage where can be seen the runs for the window shutters which were in place before glass was used. Above all, there is a thriving village store which is up-to-date, well stocked and where the service is friendly.

Hengrave 🐝

About four miles west of Bury St Edmunds, on the north-western side of the river Lark, is the parish of Hengrave. Bisected by the A1101 Bury to Mildenhall road, it is nonetheless compact and picturesque with charming old world thatched, and sometimes flint-stone, cottages. Less than a mile long, within its boundaries are a variety of dwellings: cottages, bungalows, houses and five farms, the majority of which have been built on one side. The other shows the long low flint-stone wall enclosing Hengrave Park and Hengrave Hall, a house with ornate, white metal french windows, and a row of four cottages (the Kytson almshouses, only let to villagers over 65).

The village does not straggle, but has on the shorter side of its L-shape 13 dwellings, three of which are farms, and a livery stable. It ends just beyond the bridge across the Lark. In 1674 the village contained only seven dwellings, now it is 50.

Parts of the village of archaeological interest are now protected. The geography of the land, crop markings, clearly delineated in aerial photographs, also a certain number of coins and other metal work found within the parish, indicate very definitely former occupations of the area. It is known that as far back as 3,000 BC Neolithic and then Bronze Age man lived there.

The river Lark, now reduced in size, was once a thriving waterway, made navigable from Mildenhall to Bury by an Act of Parliament in the 11th century. The river was once nicknamed 'Coal River'. When annually dredged, lumps of coal are still hauled up onto the banks.

The village's crowning glory is Hengrave Hall, a delightful Tudor mansion built between 1525 and 1538 by Sir Thomas Kytson, a wool merchant. For nine generations Hengrave remained in the possession of the Gage family. The 'greengage' or 'gage plum' was first planted in the grounds in 1724, and its descendant is there to this day. When the estate was sold in 1952, the house became the property of the Assumption

Nuns. It is now administered as an Ecumenical Conference and Retreat Centre by the Hengrave Community.

There is an ancient church in the grounds with a curious round Saxon tower. In 1589 the parishes of Hengrave and Flempton were amalgamated and the church became a family mausoleum. It contains a profusion of monuments. Sir John Wood, 1897–1952, had the church restored and used as a private chapel. It is now called the Church of Reconciliation, and services of all denominations may be held there from time to time in addition to the daily worship of the Hengrave Community.

East Anglia is rightly renowned for its wide sweep of land and sense of space. Hengrave reflects these qualities, together with its varied bird-life. On clear nights the huge canopy of midnight blue, star-studded skies lend a different enchantment.

Henley 🐦

Henley is listed in the Domesday Book of 1086 as 'Henlaie' with two churches and a tithe barn. The present church dates from 1300 with later additions. There are no traces of a second church, and the tithe barn, while appearing on 20th century Ordnance Survey maps, is no longer in existence.

The church, dedicated to St Peter, stands at a central point of the village where roads lead off in five directions. The adjacent vicarage and Henley Hall were demolished within the last 20 years and houses have been built on the sites. During the 18th century the living of Henley was held by the rector of Coddenham in plurality. He seems to have spent most of his time enjoying the hospitality of Shrubland Hall, where he was frequently wined and dined, and completely neglected his flock in Henley.

In 1848 a large vestry was built on to the church to provide a schoolroom for the children of the village, and this could have been the beginning of their formal education. Their playground was the graveyard! The present school was built in 1875 and has been extended since. It is still in use as a primary school, and children from some neighbouring villages are also brought in by bus.

As one would expect in rural Suffolk work was largely agricultural; and one can imagine the bitter start to those winter mornings for the man who looked after the horses and for those who milked the cows. Hopefully there was compensation in those long summer days in the harvest fields and especially in the harvest supper? There was work for other craftsmen, the cobbler, blacksmith, wheelwright, all very dependent on the farmer; and a carrier, a Mr List, went to Ipswich regularly.

An important source of employment in the mid 19th century was the flax factory situated near the infant river Fynn. This factory had been moved from Ipswich on account of the vile smell created by the processing of the flax. In 1861 there were 30 girls employed who apparently came out from Ipswich. The factory was burnt down once and rebuilt: then burnt down again. Was it an arsonist who could no longer bear the awful smell? Another victim of fire was the windmill, a very high post mill, burnt down in 1844.

An Anabaptist church once stood just south of the present Cross Keys public house, and was used for services. It is no longer there. From time to time old houses have disappeared, but some lovely old period farmhouses and cottages have remained over the centuries. Henley is fortunate in still having a very good village shop.

Hepworth 🐑

Hepworth is mentioned in the Domesday Book, but there is evidence of much earlier occupation. In a field near the church were some stone pits in one of which was found a hand axe which has been dated at 300,000 BC. Three axe heads dating from 7,000 BC have also been found in Hepworth, one in a newly dug grave in the churchyard.

The church, mainly Norman but with Saxon features, was at one time thatched, but St Peter's was nearly destroyed in a disastrous fire at Easter 1898. There is an eye witness account written by Emma Louise Osmond, nee Hill, who was staying with her parents at the time. She recalls how one fire appliance was late arriving owing to being pulled by uneven horses. It was due to her that the massive church door was saved. Also saved was the 14th century carved wooden font cover which is the church's greatest treasure.

There used to be three public houses in the village – the Black Horse, which is now a private house; the Half Moon which is in the centre of the village, and the Duke of Marlborough, commonly called 'The Mulberry', which stands on the old turnpike or the Diss to Bury St Edmunds road. A weekly market was held here and Hepworth boasted three forges or blacksmiths to cope with the horse traffic generated by the market. At various times there have been four shops in the village, one of which was burnt down together with a small row of cottages in October 1937. There is still a small post office shop remaining. At one time, if there were letters for people residing on the outskirts of the village they were put in the post office window until someone who could read, and was going in the right direction, could deliver them.

There were two commons, North Common and South Common, both incorporated into farmland during the Second World War. There was also a mill on South Common until about 1900 and the remains can be seen as a large shed in the garden of Mill House on the Turnpike Road.

Hepworth has three charities, one dating from the 16th century when William Brundish left a piece of land to provide money for the poor and needy. A Mr Asty also left money for this purpose, and there are also the Town Estates. The charities are now administered by trustees and money is given each year to pensioners and widows.

There is a thriving community spirit in Hepworth though there is only one small post office shop and the school has recently been closed. As Hepworth is designated a no-growth area in the local plan, very little housing has been built since the 1960s. However, two derelict barns have been converted into houses and there are plans for a low cost housing scheme.

Hintlesham 🐚

Hinkle, a Dane, made his home here, and over the years the 'k' has been softened to 't' to become Hintlesham – Hinkle's home. Its claim to fame, however, is the beautiful Hintlesham Hall, with its Queen Anne front, Tudor rear and cavernous cellars which are probably even older and perhaps belonged to the original Hall of the 14th century.

It is now a famous hotel and restaurant with beautifully appointed rooms designed by the last owners. The new golf course has meant several fields being taken into the course and the diversion of a footpath, but a multitude of trees has been planted and in time it will prove beneficial to the landscape and help enhance the rural aspect of the village.

The parish church of St Nicholas is an ancient one, with some 13th century work. It has six bells and an enthusiastic team of bell ringers. The interior is cool and quiet, with a squint and a rood loft staircase, but, like so many country churches, funds are desperately needed to put it into good repair.

One of Hintlesham's oldest houses is the Priory, which was a cell of the convent of Wix in Essex, and was much used as a residence by the prioresses. They were devoted to such sports as hawking and hunting and it is said that in the reign of Henry II the prioress was fined because, accompanied by the vicar of Chattisham, she had killed a buck in the park. The prioresses often fought with the rectors of the parish because they would insist on bringing their hawks to church and putting them on the high altar.

Hintlesham is not a particularly handsome village. It is long and drawn out, with houses flanking each side of the main road, George Street, and extending into Duke Street, which was once part of the main road with the houses there being called the hamlet of Duck Street. The main road now curves away and takes a different route to Hadleigh, while the farmsteads and their cottages are scattered throughout the parish. Two large private woodlands soften the undulating contours of the fields. For years almost all of the village was part of the Hintlesham Hall estate, but with the sale of the estate in 1909 the village has been gradually changing and there are few now who are agricultural workers. A large proportion of the 600 or so inhabitants work outside the village. Most commute to Ipswich or Hadleigh. At the turn of the century there were at least four shops and now there is one, fighting hard to survive. The village public house, the George, which is not a very old building, has been completely altered and is now a restaurant with a large open-plan bar, still welcoming though.

Holbrook

William White's description of Holbrook in 1855 as 'a large and pleasant village' is still an apt one today. Travel through the village on the B1080 road and you can appreciate its size, even if much of the new development as well as The Street lies away to the west of the main road.

In the heart of the village stands the Compasses, one of the two remaining public houses of the four there used to be not so many years ago.

Just a little further on is All Saints' church at the top of Church Hill; at the bottom of the hill runs the brook from which Holbrook is named. For centuries the waters of the brook, stored up in the mill pond on the right of the road, powered the mill that still overlooks the stream as it makes its way through lush pastures to the river Stour at Holbrook Creek. Older residents like Mrs Cecily Godbold and Mrs Florence Pennell remember seeing sacks of meal being slid down into the horse-drawn miller's cart waiting to carry them to Ipswich.

Beyond the mill the road turns abruptly, and Primrose Hill climbs out of the valley through a wood decimated in the 1987 hurricane but still carpeted with snowdrops early in the year. At the top of the hill is the impressively laid out Royal Hospital School, a boarding school for the sons of seafarers whose main building with its lofty tower dominates a wide sweep of countryside.

Holbrook is a good place to live. It serves as a centre for the Shotley peninsula, lying between the Stour and the Orwell, and although there have been changes it retains facilities such as a Co-operative supermarket, a post office and a corner shop which are used by people from other nearby villages.

Lower Holbrook, which lies some distance from the village towards Harkstead, is in an Area of Outstanding Natural Beauty which extends westwards to include All Saints' church and the mill, now a restaurant. Even away from the river, which itself can be seen from various vantage points, water is a prominent feature of the local landscape. The road to Lower Holbrook is built on an embankment which retains water in The Fishponds, one of a series of ornamental lakes the earliest of which dates back to the 18th century.

Between the new houses and The Street is the Reade Field, owned by Greenwich Hospital Estates and let to the parish council as a playing field at a peppercorn rent – a single reed handed over each year to the agent. The village sportsmen make good use of the Reade Field, and of the village hall grounds on the other side of The Street where steel quoits and bowls are played.

The elderly are well provided for with a new development of well-designed bungalows that now complements the earlier group in Clench Road, where there is a day centre for old people attached to Clench House, a council home for the elderly. Clench House is named after Judge John Clench, the first Recorder of Ipswich, who died in 1607. His effigy reclines on the family tomb that dominates the south aisle of All Saints' church.

Hollesley 🐝

Hollesley village is a mixture of buildings, some very new, others quite old. The most important old building in All Saints' church. It has a very fine set of eight bells, which give one of the finest peals in East Anglia. Another exceptional feature of the church are the beautifully carved pew ends. Some half dozen are of the 13th/14th century and their design was copied for the pews in the main aisle which were carved in the early 1950s by Harry Brown, a cabinet maker who worked for the firm of Barnes of Ipswich who made the pews.

Many new houses and bungalows have been and are being built. These have attracted newcomers to the village, many of whom work in Woodbridge or Ipswich. British Telecom at Martlesham Heath employ a number of residents.

Another historical building is St George's House, Hollesley Bay Colony, which was built in 1887. This building and its surrounding farmland was used as a college to train 'young gentlemen farmers' who, after a period of training, went out to farm abroad in the British Colonies – hence the name 'Colony'. In the early 1900s the Colony then changed to a place of training and providing a new start for the London unemployed. In 1938 the Colony became a Borstal and was also one of the first 'open' prisons for young offenders in the country.

The village amenities are all well used. There are two village pubs – the Shepherd Dog and the Fox, a delightful bowling green, a large village hall built in 1959 and a very good recreation field. Hollesley is fortunate in maintaining a flourishing village school, and in having its very own police constable, headmaster and rector. The local shop is now a mini supermarket with a post office.

'Beating the Bounds' is a tradition of walking the village boundary which is marked out here and there with mounds of soil, called by some villagers 'Dill Heaps' and by others 'Dual Heaps'. Villagers armed with spades go round each mound in turn and renew each heap of soil thus keeping the heaps well topped up for easy identification. After each 'mounding' small boys of the village are then 'bounced' on top of each 'Dill' or 'Dual' heap. To preserve the open footpaths the parish council also organise a walk of all the footpaths every other year.

A Hollesley Commons Management Association has been formed to maintain the commons and improve the habitat of animals, birds and plants. A number of villagers are registered 'Commoners'. Many birds nest on the common and among them is the rare nightjar which nests on the ground. On selected evenings groups of interested people are conducted into the forest to watch and listen to their song.

Shingle Street is a small hamlet by the sea adjacent to Hollesley. During the Second World War the inhabitants were evacuated and the area used for Ministry of Defence operations. A Martello Tower, built in the Napoleonic Wars, still stands and is now a private residence. On the way to Shingle Street is a renovated house called Dumb-Boy Cottage. It is said to have been a place used by smugglers.

Holton St Peter ⚘

The village of Holton St Peter still retains two of its original attractions – the church and the mill.

The earliest part of St Peter's, the lower two thirds of the round tower, is a thousand years old, and the 52 ft round tower is one of 42 in Suffolk. The beautiful octagonal font has early 15th century stonecarving.

Holton Mill is a post mill, which means that the wooden body ('buck') turns to the wind on a large central post supported on quarter beams, which in turn rest on brick piers inside the brick roundhouse. This has two floor levels, one of which is below ground level. The mill stands on a low hill overlooking the village on the B1123 about one mile east of the town of Halesworth, and was evidently built by John Swann in 1749; the name and date are carved on one of the old beams inside. It was working until the early 1900s and had deteriorated sadly until restored in 1966–1968.

Holton, like many other villages in the past, had its own butcher, dressmaker, tailor, shoemaker, carpenter, wheelwright and blacksmith, the forge being a meeting place for all the local farmers and village characters. The friendly smith shod the working horses and used hand bellows to raise the roaring flames to heat the horseshoes, which were then nailed hot on to the horses' hoofs. The smell of scorched hoof often lingered on the cool morning air. Inside the forge was a conglomeration of ancient and modern tools awaiting repair at a later date. Sadly only memories remain of that colourful past. A pleasant bungalow has replaced the ancient forge in the village centre.

Holton Airfield was chosen as an operational base by the USAAF because it was the closest airfield to the English Channel, being only eight miles from the coast. The 489th Bomber Group Headquarters was stationed there from April to November 1944. On 6th August 1944 Glenn Miller came to town and local people joined with the GI's in a giant hangar and danced to the strains of *Moonlight Serenade*. In 1983 an Airfield Memorial was dedicated at Holton.

Honington 🐝

Drive along the A1088 from Thetford or Ixworth and you could easily miss Honington. Yet take the trouble to turn off down Malting Row or Sapiston Road and you will find an interesting little village of over 100 houses, dominated by All Saints' church.

It was at the top of Malting Row where the local Methodist band used to meet before marching to the chapel on the A1088. The chapel is now a private house but as the road is a busy traffic route between Kings Lynn and Ipswich and Harwich, it is difficult to imagine anyone marching along its length, albeit for only a short distance.

Most of the villagers use Malting Row regularly as the church, the school and the post office are all located here. Still used for weekly services, often ecumenical, the church at present is in the charge of a lady deacon (one of the first in the country). It has a Norman doorway, poppyhead pews and a noteworthy font inside. A plaque to Honington's famous 'son', Robert Bloomfield, the Pastoral Poet, can also be seen here. Outside in the churchyard, the graves of his parents and also of 57 war dead can be found.

Stop and admire the doors of the post office. They were rescued from the Old Rectory which was destroyed by fire in 1783. This fire was said to have caused much damage in Honington and Mrs Bloomfield (Robert's mother) apparently took her clock and the deeds of her house and sat out in a nearby field until all danger was passed. Her house was saved and you can see it still at the junction of Mill Road and Malting Row. Robert Bloomfield was born and spent the first twelve years of his life here before moving briefly to Sapiston and then on to London. It was life in these adjoining villages which inspired his most famous poem *The Farmer's Boy*.

Beneath your feet, set into the pavement at the same junction, you will see a large metal tyre shoe once used by the local wheelwrights.

Honington has, in the past, been self-sufficient with wheelwright, blacksmith, baker, hurdle maker, farmer and, within living memory, three shops, a butcher and a garage mechanic. The nearby RAF station, a Tornado base, provides work for many and boosts the village school's intake, so despite the aircraft noise there are advantages to the RAF's proximity.

Hopton 🐝

Hopton is an attractive village which has grown up around a crossroads on the northern border of the county. The Little Ouse forms the northern boundary as it begins its journey westwards from Redgrave Fen to the Great Ouse and thence to the Wash.

Hopton Steam Mill

Hopton still has over 30 acres of fenland to the north-west of the village. This is of great interest to naturalists and it has been designated an SSSI. The new 'Angles Way' passes through the eastern edge of the fen on its way to the coast. Reeds are still cut from the fen and in the past it was a very important source of roofing material.

All Saints' church is an interesting combination of styles and dates. The main fabric of the building is 14th century, but there have been several alterations – the clerestory being Tudor red brick. The village also supports a Methodist chapel and High Street chapel and all three play an active part in village life.

In common with many other large villages, Hopton had its own maltings, during much of the 19th century owned and run by Mrs Isabella Button and family. This building is to be converted into dwellings.

Many millers have been mentioned in the record books and at one time at least three windmills existed. By the end of the 19th century there were two postmills working on Hopton Common by the Little Ouse. These were demolished around 1910 as the then miller, Oscar John Sayer, had already constructed a steam mill to the rear of his mill house and bakery. This was working until 1936 and in fact was not demolished until the 1960s. The only remaining feature is one of the millstones.

From the early 1900s Hopton had its own fire engine which also served the nearby villages. It was housed next to the Commercial inn. The engine at one time was pulled by the miller's horses and during the summer when the horses were grazing on the outskirts of the village they had to be fetched before the rescue apparatus could set out for the scene of the fire.

Over past centuries Hopton was primarily an agricultural community, as a high proportion of the surrounding land is fertile and productive. Certainly during the 19th and early 20th century there was a thriving village community which included harness makers, wheelwrights, carpenters and a thatcher amongst others. There was a wide variety of craftspeople and shops providing clothing, food and hardware.

Now the majority of the inhabitants travel to such places as Diss, Thetford and Bury St Edmunds for employment. Despite this, the village still retains a community spirit which is often lacking today.

Horham ❦

Horham is no longer the 'muddy enclosure' of Saxon origin, but a winner of several Best Kept Village awards. The churchyard of St Mary's won a conservation prize in 1990, the profusion of wildflowers feeding the bees to produce a profitable contribution to church restoration, by the sale of honey.

The Norman building, on the site of a former wooden Saxon church, has had its distinctly Suffolk tower strengthened to rehang the retuned peal of eight bells, believed to be the oldest in the world, heard for the first time after 80 years in 1990.

The only building left of the old manor is thought to be its Lady chapel. As a post office and general store it has had many proprietors well known and loved in the village. After the Second World War twelve houses and bungalows were built by the council and named Manor Park. In 1989, six bungalows were built on church land, called St Mary's Close. Many modern houses have been erected along The Street, infilling within the village boundary.

The Horham stocks, used for petty lawbreakers, were removed and are now on show along with the Green Dragon pub sign and the Horham station nameplate, in the old school building, now a social club.

The single-line, standard gauge, Mid-Suffolk Light Railway was laid in 1902. Mr Albert Borrett became stationmaster, clerk, shunter, porter and signalman at Horham in 1918. He was still there when inevitably, on 26th July 1951, the last train was run. The deteriorating station was recently rescued and transported to Mangapps Farm Railway Museum, Essex.

During the Second World War the American aerodrome took over much of the farmland and the village itself was part of the dispersal airfield. The 200th mission was celebrated in style with entertainment by the famous Glenn Miller, in person, with his band.

Another composer of a different kind, Benjamin Britten, arranged folk songs that evoked the 'atmosphere of the village and countryside'. He founded the Aldeburgh Festival and lived here, composing in a room built at the bottom of his garden overlooking Horham fields.

There used to be two public houses in the village, the Eight Bells closed in about 1918. The Green Dragon was the regular meeting place. Mr H. W. Baldry took over from his grandmother as licensee. He was a craftsman, who also carried on business as builder, wheelwright and agent for agricultural equipment, as well as undertaker. Many cottages were very small, so deceased relatives were fetched by Mr Baldry to be laid out in a room partitioned off from the chatting and drinking in the bar. Both properties remain as private dwellings.

As people could buy ready made boots as cheaply as having their old ones repaired, the two shoemakers joined the mill, the school, the blacksmiths and the railway station; all overtaken by progress.

Horringer 🐑

The attractive village of Horringer is situated two and a half miles from the market town of Bury St Edmunds, on the A143 Bury to Haverhill road.

Dominating the village green is the flintstone church of St Leonard. Beside the church are the gates of Ickworth Park, now owned by the National Trust. Ickworth House is part occupied by the sixth Marquis of Bristol whose family dates back to the 15th century.

Adkins Wood forms an attractive background to the thatched and tiled timber-framed cottages along one side of the village street. On the other side is the old guildhall, formerly used as a workhouse, then a village school and now converted to attractive houses. The porch of the infants school where children hung their clothes still remains.

Horringer now has a modern single-storey school, opened in 1989, taking pupils from three other villages. This building stands in St Leonard's Park estate, off the main street. Planned in the 1960s, the estate has a grocery store and taxi hire service. All the houses have Georgian style windows and open plan gardens, blending well with the rest of the village and bringing the total number of houses in Horringer to 400. The post office, tea rooms and two public houses are located in the main street.

In 1901 there were two blacksmiths. One forge stood on the village green where, during a dry summer, the foundation marks of the building may still be seen. The newer forge is now a private home, but was previously occupied by the blacksmith's widow, who never ceased to tell everyone her birthday was the same day as that of the Queen Mother! This lady's 90th birthday party was held at Horringer House. Horringer House is also the venue for the Strawberry Tea which is held in aid of the church each year and the bonfire night celebrations.

There are very few farms and no farming livestock, only arable land for wheat, barley and sugar beet. This is grown for the local sugar beet factory in Bury St Edmunds, which is the largest in Europe. Poultry is kept and recently stables were built and paddocks made for horses which take part in the Horse Show held every August in Ickworth Park.

Hoxne 🌾

Steeped in history, the village of Hoxne (pronounced 'Hoxon'), situated in North Suffolk along the banks of the river Waveney, is a very attractive and desirable place in which to live.

As long as 300,000 years ago, people lived here around the edge of a great lake. The site of the lake today is owned, and has been for several generations, by the Banham family. Until just after the outbreak of the Second World War, they made many of the bricks used for building the houses in the village.

Hoxne is well known for its links with King Edmund, who, it is believed, put a curse on the Goldbrook bridge. Legend has it that he was betrayed to the Danes in AD 870 by a couple who, when they were crossing the Goldbrook bridge on their way to be married, saw the reflection of his golden spurs in the water as he was hiding under the bridge. Subsequently he was captured by the Danes, securely tied to an oak tree and put to death by a volley of arrows. Nearly a thousand years later, in 1848, the oak tree to which he was supposedly tied, mysteriously fell to the ground in August, on a calm windless night while still in full leaf. A monument stands on the site today, and is a great tourist attraction. Even now, after all that time, brides make long detours to avoid the bridge on their wedding day.

In recent years much more pleasant customs have evolved, one being the Harvest Breakfast which follows the morning service held in the magnificent 13th century church dedicated to St Peter and St Paul. The congregation and clergy process down the hill to the village green at Low Street for a full traditional breakfast.

Cross Street and Heckfield Green are situated at the top end of the village where, since the end of the Second World War, many new houses have been built, including a well equipped, sheltered housing complex. Residents are well served by three general stores, which include two sub post offices, motor repairs and petrol station.

The Grapes public house in Cross Street still offers friendly hospitality to its customers, and on a crisp winter's day when the local hunt receive the stirrup cup from mine host prior to their activities, transports the onlookers back to Dickensian times.

Hundon 🌾

Hundon, called 'Hundendana' in the Domesday Book of 1086, is the second largest parish in West Suffolk. It is a scattered village which includes the hamlets of Scotch Green, Babel Green and Brockley Green, and is situated about six miles from Haverhill and four miles from Clare, with its main north–south street centred around the church of All Saints and the United Reformed church which was built as an Independent chapel in 1846.

In the 1890s most Hundon people worked in or around the village as corn millers, tailors, wheelwrights, bootmakers, saddlers, blacksmiths, farmers, butchers and bakers. Today this is the exception, people travelling sometimes as far as London on a daily basis; gone is the horse-drawn farm equipment and the driving of herds of animals to market on foot – all is now mechanised. In the 1930s there were eight public houses or alehouses in the village – there are now only two; but unlike many villages Hundon has retained two shops and the post office.

All Saints' church, whose register dates from 1642, suffered a severe fire in 1914, losing five of its six bells, and was rebuilt in 1916. In 1929 Canon Arthur Wasket came to All Saints' as his first living, and remained here for 52 years until his death in 1981. During his time in Hundon he published a book of poems, and was an accomplished water-colourist. In 1687 the church sexton, while digging a grave, unearthed 200 Anglo-Saxon coins, each worth 4d. Jackie Blackcap was a 'gentleman of the highway' whose round included Hundon, and it was not uncommon for him to sleep in the church porch.

Some of the oldest surviving houses are Hundon Hall; 'Thatchers' which was originally a hall-house; Pinhoe Hall, at one time a moated house; and Workhouse Yard which was built in 1737. There are houses of every period in the village, including an unobtrusive modern development.

The approach to the hamlet of Scotch Green is called Steeplechase Terrace, which is reminiscent of the horse-racing which took place in the 1730s for the prize of a pair of silver spurs. This must have been quite a festive occasion, for footmen could run for a prize of ten shillings, and also ten pairs of gloves could be won by young men in a football game.

In 1936 much of the parish was bought by the Air Ministry for the building of an aerodrome. This was opened in February 1938, and was named RAF Stradishall (Hundon) to avoid confusion with the existing RAF Hendon. RAF Stradishall closed in August 1970, but a few years later the buildings housed the refugee Asians from Uganda. The establishment is now Highpoint Prison.

Until the building of the village hall in 1956, the school provided the venue for many functions. Built by local volunteers with help from the Quaker community, the hall now accommodates all the village organisations from the play group, through all ages and interests, to the Evergreen Club.

Icklingham

Icklingham may seem at first sight to be unremarkable. The more interesting of its two churches, All Saints', has been declared redundant, the village school has closed, there is no longer a shop, and the busy traveller on the A1101 will pause not to comment on the beauty or historic interest of the village, but rather to mutter that he is delayed by the 30 mph restriction and the sharp bends at the west end of this straggling group of houses.

But the village has a fascinating history. The unremarkable face the village presents today contrasts markedly with its profile in former times. From the earliest age Icklingham has shared with Lackford the guardianship of the lowest fording place on the river Lark: the spot where the Icknield Way, part of which is now the eastern boundary of the village, crosses the river. Ancient Britons, Romans and Saxons all lived on the site now occupied by the village, choosing this 'shelf' of land between the fertile fen bordering the river and the barren breckland as a good place to settle. Abundant relics of life in prehistoric times surface regularly for archaeologists to study. Among these the so called 'Icklingham Horde' of pagan bronzes is currently exciting much interest.

Common travellers rode a risky track as they came south from Norwich to cross the Lark and there are many tales of ghostly riders. A mound in the old roadway is said, even today, to make the quietest pony shy away and dogs and cats avoid the area at night. The Normans introduced warrening as a way of utilising the breckland and the rabbit has since become the star of folk stories. A white rabbit is often seen at dusk walking a certain path as the familiar of a witch. Sight of her has caused horses to bolt and men to die and the well worn path she uses to cross a track and pass into a field through a gap in the hedge which cannot be closed covers the site of an early cemetery.

The centre of the village today is the churchyard of the active church of St James, and records in that church show the changes of ownership which the manor has undergone since it first belonged to the King at the time of the Domesday Book. At the Dissolution of the Monasteries it returned to the king after 300 years as part of St Edmund's abbey's land, and then it passed from one landed family to another until the present day when the largest owner is the Elveden estate, belonging to Lord Iveagh of the Guinness family. It is this sense of continuity kept alive miraculously amongst a fairly mobile population that gives the village its identity.

Sadly this may not be apparent to the passerby, but rest awhile at the Plough inn, a house with a long history of its own, and the character of this unique village may be, in part, revealed.

Ilketshall St Andrew 🐄

Ilketshall St Andrew has seven commons, which during the 1930s were grazed almost daily by animals – usually cows – from the surrounding farms. There were several small enclosures which were known as 'pounds' and used by smallholders to confine a pony or cow during the hours of darkness, when grazing was not allowed.

At that time gipsy travellers would spend a few weeks each year with their caravans parked on a small meadow. Some families stayed long enough for their children to attend the local school – now closed – whilst the men folk took seasonal work before moving on to the fen district for the potato harvest etc. A few could be seen sitting near their caravans making clothes pegs to sell to householders. Naturally each caravan had a horse for pulling and maybe a few extra, which greatly increased the numbers on Great Common.

With the arrival of tuberculosis testing of all bovine animals, which at first was voluntary, the number of farmers exercising their grazing rights decreased. Herds which had passed could not mix with non-TT herds. In time all were required to become tuberculosis free, but grazing became less popular; mainly because it was very time consuming. With three exit roads from each common it was necessary for owners to be on constant watch.

When grazing almost ceased the commons took on a look of neglect, becoming overgrown and a fire hazard. With bushes fast taking over, some areas appeared ideal for courting couples to park their car. They thought little about the very wet land until they wished to return to the highway. Next came a walk to the nearest farmer for help and a tractor to pull the vehicle out.

Following the registration of common rights in 1965 an association of Common Right Holders was formed to restore and care for the grassland. Each member tends set areas throughout the commons by grazing or cutting and therefore contributing to very pleasant rural scenery.

Ilketshall St Lawrence

One of eleven villages known as 'The Saints', the parish of Ilketshall St Lawrence stands on the old Roman road that runs between Bungay and Halesworth; a sausage-shaped village, with the church at one end and the school two miles away on the other end. Halfway along the sausage has burst, spilling out into a green round which some small farms are grouped.

The church stands on a mound which is reputed to be an old Roman staging post, and certainly there are some Roman bricks built into the end wall of the chancel. It is a simple 12th century building, much restored.

Two red brick cottages made up the Methodist church until 1937 when a new wooden one was built. These cottages then became a private dwelling. Recent occupants dug up a tombstone in the garden of one John Knapp 1798, and they declared that they often heard someone walking about the house and articles being moved, and they were sure it was the ghost of John Knapp.

The village green is owned by the Duke of Norfolk and those farmers who have grazing rights on it should pay a yearly rental of two peppercorns, though needless to say this is never collected. The people who make use of these 'goings' turn cattle out to graze, keeping them in with an electric fence, and also cut the grass for hay, so the green is in good condition. Alas, the local pub is closed, but the village primary school flourishes with over 100 children on the register.

The name Ilketshall, borne by four of the saints, indicates that they were once part of the lands of Ulfketill. After the Norman Conquest the village became part of the Bardolphs manor and the family held it for many years. Today, though some old cottages have gone and a few new houses have been built, the inhabitants still number about 150 and the village is still very rural despite the traffic that thunders through on that straight road built by the Romans.

Ilketshall St Margaret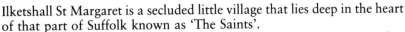

Ilketshall St Margaret is a secluded little village that lies deep in the heart of that part of Suffolk known as 'The Saints'.

The village has a recorded historical past dating back to 1062, with a Danish lord as occupier of the manorial seat; however there have been archaeological finds that suggest a much earlier settlement, such as a Neolithic axe and pieces of Roman pottery. The village is settled in two separate areas one and a half miles apart. One reason given for this is that when the plague struck in the Middle Ages the whole population abandoned the settlement that was built around the church and moved two miles away.

A farming area, the large modern prairie-type fields have evolved from the small strip farms of the past. However, many of the original footpaths still remain that link St Margaret's to the surrounding villages and the nearest town of Bungay, and join up with the well known Bigod Way. Ramblers and hikers visiting the village can enjoy walking these paths, some of which take them past interesting 16th century timber-framed farmhouses and barns.

The most visited building in the village, is of course the church. The main structure of the church is Norman but the round tower constructed of flint and rubble is thought to be Saxon. The tower houses three bells. Bells one and two were cast in approximately 1390–1410 and were probably by William Dawe of London. The third bell has the marks of Richard Brasyer of Norwich and was cast about 1480. The Brasyers were a well known Norwich family who were famous for their bell making.

The original village school dated 1847 is now the village hall, and is used to the full. The oldest established fruit, vegetable and flower show in the area is still a regular feature of summer activities, held on the third Saturday in July.

At Christmas time, the poor, the widows and the retired of the parish receive a gift of winter fuel, a gift from the Henry Smith charity. Henry Smith, an alderman of London, decided in 1619 to distribute the income from some of his tenanted farmlands to the poor and needy villagers of Essex and Suffolk. Which villagers were to be given this money was decided by Henry Smith himself; disguised as a vagrant he wandered from village to village; according to the kind of treatment he was given by the inhabitants he allocated the amount of money each village deserved. Some villages didn't receive any gift at all! However, Henry was not a true philanthropist, he excluded those villagers who were guilty of excessive drinking, profane language, swearing, pilfering, vagrants, or any other idle persons.

St Margaret's must have been a friendly, caring and sober village then, as it is today.

Ixworth 🐟

Ixworth lies six miles north-east of Bury St Edmunds, at the crossing of roads from Bury to Norwich and on to Yarmouth, and from Ipswich to Thetford. From earliest times its history has been influenced by roads, since it lay close to the Icknield Way. Ixworth was one of the Iceni tribe's headquarters settlements. When the Romans came to Britain they developed the Icknield Way, and built Peddar's Way which runs from Colchester through Ixworth to Holme-next-the-Sea in Norfolk. The Romans built an important fort here and there was a substantial civilian settlement including three villas.

In the late 12th century the Blount family founded a priory for the canons of St Austin (St Augustine). Remains of it, including an interesting crypt, have been incorporated in the much later house known (muddlingly) as Ixworth Abbey, which lies hidden among trees on the north bank of the river Blackbourne.

The river marks the southern boundary of Ixworth, and after crossing it the road curves through the old heart of the village. Many of the houses were built during the Middle Ages – the oldest in the late 14th century – and are timber-framed. The very fine church of St Mary, decorated with flint flushwork, dates from the 14th century with additions in the 15th, 16th and 19th centuries; it sits slightly back from the High Street in the peaceful old churchyard.

Clearly Ixworth prospered in the late 18th and early 19th centuries. It was a thriving, self-contained place with a population of about 1,000. Many trades and shops supplied the needs of the inhabitants and no less than 13 farmers cultivated the land. Transport was much better then than now, with daily coaches to London, Bury and Norwich.

Ixworth's High Street can have changed little in appearance during the next hundred years, for the decline in agriculture in the later 19th century meant that its population dropped to 856 by 1901 and by 1931 was only 776. Few new houses were built. A notable exception was the building of four pairs of council houses erected in Stow Road in 1894 – the first such houses in the whole country.

New buildings sprang up rapidly after the Second World War, though most are not visible from the High Street; by 1971 the population had risen to 1,187 and by 1981 to 1,377. Now the roads which had brought prosperity to Ixworth over the ages began to be a problem. A bypass had been mentioned in the 1920s but not until 1986 was it at last accomplished. This, in its turn, has brought changes to Ixworth. The High Street is now a pleasant place in which to shop and linger, and in summer its houses – many freshly repainted – are bright with window boxes and hanging baskets. The price of the bypass has been the building of new housing estates on the village perimeters, and the population has grown to about 2,500.

The village is well served by several shops, a post office, two pubs, and primary and middle schools. Today Ixworth is a community in the true sense of the word. Community spirit is very strong. It is a pleasant, busy place with 40 small businesses belonging to the Trader's Association.

Kedington ✖

Kedington, formerly known as Ketton, was a small, quiet village until the Haverhill overspill scheme began in the 1960s. Since then housing estates have covered several large areas of farmland and the village is now a busy, thriving place, with its community centre hosting a variety of clubs and sports.

The church of St Peter and St Paul is well known to tourists and has been called the 'Cathedral of West Suffolk'. It has many interesting features, including a 15th century font and a 16th century oak chancel screen. A Saxon cross, originally found in the churchyard, was later removed from the eastern gable point and installed in the chancel window. There is a three decker pulpit believed to have been used by the great Protestant preacher Samuel Fairclough, a wig pole, a sermon timer rather like a large egg timer and many Barnardiston tombs. This family dominates Ketton history.

Behind the church is a row of ten elms said to have a dead knight buried beneath. When one of the trees blew down, legend has it that a skeleton was found at its roots, but no ghosts have been seen. One old lady did go round to inspect a newly dug grave and slipped into it. She was rescued after some time by nearby gardeners who heard her cries.

Church Walk was a lovely route up to the church, with alternate limes and chestnut trees. It has lost some of its charm by extra usage but the new school fits neatly into one side of the walk. The nightingale no longer sings in the walk and the nightjars, cuckoos and jays have left the Dash End area, where the old village pound is now filled with council houses.

There is a strong community spirit in Kedington. This is especially noticeable at the annual Meadowlarks in June, when all the clubs and associations in the village join together to keep their community centre solvent. Haverhill Meat Products employs a large number of village people and are generous to local good causes.

From being a sleepy backwater, Kedington is now a pleasant place to live, complete with a beautiful church, happy school, good library and playing fields and two welcoming pubs.

The bells of the church rang out the old year and rang in the new for the first time for 30 years in 1991 – thanks to a keen team of eight bellringers.

Kelsale ✿

It quietly sleeps away its history, a gentle village with its church on the hill, lovely as only Suffolk churches can be. Past the village hall a straggle of cottages along Bridge Street speak of change in ways of living as they contrast with the houses in the smart close called The Vines, but the vineyard which gave it its name, and the lovely apple orchard which existed across the road ten years ago, are gone. The Street settles into a countryside of trees, meadows and ditches, with lanes meandering to the hamlets of East Green, North Green and Curlew Green.

The five smithies, eight bootmakers, tailor, toffee maker, laundress and the three windmills of the 19th century are but a memory of older villagers who learnt of them from their parents. The vast grain growing area of times past can now boast only seven farms. No longer disturbed by the noisy A12 road, now away to the west, the large Eight Bells inn is shuttered and empty, awaiting yet another metamorphosis.

Centuries ago Kelsale was of great importance, larger than Saxmundham, with a thriving market between the Guildhall and Kelsale Court. The Guildhall was not a trade hall, but that of the Order of St John the Baptist, with a priest in charge, acting as an adjunct to the church, receiving monks from the many local monasteries, keeping order and law in the market, dispensing absolution, and help to the needy, for the market served all who came to buy and sell.

The Court House, afterwards enlarged with a fine rectory, played its part in housing a series of philanthropic rectors, but in the 12th century its ecclesiastical connection was with the courts at Dunwich, from whence miscreants were brought to be housed in the dungeons below, which are still there amongst the labyrinth of cellars. The Court House has now become a retirement home for the elderly.

The manor house, moated since medieval times, almost hidden beyond the church, has a now neglected garden originally designed by Gertrude Jekyll. No longer can the cry of peacocks be heard on its terrace.

In the early part of the 19th century, to the church's good work was added that of Methodism. Farmers with their families would congregate for whole days to picnic in the open and listen to sermons from morning until night. Preachers worked in relays as they tired. Perhaps the most famous preacher was Mr Joseph Arch, who founded the farm workers' union.

It is apt that Kelsale is now Kelsale cum Carlton since Carlton once housed a convent which was responsible for the building of the 11th century church. It came under the patronage of the famous Garrett family of Leiston who did much for the village. After her husband's early death, Mrs Garrett founded and taught in her own school.

Although places of work, in this age of cars, may take its people considerable distances, the spirit of the village lives on.

Kesgrave 🐦

In the Saxon-Danish period a settlement called Gressland or Kesgrave was established on the heathland, on a route half way between Ipswich and Woodbridge, now the busy A1214.

For 700 years Kesgrave was a small agricultural community, with a church dedicated to All Saints, an inn named the Bell and a few farms. After 1921, with the development of Martlesham aerodrome, changes began in the village and many small dwellings were built, chiefly bungalows.

The Ipswich Eastern Fringe Local Plan, published in 1984, proposed some 3,000 new houses on the Grange Farm area of the village, using 378 acres. At present, the total area of Kesgrave covers roughly 800 acres, over half of which is residential, mostly bungalows still. The remainder is private woodland and agricultural.

In 1966, to commemorate their Golden Jubilee, the Women's Institute commissioned and presented a village sign to the parish council. It depicts one of the fine cedar trees which were a notable feature of the churchyard. Sadly several since have had to be removed as they were unsafe.

Ranulf de Glanvile, whose name is commemorated by Glanvile Place, was a lawyer, soldier and native of Suffolk. He founded a priory at Butley in 1171, and the parish church of Kesgrave was one of those who had to pay tithe to the priory. Ranulf was killed in 1190 whilst accompanying Richard I to the Holy Land. The Puritan William Dowsing and his men visited Kesgrave church in January 1643 and took down 18 cherubim and removed six stained glass windows. There are lead pellets in the door, reputed to be from that incident.

In the northern part of the parish is an area known as 'The Sinks', where stands a small pump house. During the Second World War a Canadian soldier painted St Francis feeding the birds on one side and St Christopher carrying the Christchild on the other – with the words 'Pray for Peace' 1944.

John Dobbs was a shepherd who lost a sheep and reputedly hanged himself, for fear of transportation. He was buried at the meeting of the footpaths from Martlesham, Foxhall, Kesgrave and Bealings. His grave has small stone head and foot markers and is cared for by the county council.

There is an original London–Yarmouth milestone near Kesgrave High School (1818). It was broken by a snowplough some years ago, but is being restored by public subscription.

Kessingland Beach as it looked in the 1920s (by kind permission of Mark Utting)

Kessingland

Kessingland is a seaside village bordered by the North Sea to the east and to the west by the A12, which formerly ran through the village street until the recent bypass was built.

The Domesday Book records that in the reign of William the Conqueror the village had to pay the lord of the manor 22,000 herrings. So, there were fishermen in those days and in medieval times Kessingland was a thriving port. The port decayed and later became only a smugglers haunt.

The first lifeboat was presented to Kessingland in 1870 by the people of Bolton in Lancashire. The last lifeboat was taken away in 1936. The crews were made up mostly by the men who fished in small boats, called longshore boats. These men caught various types of fish and also shrimps, which were boiled in a copper pan on the cliff-top.

The other types of fishermen in this fishing village were those who went out of the port of Lowestoft; firstly in sailing smacks and later steam drifters and trawlers. The main catch the drifters went for was 'King Herring'. If catches were good in those old days, the man of the house would come home with his pockets jammed full of sovereigns and at this time there would be highway robbers who lay in wait for the fishermen as they tramped some lonely road homewards. The fisherman's wife on the arrival of her husband had to get down to scrubbing the clothes, thick and heavy, greasy with herring scales and ridden with salt.

The fishing industry had a great support industry and Kessingland was at one time reputed to be the richest village in England. In large two storey sheds, built of wood with slate roofs, called 'beating' sheds, the women and girls called beatsters mended the nets, this being hard and tedious work.

There was a great deal of bravery amongst the fishermen, and one of them won the Stanhope medal for the most courageous life-saving deed of the year. It was in 1926 when Harry Smith won that award and he became 'pride of the village'.

There were many superstitions in the fishing community, one being that pigs must *never* be mentioned on board as they were considered the unluckiest of animals.

The 96 ft towered church of St Edmund has been a landmark for seafarers since Agincourt. The church was supported by the nuns of St Clare until the Dissolution of the Monasteries.

Kessingland has been a holiday centre from far off days and Sir Henry Rider Haggard, a famous past resident, had his holiday home at the clifftop house he called the Grange from the 1880s to 1925. Rudyard Kipling stayed there frequently and older folk could recall he and Sir Henry walking the cliff-tops together. The property was developed into Catchpole's Holiday Camp in the late 1920s and the Denes was begun just before the Second World War.

Once there were eight farms but only three survive, and there were numerous shops which supplied almost every need. The village, although it has grown to enormous proportions, has not the same kind of service. Kessingland has become a dormitory for Lowestoft, with folk commuting to work in factories, shops and offices. Many men are now employed in the oil industry, and some light industry is in the village.

Kettleburgh

The village is situated two miles from Framlingham. It once lay on the outer borders of the kingdom of the Iceni tribe, who were enslaved by the Romans after the uprising led by Queen Boudicca. Pieces of Iron Age pottery have been discovered, together with human remains, a seal, and an ancient stirrup decorated with jewels. Several Roman coins have also come to light. Most of these finds can now be seen in Ipswich Museum.

The village is bisected by a crossroads and the church is no longer the centre of the village, but is reached up a pleasant lane off the Framlingham road. The school house on the corner of the lane was closed in 1968 and is now a private residence. Passing houses, and through a farmyard, St Andrew's is on high ground overlooking fields. The tower was built in the 14th century and the nave and chancel in the 15th century. William Dowsing came here between 1643–44 and with Puritan zeal destroyed 'six stained glass pictures and leveled the steps'. However, there was major restoration in 1882 and seating was provided for over 200 people. Due no doubt to the church being sited on a hill the earthquake shock of 1884 was felt here.

In the churchyard and indeed elsewhere in the locality, there are some gems of tombstone poetry. They were written in the 1840s and 1850s by the poet Samuel Hart. He earned his living as a shoemaker and blacking seller and practised as a herbalist. There is now no school in Kettleburgh, though once there were several, including dance schools and Sunday schools. One tombstone records Mary Skulthorp who died in 1839 aged 83 – 'She kept a school in this parish for 43 years'.

Continuing down the Framlingham road on the left hand side, can be found the village hall. In 1957 the Kettleburgh Village Produce Association was formed and holds here a well attended Annual Produce Show and Competition.

Near the crossroads is a thriving post office and shop, and on the road to Easton is the Chequers inn. The original building was burned down in the early 19th century and was rebuilt in 1912 in Tudor style.

Kirton & Falkenham 🐚

'Kirton – held together by rivets'. So it was said in the local White Horse inn. There were more families with the name of Rivett, at one time twelve in all, than any other name in the village. Kirton and adjoining Falkenham lie near the mouth of the river Deben, about four miles north-west of Felixstowe.

There was a thriving port called Guston at Kirton Creek which was part of the area called Goseford, a focal point of the old Hundred of Colneis which included Walton, Felixstowe, Kirton and Falkenham. King Edward I and Edward III are reported to have been lords of the manor at Walton and used Kingsfleet as a haven for their ships, also to have enjoyed deer hunting in Falkenham Woods! The Anglo-Saxons used a ford over the river at Kingsfleet and called the area Goseford – a ford haunted by geese – so descriptive even today of the lonely valley with its wide horizons and the welling tide running in over the land to higher ground.

Fishing was the main industry of the ports in the estuary. The local method used was by means of weirs. The rent for a weir was 4d a year payable to the lord of the manor who was entitled to a 'preferment' of the fish caught. The weirs mostly had names of the local tenants such as Waller. Kirton was surrounded by three hamlets, Guston, Croxton and Strewston which over the years merged into one village. The names still survive as street names for various new developments.

Kirton has a population of approximately 1,100. Many old cottages have been demolished and replaced by modern houses. The village green is still a focal point of the village with a village sign designed by Mrs J. N. Metcalfe depicting the church, river Deben and ears of corn. It was made in wrought iron at the village forge by local craftsmen Alec and Winston Jacobs. A tree planting scheme has been in force for several years to replace heavy losses in the 1987 hurricane.

There are two churches in Kirton and Falkenham, St Mary and St Martin at Kirton and St Ethelbert's at Falkenham. The community included two chapels, one of which, the active Methodist church, celebrated its centenary in 1986, but the disused Congregational chapel was demolished in 1982.

Kirton and Falkenham are very lively and busy villages with the majority of people working at Felixstowe docks or British Telecom, but there are still several local employers. There is a thriving electronics factory, the forge, two general stores, one of which is the post office, several builders, decorators, painters etc, not forgetting the local farmers who still employ a number of local people. As for the social side of village life – it has been said of Kirton that it has never been known for a village to have so many thriving organisations!

Knodishall ॐ

'The Common' is the main feature of Knodishall. This wide area has a wealth of heathland flora and fauna. The twice-yearly flowering gorse and elegant broom thrive amidst silver birches, young oaks, bracken and heather. Walkways and paths criss-cross and meander this way and that.

Here and there may be seen tethered goats cropping the young shoots ('Commoners' rights are still exercised here). The river Hundred which, in the past, has given many problems with flooding, has been dug out and deepened. It takes surface water from roads and farmland, and over recent hot, dry summers has dried out completely in places. Passing along the edge of the common, it widens into a picturesque pond. Domestic ducks and geese are often seen there. Two footbridges lead onto the common whilst a renovated road bridge spans the main road. A children's play area with swings, is in a secluded corner of the common.

On the skyline stride pylons, over the busy road linked to the major construction site at Sizewell 'B' and the original Sizewell 'A' power station. Many local people work there. Others find employment in schools or small businesses, or at one of the American bases nearby.

One hundred years ago Knodishall had 442 inhabitants and covered 1,843 acres. Its population now stands at 870. The parish also included Buxlow, then Buxlee, which previously had a separate parish with its own church – the site of which is now a garden with a few stones only remaining. That particular area is still referred to as Buxlow. It features on the path of one of Knodishall's two circular walks. Also to be seen is the old school, now two private homes.

The church of St Lawrence, situated about a mile out of the village, had a complete renovation in 1983, following the sale of a valuable painting, *Jacob and Rachel (The Meeting)* by William Dyce RA, which had been donated to the church by William John Burningham.

Amazingly, the Cold Fair, established in 1312 and traditionally held in a part of Knodishall called Coldfair Green, was revived in 1988. It is now held in nearby Leiston in mid December.

On the main road there is still a reminder of the gipsies who used to camp in Knodishall for the fair. It is a square, flint building, thatched and with quaint, old-fashioned windows, called 'Romany's Rest'. Mill House marks where a mill stood, but it was sold and dismantled in 1911.

Lakenheath 🐝

Lakenheath is still called a village, but with a population of over 5,000 it is getting rather large now. The name is derived from an Anglo Saxon named Lak, who landed at a hythe said to be the small quay which has now become Mutford Green. It became a quite important market place, causing rivalry between the Abbots of Ely and Bury, and the name was mentioned in the Domesday Book. The cottages were built of chalk and flint – the stone of the area. Right up to the 20th century the land remained the main occupation, there was no other industry.

In the centre stands the parish church of St Mary – this has to be the main feature of the village. A fine building with a Norman arch to the chancel, and a wealth of carved pews – not built for comfort! The fine hammer beam roof, with the angels' faces multilated by Cromwell's soldiers, is worthy of comment, as is also the font and pulpit. The family of Earl Kitchener, a hero of the First World War, resided in the village; there is a memorial tablet to him in the church, and several gravestones to his ancestors are in the churchyard. The church is still loved and cared for today as it must have been for 900 years – recently a parishioner made, by hand, some handsome oak doors for the west entrance.

The greatest change was the coming of the Americans in the Second World War. The base became the main employers of the area and many new housing estates have been built to accommodate them. They do not contribute a great deal to the social life, having all their own facilities on base, but their presence is always evident and many people have formed close friendships. The new estates also accommodate many new people – notably retired town folk.

In living memory there were nine public houses, but now only five remain. On the whole the village is well catered for with shops. The spiritual needs of the community are well served as there are three Nonconformist churches besides the parish church. A home for the elderly has been opened at the Old Vicarage, called The Lakenheath Village Home and Christian Fellowship Enterprise. The residents are very happy and well cared for, and a group of 'friends' work tirelessly to improve it all the time. While never claiming to be a picturesque village, Lakenheath has nevertheless quite a lot to recommend it, a certain character which the old inhabitants love, and hope that the newcomers do too.

Lavenham 🐝

The magnificent tower of the church of St Peter and St Paul greets all who approach Lavenham, whichever route they travel. Built of flint, at a height of 141 ft it is reputed to be the highest church tower in England and can be seen for miles, its massive shape dominating the sky-line against a Constable sky. The church, almost of cathedral proportions, was mostly rebuilt between 1485 and 1520, just the chancel being of an earlier date. Rich clothiers bequeathed large sums of money for the rebuilding.

At the time of the Domesday survey in 1086 Lavenham was already a well populated place, with two manors, a church, and even a vineyard. The first lord of the manor was Aubrey de Vere, brother-in-law to William the Conqueror. The de Veres were a powerful and influential family who later became the Earls of Oxford. They were lords of the manor for nearly 600 years until the 17th century, when Edward, the 17th Earl, sold his inheritance. A colourful character, he wrote poetry and music, founded a company of actors and was in attendance at the court of Queen Elizabeth I. He is thought by a number of people to have been the true author of Shakespeare's plays, so perhaps Lavenham is really Shakespeare country!

Lavenham's heyday was the medieval period when the making of cloth was its fortune. In 1524 it was the 14th richest town in the country. Wool was dyed – hence 'dyed in the wool', and then woven into a thick cloth, which was sold both at home and abroad. The superb houses built by the wealthy men in the cloth trade can still be seen today, a joy to behold with their massive timber-frames and delicate colour-washed plaster.

The incredible thing about Lavenham is that it is all still there, with the Market Place, complete with market cross, and medieval street pattern still intact. The Guildhall, built in the early 16th century (now administered by the National Trust) stands in the Market Place surrounded by a medley of beautiful buildings. The Guildhall was left to the people of Lavenham in perpetuity by a benefactor and is still used as a meeting place for many local organisations including the WI.

Older residents like to reminisce about the early days of the 20th century, recalling the railway, the gas works, the horse-drawn fire engine hurtling through the streets with the men desperately hanging on, and the blacksmith with a long queue of horses down Water Street waiting to be 'frost-nailed' so that they could walk on icy roads. Lavenham also had the first sugar beet factory in the country, though it was short-lived due to a disastrous fire which gutted the building.

A delightful saying is remembered by a 90 year old.

Eight bells in the belfry
Eight stars on the steeple
In the churchyard, eight trees in a straight line
And eight steps to the church
Eight streets in the town
And eight pubs upon those streets
Eight letters in its name
And eight rich burgesses

The stars represent the de Veres. Sadly the magnificent lime trees have been felled, but now replaced with saplings. The pubs have dwindled to four, the others now homes, their names echoing their past, like Lion House and Blackbirds. Burgesses no longer run the town as they once did, but today Lavenham is surely 'the finest medieval town in England'.

Lawshall Parish Church

Lawshall

The parish of Lawshall is situated in West Suffolk, six miles to the south of Bury St Edmunds. The village appears to be made up of four separate centres and must be one of the most spread-out villages in Suffolk. According to the local postman, there are seven miles of the village!

The earliest documentary record of Lawshall was in AD 972 when it was known as Laushella. However, there is evidence of man in the village in pre-Roman times. A Bronze Age sword was found in a ploughed field which has been dated at between 800–600 BC and can now be seen in Bury Museum.

The most prominent feature of the village is the church of All Saints, which is situated on one of the highest points in Suffolk. Most of the building dates from the Perpendicular period, but traces of the Early English style can be seen in the chancel.

Near to the church is Lawshall Hall which at one time was owned by the Drury family, who entertained Queen Elizabeth I at the Hall in August 1578. The Catholic Rookwood family lived at nearby Coldham Hall and tried to persuade the Queen to visit them, but were only rewarded by one of them being thrown into prison in Bury, where he later died. His Catholicism appears to be the reason for his imprisonment.

In 1605 Ambrose Rookwood was involved with Guy Fawkes in the famous Catholic Gunpowder Plot to blow up James I and his Parliament. He had one of the finest studs of horses in the country, and was invited to join the conspiracy as his horses were to be used for a swift retreat. He was subsequently arrested, imprisoned in the Tower of London, and executed.

Like many of the villages in Suffolk, Lawshall has gone through many changes. It was once a self-sufficient community and indeed, during the middle of the 19th century was starting to provide goods and services outside the village. The major 'exporter' at this time was the horse hair factory. There were also rake and hurdle manufacturers.

A monument was erected in the form of a well cover at Lawshall Green, in memory of Charles Tyrwhitt Drake from nearby Shimpling. Charles Drake died in Jerusalem in 1874, whilst working for the Royal Geographical Society. After many years of neglect this fine monument, which is known locally as the 'Wishing Well', has been restored to its former glory.

In 1872 the village school was completed, which replaced five schools dotted around the village. This is the same school that is still used today after extension and improvement in 1989.

Today, Lawshall is a thriving community with about 900 inhabitants but with significant changes. Most of the working members look outside the village for employment. There is now only one public house (at one time there were seven!) and three churches of different denominations. There is still a village shop and a post office, which are centres for meeting old friends and keeping abreast of the local news.

Laxfield 🐏

Laxfield at the time of the Domesday Book was well over twice the acreage it is now. It was not wooded; out of 8,600 acres only 43 were woodland. Now in a parish half the size there are still 20 acres of woodland. Using the accepted formula to calculate the population, then it was about 250, it is now almost 1,000. Statistically the greatest change in a thousand years seems to be the pig population, up from 40 to just under 8,000 now!

Laxfield today is a good working village, not really pretty in the picture-book way, but with a considerable number of attractive buildings in the wide main street. The village functions well, there are many amenities lost to smaller villages. Four shops, one with a post office, a primary school, two pubs, a garage and no less than 21 social and special interest clubs at the last count. There is a 14th century church, All Saints, which Pevsner describes as having a 'surprising interior', the nave having a 36 ft span with no side aisles.

The handsome Baptist chapel built in 1808 has a memorial stone to one John Noyes, a martyr of the Marian persecutions. Perhaps the most important building in the village is the Guildhall of the Guild of St Mary, built some time very early in the 16th century. After a chequered history it now houses a delightful local museum, which is open on Saturday and Sunday afternoons in the summer months.

The King's Head public house, affectionately known far and wide as 'the Low House', is a small hostelry which as yet is totally unmodernised, just benches around a fireplace, with beer from the kitchen, not a juke box or even a bar . . . secrets like this one just cannot be kept.

Leavenheath 🐝

Leavenheath, halfway between Colchester and Sudbury, is a comparatively new village. Early in the 19th century steps were taken by the inhabitants of scattered farms and cottages in the area to become a settled community. This came about by an Act of Parliament in 1815 – the owners of various estates and land in the five surrounding parishes wished the land to be divided and allotted.

In 1835 a school-chapel was built, also a house for the minister, all by voluntary subscription. A Primitive Methodist chapel was built in 1861 at Honey Tye and was used for services until 1982 when the chapel was closed – the building still stands today. A new National school was built in 1874 and was well used through the years until the property was sold in 1950. Now the buildings have been joined and converted into an attractive family home.

Leavenheath became a civil parish in 1952 with the right to elect its own parish council. By December 1990 the inhabitants numbered over 1,000 and will continue to increase as there is more development.

St Matthew's church is a small Gothic structure in the village, restored in the late 19th century. It is a charming place of worship. There are several listed buildings – Honey Hall at Honey Tye, Rosehill Farm and Greens Farm to name but three.

On the village green is a cricket square, with matches most summer weekends, a football pitch and a fenced off children's playground. Part of Leavenheath is included in the Dedham Vale 'Area of Natural Beauty' and a further section may soon be included in the Stour Valley extension to the Dedham Vale.

The village is in three parts, almost like the three points of a triangle – one part with mostly long-established and listed property and the other two parts with established and new development. Today Leavenheath is given over mainly to arable farming and also fruit farms. St Matthew's church is in use every Sunday. There are two garages, two public houses and one village store with post office.

Levington 🌿

Levington is a small village on the banks of the river Orwell. St Peter's 12th century church stands overlooking the river. The Ship inn is an old smugglers' haunt – where Margaret Catchpole used to meet her lover. It is a true country pub where folk in olden times would gather for an exchange of news and gossip, as well as for the real ale. Nowadays it is used mainly by the sailing fraternity from the marina and for local office workers who meet there for the excellent food and to relax over a pint.

Levington Hall was the Squire's residence, with the lodge cottage for the gardener. Hilltop Cottage, opposite the pub, has a thatched roof and groceries could once be bought there from the shop adjoining. There were 42 cottages in the village altogether. There was a wheelwright, a watchmender and a sexton. Of course there was a post office, but when the elderly postmistress died the post office disappeared. There were three farms in the area, mostly arable, a village hall and a Baptist chapel, built in 1839 but made redundant in 1984. Barges used to come up the creek in the 1920s, and the children had great fun playing with the wood which was delivered there.

In 1956 Fison's built their research station and eventually produced the now famous Levington Compost. At that time they also built 17 houses in a half-circle to house their workers, agricultural and horticultural alike. It not only provided work for villagers and people from outside the village but it also improved the bus service from Ipswich to Felixstowe, which includes Levington village.

The Suffolk Yacht Harbour has now expanded greatly so there is a lot of traffic through the village. It is to be hoped that Levington can still remain 'a village' in spite of the port of Felixstowe creeping up the river and industrial buildings and supermarkets encroaching on the countryside.

Linstead Magna 🌿

Linstead Magna is a parish consisting of a few scattered farms five miles west-south-west of Halesworth.

The church of St Peter stood in the centre of the parish in an enclosed piece of land surrounded by fields. It was an ancient flint building, Early English in style, consisting of chancel, nave, south porch and embattled western tower containing one bell. In 1900 services were held in the chancel, the nave being almost in ruins and unfit for use. There are now no remains of the church or churchyard.

The following is a letter taken from the *East Anglian Magazine* 1965 written by Mr Peter Northeast: 'I am rather surprised that the passing of the Linstead Magna church near Halesworth has gone unmourned in your columns, In *EAM* July 1953 L. Sewell stated that it had been sold for demolition in 1924 but that public protest stopped this – it had been fast decaying all the years of this century. In August of last year (1964) the remainder of the brick tower had become unsafe and was demolished. On visiting the site in that month I found a rather pitiful scene. The sole reminders of this church are now a 15th century font and a medieval bell preserved in St Augustine's church in Ipswich.' A picture with this article shows just a heap of rubble where the church had stood.

Linstead Parva ▒

Linstead Parva is a village four miles west of Halesworth, mainly a farming community. There were three village greens known as Blacksmiths, Morrell Haugh and Collipys Green. These have all been taken into farms.

A school established in 1869 and attended by about 30 children was held in the Literary Institute, which was built in 1852 by local effort. It had about 250 volumes and 30 members who each paid a shilling a year. This building is now part of a cottage.

There is now no village shop, this closed in the 1970s; the public house closed in the 1950s. The blacksmith was still working in the early 1970s. The old school closed in 1913. Where the blacksmith's was, there is now a garage and petrol pumps, a garden machinery showroom and workshop, and also Linstead Ironworks which is a separate concern. These are situated on the main road through the village.

Linstead has a village hall, built in 1927, and like the Literary Institute the money was raised by the efforts of the local people. Miss Adams, retired teacher of Old School House, trained the village folk for concerts! Great fun they were, the stage was made with barn doors and beer crates loaned from the local pub, the Greyhound.

The church (St Margaret) is a small flint building with a western turret of wood containing one bell. In 1973 Linstead church was the venue of the wedding scene in the *Requiem for a Village* which was filmed in different villages in the area.

Little Saxham ▒

It was called Saxham Parva in years gone by, when the village consisted of two farms, several tied cottages, mostly thatched, an inn and a beautiful old Hall. A claim to fame is that Charles II often visited the Crofts family here, as King Charles' son, the Duke of Monmouth, was brought up here until he was 14 years old. Charles II once visited the church and listened to a very long sermon, which he had printed. Sadly, the old Hall was pulled down in 1773. The moat remains and when it dried up in a very dry summer, hundreds of oyster shells were found in

St. Nicholas' Church, Little Saxham

the mud. Were they eaten by the nobility when the King visited or were they the regular diet for the Crofts family and the young Duke?

The flint church of St Nicholas, with its lovely round tower and Norman superstructure, is said to be the best unspoilt example in the region.

In the 19th century, a parson was so infuriated by the continual traffic of carriages and horses and mud which passed his front door (next to the church) that he caused the road to be moved. He cut across the village green, knocking down a couple of old cottages and meeting the Barrow road behind the church – creating a very dangerous corner for the faster traffic of today.

In 1947, a very beautiful old barn with four bays blew down in a gale. The thatch blew off and down it came, there was not one single nail in the construction of it. At the same time a very old tree blew down and the roots were torn up. The ground beneath was sand and many beautiful fossils were found. This land must have been underwater millions of years ago.

Even 50 years ago, there were many red squirrels here and hundreds of rabbits. Fourteen Suffolk Punch horses worked the farm. Now tractors

151

and combines do the farm work and Honey Hill Farm has diversified to include a horse riding stables. A small tractor business grew into a major industrial estate nearby, and in a converted garage is a world renowned embroidery centre. Grey squirrels have taken over and rabbits almost disappeared.

During the Second World War the village lived under a constant drone of heavily laden bombers. One night over a thousand passed over. Many of the women here took Red Cross lessons and prepared to do their best, should one of the planes come down as it came limping home. When the war ended, the silence was something which words can hardly explain.

A sad change for the village came with the closing of the tiny village school of about 15 children, aged from five to 14. The children were sent to Bury and eventually benefited from the change. A change of rector brought the Sunday school to an abrupt end and the church choir ended when the boys grew up and left home.

How times have changed! No-one can really long for the old days of water wells, prehistoric sewerage systems and oil lamps. Yet the place was peaceful and close knit in sorrow or in happiness. The church still stands on the corner in solemn splendour.

Long Melford ✺

Julian Tennyson, the gifted young writer so tragically killed in the Second World War, described Long Melford as his favourite small Suffolk town, and the most romantic of them all. Although he describes it as a town, it is still known as a village; its population is now about 4,000. Its long history dates back to Roman times when the river Stour on which it stands was still navigable. The main street probably follows the course of a Roman road and was crossed by an important east–west road. Many exciting finds were made in 1958 when a mechanical digger cut into a tessellated pavement. Among them was a blue glass Roman vase, now in the British Museum.

Its name in Roman times is not known, but the name Long Melford derives from the great length of the village and the mill ford in the centre, now crossed by a bridge. Before its demolition in the 1950s this watermill lay at the lower end of the splendid green. The church is at the upper end and dates from the 15th century; in the Domesday Book an Anglo-Saxon church is recorded on the same site. It is known as a wool church, built with the wealth created by the medieval wool trade which brought so much prosperity to East Anglia. It has been described as the most beautiful church in Suffolk, to which visitors come from all over the world. Looking up the green, in front of the church, one sees the attractive brick-built almshouses, the Hospital of the Holy and Undivided Trinity, founded by William Cordell in 1573 for twelve poor men. The building was reconstructed and improved in Victorian times and enjoys the finest position in Long Melford.

Long Melford had a close association with Bury St Edmunds Abbey as the abbots had their hunting lodge and a large estate here. Afer the Reformation this was granted to William Cordell, a lawyer, who became a knight and Speaker of the House of Commons in Queen Mary's reign. As Sir William he welcomed Queen Elizabeth to Melford Hall when she made a Royal Progress through Suffolk. Sir William's magnificent tomb is in the chancel of the church.

Kentwell, Melford's other Tudor Hall, was the home of the Clopton family, mainly responsible for rebuilding the church as it is now, except for the tower, rebuilt in Victorian times.

Melford's annual Whitsuntide fair, granted to the village by King John, is held on the green. It became a horse fair, and is now merely an amusement fair.

After the decline of the wool trade, new village industries included mat making, horse hair weaving and an iron foundry. There were several maltings, three of which are now converted to other uses. There is also a caravan factory and a flourishing factory for horse rugs and sports clothing. Agriculture, which used to give the most employment, has diminished in these times of modern farming. There were always plenty of shops and public houses, the best known being the Bull, now a Trust House hotel. In 1648 it was the scene of a murder when a Roundhead slew a Cavalier there.

Over the years the tourist trade has greatly increased, owing to the many attractions this corner of Suffolk has to offer, and the recently opened bypass has allowed the village to return to a more peaceful life now that commercial traffic no longer thunders through the main street. The many different organisations in the village are well supported, making the village a good place to live where old and new mingle, and people make a happy life together.

Market Weston 🐑

The village of Market Weston lies amidst farmland off the main road network two miles from the Norfolk/Suffolk border. It is a small community which recently unveiled a new village sign depicting life in the 13th century with the church and the, long since demolished, windmill overseeing a colourful busy village market scene. The village was granted the market charter in 1263.

Today life is much quieter, apart from the roar of RAF Tornado aircraft overhead. There are nine owner-occupied farms and three rented from the county council. All the farms are worked by the families occupying them, growing wheat, barley, oats, sugar beet and grass. The sugar beet is processed at the factory in Bury St Edmunds. The grass is for hay, silage and food for the cattle, sheep and pigs raised locally.

The pattern of housing follows that of a ribbon development along the three roads and their branches. These converge at the village hall, in the centre of the village, which until 1961 was the school and therefore the focal point for the inhabitants.

The church of St Mary stands in open fields and can be seen afar. It has original Victorian furniture and oil lamps converted for electricity. There has been a great deal of fundraising required for the restoration of the roof and clock tower.

There is no longer a village shop or post office, which closed in 1986 with the retirement of the postmistress. Villagers must travel to Hopton and Barningham for these services or further afield for larger supermarket shopping. Market Weston is, however, well served by mobile shops, particularly useful to the elderly and housebound.

Country walks are a favourite pastime of the local people and visitors, many ending at the Mill inn where bar snacks and full meals are available as a perfect ending to an outing. One of the many rights of way traversing the village leads down to Market Weston fen which is one of the best remaining examples of the valley fens along the Little Ouse and Waveney valley. It has so far escaped the drainage and bore extraction which is so harmful to valley fens. The fen was sold, by the parish, in 1981 to the Suffolk Trust for Nature Conservation.

Market Weston is no longer the bustling medieval market village it once was and must now look beyond its boundaries for the majority of amenities but it has a wealth of natural beauty resources and retains a good community spirit.

Martlesham

Martlesham is a large village stretching from Woodbridge in the north to Kesgrave in the south and from Bealings in the west to the banks of the river Deben in the east. The village has developed from a settlement on the creek joining the river Fynn to the river Deben. The earliest hamlet was probably where the church is now, on a promontory overlooking the river Deben. Flint implements and spearheads found in the area and also tumuli still remaining on the heathland point to early settlements.

Later the village moved inland around a crossing place over the Fynn, first by a ford and later a hump-backed bridge, which served the traffic on what was then the main road between Norwich and London via Ipswich. The tollgate house has gone and the hump-backed bridge has been replaced by a modern one but the old Red Lion inn still stands nearby, its restaurant a popular eating place. It proudly sports as its sign a brightly painted ship's figurehead said to have been taken from a Dutch ship at the battle of Sole Bay in 1672.

Opposite the Red Lion, School Lane parallels the Fynn and leads to Church Lane. At the end of this winding leafy lane stands Martlesham Hall and the parish church of St Mary. St Mary's is a typical Suffolk church with knapped flint walls and a square tower, the churchyard surrounded by tall trees. The pulpit has the date 1614 inscribed and there is a medieval wall painting of St Christopher carrying the Christchild on his shoulder.

In Top Street to the north of the Fynn, Mr and Mrs O'Brien Baker established Home Meadows Nursery in 1938. With the help of their son they still carry on the business, specialising in Iceland poppies and chrysanthemums and exhibiting regularly at the Chelsea Flower Show. Across the road from the nursery Mr Finch plied his trade of blacksmith until very recently. Also nearby is a thriving market garden and a garage giving friendly service.

South of the Fynn, Lamb Barn Hill rises steeply to heathland and during the First World War part of the heath became an airfield. For the next 50 years the Royal Air Force used the site to test all types of civil and military aircraft. During the Second World War it was a frontline fighter station, first for the RAF and later the United States Army Airforce (USAAF). It has today become a new development – Martlesham Heath.

By 1936, houses had spread up the hill and beyond and a Miss F. E. Jermyn opened the Black Tiles cafe, which was renowned for homemade cakes and pastries as well as its gleaming rooftiles from which its name is derived. During the Second World War it was a haven for men from all over the world who were stationed at the airfield. The Black Tiles is now a licensed inn and serves Suffolk beers.

With the growth of the east coast ports of Felixstowe and Ipswich to the south and the expanding holiday resorts of Lowestoft and Yarmouth to the north, the road through old Martlesham became more and more busy and dangerous. Life on either side of the road was intolerable and people crossed the road at their peril. Thankfully a bypass was built in 1987 and peace has returned.

Martlesham Heath 🐝

This unusual village was built in 1975. Before that no one but the RAF had lived on the site since Bronze Age man left evidence of its use as a burial ground. Converting an airfield with gorse, heather, and concrete runways into landscaped gardens meant that many bullets, bits of aircraft and even unexploded bombs were dug up!

The village won an award for its design of individual hamlets (separated by open areas of heathland) radiating off a single spine road around a village green. Some people call it 'Legoland' because of the variety of colours (including Suffolk Pink!) used for the houses. The old wireless station is the only RAF building converted to a private dwelling. External TV aerials and telephone wires are not allowed, so underground cables are used, giving a five channel cable TV service. Martlesham Consultants Limited, of which all houseowners must be shareholders, manages and maintains the open spaces for the benefit of residents.

The shopping centre (including post office and doctor's surgery), designed to resemble old Suffolk maltings, is next to the village green.

The local primary school, Birchwood, built in 1989 to an unusual design, with pairs of classrooms radiating from a central atrium area, is also used by the Brownies and other local organisations. The new church of St Michael and All Angels, which opened in 1991, built using money raised by the villagers over a number of years, is dedicated to all the airmen who flew from 'The Heath'.

Sir Douglas Bader flew from Martlesham Heath, 17th December 1940–18th March 1941, as a member of 242 squadron. Although a teetotaller, he opened the public house named after him in 1979. The final plane flew from the runways in spring 1980, and they were finally built over in the mid 1980s with the completion of the spine road. The only remaining piece of runway is opposite the British Telecom Research Laboratories, although the car park and forecourt of the Douglas Bader pub are actually pieces of runway covered over! The original control tower (used by the playgroup), wind sock and an old hangar, still remain to the west of 'The Heath'.

There is still heather, gorse, and silver birch, maintained by the local conservation group. 'The Heath' was part of the old sandlings stretching right up the East Anglian coast at one time. The 'Western Corridor' has therefore been set aside as a site of special scientific interest (SSSI), being one of the last remaining natural habitats of the silver studded blue butterfly. There are many footpaths and cycle tracks for exploring.

Many villagers work at the British Telecom Research Laboratories or the Suffolk Police HQ, which are both just a quick stroll away. Others are employed by Heath Road Hospital, the Port of Felixstowe, Hollesley Bay Colony, or are Americans from the local bases. Many of the US airmen buy houses here, rather than living on the base, and integrate into the local community, sometimes so well that they stay at the end of their tour of duty. As a result, the accents on the Heath are varied, with people from all over Britain, if not the world. This is certainly not a typical Suffolk village!

Mellis 🐚

Here is one of the largest open commons in the country – a vast expanse of grass full of wonderful wildlife. Mellis Common during the Second World War was cultivated to produce potatoes and grain – with the proviso it would be returned to grassland at the end of the war.

How does one assess the progress of a village? The population has certainly not seen a steady rise. In 1086, at the time of the Domesday Book, there were 12 people living here. In 1851 the number was 610, but 100 years later in 1951 it was down to 347 and by 1981 it was still decreasing.

Mellis is still an agricultural village. However, in 1831 85 people were employed in agriculture and by 1912 the figures were down to nine farmers and two farm bailiffs: mechanisation had a lot to do with these numbers. Records show that there was a miller in the village in the 19th century.

All villages have their 'characters'. Mellis is no exception. In St Mary's church is the tomb of Francis Yaxley, a diplomat of the 16th century and a 'foolish prating knave' who was sent to the Tower for giving away State secrets. On his release, he went to Spain on behalf of Mary, Queen of Scots to ask for aid against Elizabeth I. He drowned on the voyage home. Fortuitous perhaps!

Mendham & Metfield 🐟

The village of Mendham stands on the Suffolk bank of the river Waveney, which is spanned at this point by a distinctive iron girder bridge. The bridge was built as a 'temporary' replacement for its wooden predecessor which was washed away by floods in 1912.

Standing close to the river, but never affected by the frequent flooding of the marshes, is the 14th century All Saints' church. Records say that there was a church on the site in Norman times, when it was connected with the priory of Cluniac monks founded by William de Huntingfield in the 12th century. The priory was situated on the marshes between Mendham and Withersdale, but the last of the ruins have disappeared within living memory. Many of the stones which formed its fabric were carried away and incorporated into walls and buildings in the neighbourhood.

The Red Lion public house, which stands across the road from the war memorial in the churchyard, closed in the late 1960s to become a private house. Meanwhile the village post office stores building has been greatly enlarged and turned into a country hotel. There is still a tiny post office standing in one corner of the building but it bears no resemblance to the huge, thriving general store of earlier years.

The hotel is named after Mendham's most famous son, Sir Alfred Munnings RA, who was born and raised at Mendham Mill. He had his first studio in the street. To commemorate this the row of council houses built on and around the site are called Studio Corner. The old folks' bungalows are called The Greys, after the couple Nobby and Charlotte Grey, who used to live on their site and were often featured in Alfred Munnings's paintings. His painting called *Charlotte and her pony* was used as inspiration for the village sign which was unveiled by his niece Kathleen Hadingham, a resident of the village all her life.

The mill has not operated since 1938 when it was sold and converted into a private house. More recently the land belonging to the mill has been turned into a trout fishery.

Mendham also boasts a rather infamous son, Henry Cabell, a thief who was transported to Sydney Cove, Australia. He was reputed to have been the first Englishman to set foot in Sydney Cove, having been elected to carry the ship's captain ashore on his back. Once arrived, Henry married his commonlaw wife Susannah Holmes. They went on to become respected members of the community and very prosperous, having eleven children.

Two miles from Mendham is the village of Metfield, where there was a USAAF airfield during the Second World War which was the base for P47 fighters and B24 Liberator bombers. The land covered by the airfield has been reclaimed for farming in recent years and few signs of it remain.

The Metfield church of St John the Baptist has a fine clock which was originally made with a Virgin Folio movement, but when it was restored this was replaced by an Anchor Escapement. The workings can be easily seen by all visitors to the church.

Metfield is another village surrounded by farms but the centre has been, and is being, developed for housing. Many retired people and commuters live here contentedly among the native villagers. Metfield is a growing and lively community with a village hall, shop, bakery, pub, garage and pottery.

Mendlesham 🐚

Given the rights of a market town in 1281, recorded in the Domesday Book as Melnessam, and believed to be the seat of East Anglian Kings, today Mendlesham has two main streets running parallel with an assortment of interesting houses packed together, dating back to mid-Saxon times, and is designated a conservation area. In Old Market Street, the Preaching Stone can be seen, said to have been used by itinerant preachers. Further down the road is the Old Schoolroom, bequeathed by Peter Duck in 1618 for the residence of a schoolmaster and the maintenance of a grammar school, now used as a hall.

The beautiful church of St Mary lies at the eastern end of the main streets on the site of an earlier Saxon church. One of the most interesting features inside the church is the wooden font cover made in 1630 by a local man, John Turner, who also made the pulpit. The poppy head benches flanking the nave are thought to date from 1588. Sadly, many were badly mutilated during the Cromwellian period. Beside the altar are two Mendlesham chairs made by Daniel Day who had a workshop in Front Street in the 18th century. These uniquely styled chairs were traditionally made of yew or fruitwood, the seat being of elm. Today, similar chairs are being produced by Roy Clement-Smith of Elms Farm.

Perhaps the most interesting feature within the church is the wonderful collection of armour stored since 1593 in the priest's chamber over the north porch, thought initially to have been the accommodation of the resident chaplain. Viewing is by appointment, the chamber being approached by a narrow, winding flight of stairs.

There are two other places of worship, both nonconformist. The Baptist church can be found in the hamlet of Mendlesham Green, two miles south of the main village. It is worthy of note that in a church survey on 30th March 1851, morning service at this chapel was attended by 120 people, and afternoon service by 160, but these figures were said to be low due to bad weather!

In earlier times, the Green had its own shops, blacksmith, wheelwright and public house, but now all that remains is a post office. The Street, as the main part of the village is known locally, has a butcher, bakery, post office and store, fish and chip shop, and a hairdresser. An interesting feature of the property of the latter, located in Front Street, is the long window above the shop said to have lit a weaver's loft.

Two public houses remain in The Street from an earlier six, the King's Head in Old Market Street, and the Fleece in Front Street. Outside the Fleece was one of the public pumps for those villagers with no access to a private well. Mains water was installed in 1950. Opposite the Fleece was the fire station, now a dwelling house. The fire engine, drawn by two horses and pumped by hand, was in use until 1939. The Green had two fire engines, one privately owned by Mr Arbon.

Agriculture and livestock continue to be an important source of local employment. Other major employers are based at the industrial estate on Mendlesham airfield, two miles away on the A140, a former Second World War American airbase. The local landmark, visible for many miles, is the 1,000 ft high television mast, and close by is a memorial to American airmen.

Mettingham 🐚

Mettingham is a scattered village on the south bank of the Waveney and the borders of Norfolk. The B1062 Beccles to Bungay road runs through the village, which has approximately 80 homes.

Mettingham Castle is well known today for the 14th century gateway and the ivy-clad walls. It was built in 1342 by Sir John de Norwich, an admiral under Edward III, whose service against the Scots, Spaniards and French was rewarded by permission to convert his manor house into a fortified castle. Later that century the estate passed to the Church and a college for a master and 13 chaplains was founded there. In 1842 six silver bells were found in the moat, near the ruins of the supposed belfry tower. The present house in the castle grounds was built in 1880.

All Saints' church stands on a hill almost in the centre of the village. The church is Norman, but there was a church there in Saxon times. Fierce gargoyles glower from the embattled tower. A canopied tomb in the chancel wall is thought to be of John de Norwich, whose arms are on a medallion in one of the windows. The Tudor font is richly carved with lions and angels. The lamp above was made at the local forge.

Next to the church is the Tally Ho! which, modernised and extended, is well known for the excellent meals served there. A bowling green, run by an active club, nestles between church and public house. The church rooms are run by a committee who work hard to maintain the rooms for village use.

For many years a fruit farm was run at the Red House with many local people employed to pick the strawberries, blackcurrants and apples. Once a restaurant, then an hotel, this Georgian house is now a private residence. On the site of the old Hall stands a 17th century house with distinctive shaped gables.

With the changes in farming, there is little employment in the village now. Those who are not self-employed, travel to Beccles, Bungay or further afield for their work. Some old properties have been modernised, some pulled down and the sites used for new houses, but there has been no large housing development to spoil the countryside. Mettingham remains a quiet, peaceful village. No shop, no post office, but one can post a letter or choose a book at the mobile library. One can also enjoy a walk along the many footpaths which are part of the Bigod Way.

Mildenhall

Mildenhall is a fen-edge market town, still considered a village by most outsiders, twelve miles west from Bury St Edmunds. Mildenhall was a port for the hinterland of West Suffolk. Barnack stone used in the building of St Mary's was transported through Peterborough along the rivers Nene, Ouse and Lark to Mildenhall. Navigation continued as far as Bury St Edmunds in medieval times and Daniel Defoe refers to coal, corn and iron carried by barge in 1722. The Eastern Counties and Transport Company attempted to keep the waterway clear of weeds until 1892. Today the river Lark is no longer a commercial trade route.

The great west tower of the parish church, St Mary's, dominates the landscape. The church is justly famous for the chancel's east window, the angel roof of the nave and the carvings on the spandrels in the north aisle roof. Prior to 1895 the church was known as St Andrew's. Mr Beckford Bevan discovered a document in Norwich revealing the original dedication to St Mary.

In 1042 the manor of Mildenhall was given to Bury Abbey 'that the monks might eat wheaten and not barley-bread'. It is believed but not authenticated that the Cellarius (collector of tithes for the abbey) inhabited a house near or on the site of the present-day house named The Priory in the south-west corner of the churchyard. This house was the workhouse until 1897.

Also of interest in the churchyard are the remains of the charnel house where bones were stored after disturbance by continued use of the ground for burials. The north side of the churchyard was used for feasts and ales run by the churchwardens to raise funds. A play entitled *St Thomas* was performed here in 1505.

Sir Henry North (1556–1620) built a manor house on the north side of the church. His altar tomb is at the east end of the south aisle. William

Bunbury, vicar of Mildenhall, succeeded to the manor in 1747. It was one of his descendants Sir Henry Edward Bunbury (1778–1860), who was dispatched to inform Napoleon Bonaparte that he was to be permanently exiled on St Helena. The manor remained in the Bunbury family until it was sold in 1933. The manor house was demolished and the bricks used in the building of bungalows in Church Walk.

Monewden

Monewden is situated on one of the 'high' points of Suffolk, being approximately 300 ft above sea level, and is considered to be a hamlet nowadays although there have been dwellings on the site reputedly going back to Roman times.

Throughout the Middle Ages there were connections with the de Cretingham family and references to the land being held by Thomas Seckford of Woodbridge. The house built on this land, Monewden Lodge, stood in a commanding position surrounded by a moat and with good views over the surrounding countryside. During the early part of the 20th century it was owned by a Colonel who had it blown up in the 1950s as an exercise by the Territorial Army. It was by this time derelict.

The village now contains 47 houses and many of its residents are related in one way or another. Although it used to have a school, a mill, a blacksmith's, a wheelwright's, a sub-post office and a shop, as well as the church, the church is the only one remaining in use. However, it is still a very active community. The Victorian school is now the village hall and many events are held here and throughout the village during the year. The most widely known of these is the Fuschia Festival which takes place every August Bank Holiday on Sunday and Monday.

Monewden has always been a farming community and with the closure of the previously mentioned businesses the only activities today are a local carpenter and the watercolour artist, John Western, who has his home and gallery in the village, although he was brought up in the next village of Cretingham.

The village's one claim to a 'famous' person is William Pitts whose decaying gravestone can be seen in the churchyard. In 1791 William Pitts was appointed assistant astronomer to his friend, William Gooch, to accompany him on Vancouver's voyage of exploration. They sailed in a ship called the *Daedalus*, but unfortunately Mr Gooch was murdered by natives in Honolulu and, unable to carry on the work alone, William Pitts left the ship and travelled home via Canton and then in an East India tea clipper.

The Suffolk Wildlife Trust has two reserves in Monewden. One is called Fox's Meadow and the other Martins Meadow which lies behind Rookery Farm.

Although at first glance the passerby would think this a quiet sleepy hamlet not really worth stopping in, those who live there never want to move away and many people who attend the various social events wish they could move into the community as it is 'such a friendly place'. Not one that is easy to find, most first time visitors tend to go astray and even those living within a ten mile radius have often never heard of Monewden, but once they find their way here they keep coming back.

Monks Eleigh ⚜

There has been a settlement here since Stone Age times. Stone Age scrapers and a stone hammer were found at Slough Farm. There is also evidence of Roman occupation. Documented history can be traced back over a thousand years, to Aelfgar, Ealdorman of Essex who was lord of the manor and who died in about AD 953.

No monks have ever lived here, despite the name. The Canterbury monks obtained the lordship of the manor by bequest from Aelfgar's son-in-law Beorhtnoth, and it remained the property of the prior and monks, and their post-Reformation successors the Dean and Chapter of Canterbury, right through to the 20th century. The lordship is believed now to vest in the Church Commissioners, though with no land.

Throughout its long history, therefore, Monks Eleigh has never been a squire-dominated village. The Hall, attractive though it is, is essentially a modest building, a residence for a steward or agent, rather than a squire. Its fine chimneystack bears the initials 'MB' and the date 1658. The initials are those of Miles Burkitt, the enterprising Puritan who bought it when the Dean and Chapter were temporarily expropriated at the time of the Commonwealth. He rebuilt the Hall – hence the date – only to be himself expropriated at the Restoration of the Monarchy.

White's 1844 Suffolk directory shows a self-contained village. The population had then peaked at 732, compared with 542 in 1801 and a record low in 1971 of 405. It consisted mostly of farm labourers and their families living in crowded conditions on very low wages. There were several well-stocked shops, including a grocer's and a draper's, and pubs. A church school had been built in 1834 on the site of the old parish workhouse on Church Hill. Trades represented included a vet, a blacksmith, two wheelwrights, two corn millers, a tanner, two shoemakers, two tailors and, surprisingly, an 'animal painter', J. R. Hobart.

The parish church of St Peter dates mostly from the 14th and 15th centuries, though the font is older. The church had a spire erected in 1631 which was taken down as 'dangerous' in 1845. It continued to dominate the village even without its spire, as it still does today.

The first recorded member of the Hobart family to live at 'Hobarts' was John Hobart in 1389. The most famous member of the family to be born here was Sir James Hobart, who was later to become Attorney

General to Henry VII and a Privy Councillor. Hobarts is reputed to have a ghost – one Nathaniel Lukin, a Huguenot, who lived in the house in 1688. He came to Suffolk to teach weaving. His initials and those of his wife Sarah are carved over the fireplace.

Mutford & Rushmere ✍

The village name derives from there being a moot hall by a ford in the river, and this would have been the collecting point for taxes from the surrounding Hundred. The village was important enough to have a gallows and ducking stool. A piece of land is called Hanging Piece and close by are Corpse Meadow and Hangmans Lane.

Legend has it that a parish clerk was found guilty of sheep stealing, was hanged, and buried beneath the gibbet. Later a jealous neighbour confessed to the crime on his death-bed and the remains of the ill-fated clerk were reinterred in the churchyard. A gravestone there is inscribed, 'Let all the world keep silent, God himself is Judge'.

St Andrew's church is the only known church with a Galilee porch attached to a round tower; it stands on high ground, slightly away from the village itself. The two public houses have long since become private dwellings and the village school was demolished afer 60 years to make way for modern housing. Two blacksmiths' forges have closed, although one now houses an engineering works; the village post office and store remains open. In years gone by, men earned their living from local farms or travelled to Lowestoft and Kessingland to join the fishing industry. Timber from Mutford Wood was used in the building of steam drifters at Lowestoft. Today, employment is found in nearby towns, although the local thatcher still plies his trade and a small garage is kept busy.

The river Hundred, once a navigable waterway, now shallow and overgrown, forms the southern boundary to the village. It flows on past the tiny hamlet of Rushmere, once a marshy mere where rushes abounded. Early records show a village of 30 dwellings, present-day dwellings number 32. It stands six miles south-east of Beccles and six miles south-west of Lowestoft on what was once the coach road to London.

The 13th century church of St Michael, at present unused, has a thatched roof and flint walls. Like St Andrew's, it has a round tower and inside remains the pulpit and a Jacobean font.

Tuns Cottages were once the village hostelry; rumour says the local farmer closed it down after deciding his labourers spent too much time there. His men were also expected to be regular churchgoers. The Elizabethan Hall remains the centre of a busy farm, but the nearby butcher's shop, where local cattle would have been slaughtered, has long gone.

Hannah's Green, an area covering 20 perches of land, was given by the lord of the manor for the benefit of the poor. The rent was collected and distributed as a charity. This continues to the present day, as does Brandons Charity, set up to give needy villagers 6s 8d a year.

Nacton

Anyone standing on Nacton shore today who could ignore the distant prospect of Felixstowe's dockside cranes, would see a picture much the same as it was almost a thousand years ago. The herons fishing on the margins of the mud and the shelduck keeping station in the shallows would have been there when the Danes came up the river, fought Earl Ulfketel and left their dead piled beneath the Seven Hills just outside the village.

Away from the river there were changes in the landscape in the 850 years that followed. St Martin's church was built in 1200, and the two great houses, Orwell Park House and Broke Hall were established.

The engineer of some of the greatest changes in the area was Colonel George Tomline who lived at Orwell Park House and owned virtually the whole of the area that lay between the Orwell and the Deben. In 1850, because he did not like the humble cottages and their occupants near his house, he had the village moved to its present site.

This is not to say that he did not benefit the village. He built a school at Seven Hills, started an oyster company and built the railway from Ipswich to Felixstowe, with a station at the far end of the village. He also built the observatory at Orwell Park House that is still operating.

Tomline died in 1889 and E. G. Pretyman inherited Orwell Park. Because his wife, Lady Beatrice, objected to it, the village pub was closed, and Nacton village is dry to this day.

The workhouse, which had a chequered history – rumours of starvation among the inmates and drunkenness among the officers leading to a full scale riot that had to be quashed by the local dragoons at one stage – became redundant in 1900, and today it is Amberfield School.

Mighty Orwell Park House itself also became a school, in 1937. Broke Hall passed out of the hands of the descendants of Lord Broke in 1942, and the house and its surrounding buildings have recently been restored for residential use. The railway station, closed in the Beeching cuts, has survived in a similar way, and the chapel in the centre of the village is now a shop.

What was the pub is now Anchor House, and the original shop closed in 1983 after 115 years in the same family. Now it, too, is a private residence, still lived in by a member of the Keeble family and with some of the shop fittings still evident in the front room.

The 1,250 acre Home Farm set in the Orwell Park estate is still in production, but where once 20 or more men looked after cattle, pigs and sheep, today the farm manager and just four men, using modern machinery, tend the largely arable land.

Nayland & Wissington 🦢

The village of Nayland stands on the border of the river Stour at the beginning of its most beautiful upper stretch. The original Manor stood on a moated field called 'Court Knoll', the site of an ancient settlement, of which nothing now remains. Nayland was once recorded as the 45th largest town in England.

High Street, at one time, was divided into two rows of cottages (now a central square), the 15th century Alston Court standing proud with its canopied hood, panelled front door and mullioned window. Overlooking the square is the Guildhall, also 15th century, thought to have been built for the Brotherhood Fraternity of the Guild of our Lady of Nayland, later used for local judiciary minor offences. For 200 years it was a bakery and dairy, with animals at the rear of the property, now renovated to a private dwelling.

In the early years, the wool trade and cloth making were the main industries, gradually turning to a thriving farming area. There are still weaving looms working in the old school building today. In the 1800s Nayland was self supporting, with a flour mill, brewery, tannery, saddlers, gas works, blacksmiths and basket makers. There were grocers, butchers, a slaughterhouse, bakers, shoemakers, a post office, ironmongers and a bank.

Fen Street has the mill stream running along it and a number of delightful cottages with little bridges to their doors. This leads to 'The Fens' which is a large piece of common land, bordering the river bank. The rights of these fenages were originally allocated to villagers, enabling them to graze their cattle. Today they are still grazed, but on a collective basis.

Abels Bridge was originally built in wood in the 15th century, dividing Suffolk from Essex. In the 16th century, this hump bridge was built in brick by a wealthy clothier, John Abel, for the navigation of barges transporting goods and corn to the flour mill. It was renovated again in 1959 to accommodate modern traffic. The keystone, transferred from the old bridge, bears the letter 'A' and a bell.

The beautiful building of St James' was the second church to be built on the site in 1400 and, with the foundation of wealth in the wool trade, owes a great deal of its existence to the sheep. The church is renowned for the Constable altarpiece of *Christ Blessing the Bread and Wine*. This was commissioned by his aunt who lived nearby and was painted in 1809.

Wissington is a farming hamlet with an attractive mill, a Norman church with interesting murals, and scattered cottages.

Overlooking the whole valley is the East Anglian Sanatorium, founded and built by Dr Jane Walker, to her own specifications for open air treatment of tuberculosis in 1901. After the decline of tuberculosis, the hospital was changed to care for the mentally handicapped in 1959, when it was reopened by the Queen Mother.

Nayland and Wiston are now part of the Dedham Vale in Constable Country, and have the most stunning views, enjoyed by artists, anglers, walkers and photographers.

Nedging-with-Naughton 🐾

Two hamlets combined as one for parish purposes with a total population of some 300, but supporting two separate churches within their boundaries. Despite the changing years bringing increased traffic there is still an air of tranquillity which delights inhabitants and visitors alike.

A glance backwards over the centuries shows the chilling spectacle of the ancient custom of reading the burial service at the north doorway of the churches over the helpless victims of leprosy, who were required to listen to the ceremony outside that particular door.

The continuing thread over the centuries lies within the strong farming background of the two communities, which has seen many changes and suffered severe hardships and disasters even as recent as the storm of July 1947. This devastated crops as it swept its five-mile-wide path through 60,000 acres travelling to the Norfolk border. Here in the village the severity was such that hailstones smashed windows of houses and cottages, battering to death chickens, ducks and geese.

Naughton Mill caught fire in about 1910 with firemen coming from Bildeston, Monks Eleigh, Elmsett and Kersey. The mill was immediately rebuilt, but today is used as a private dwelling. Nedging school, long since abandoned for such purposes, must surely rank as one of the smallest, being approximately 30 by 17 ft of flint and stone construction.

The story is told of a farmer who, having aided a gipsy, in return was given the secret ingredients of a special linament to ease pains in the joints. This linament was sold for two shillings a bottle in the Wheelhouse in Naughton as recently as 20 years ago. The secret cure died with the farmer!

Needham Market 🐾

Needham Market was once a hamlet of Barking. The market charter was granted by Henry III and the market flourished until the plague struck in 1665. A market has never been held since, although the right to do so still exists.

To this day, Chain Bridge to the west and Chain House Farm to the east are reminders of the sacrifices made by the people of Needham Market to contain the plague. Chains were erected across the road at these points beyond which nobody crossed. Food was exchanged for money, the coins being sterilised in a vinegar and water mixture. Victims of the plague were buried in a mass grave just outside the village on a site which is now a new housing estate. The 'sick houses' can still be seen in

Crown Street, where the victims of the plague who did not die were sent to recover.

Priestley Road, the Priestley Hall behind the United Reformed church, and the nearby Priestley Wood are all reminders of the famous scientist Joseph Priestley who was minister of the local Congregational church in 1757.

In 1744 one of the first private banks in the country was founded by Samuel Alexander in Needham Market. A bank still stands on the site today.

One of the most interesting and historic buildings in Needham Market is the church of St John the Baptist. Situated in the High Street, it is famous for its magnificent hammerbeam roof, said to be one of the finest examples in the country. The church was probably a chapel of ease or rest house for pilgrims on their way from Ipswich to the shrine of St Edmund; indeed the name 'Needham' is thought to mean 'a place of refuge'.

Needham Market is a village which has outgrown its original boundaries, and is surrounded by modern development. There is much evidence of Tudor occupation – the centre of the village has fine examples of the architecture of that period.

Modern Needham Market is a thriving community with a good range of shops, schools and a community centre. Whilst the majority of the local population seeks employment out of the village, there is an expanding development of light industry. The two largest employers are the District Council, whose offices are in the High Street, and a well known manufacturer of bakers sundries who occupy the Old Maltings.

Newbourne 🌿

Newbourne lies approximately seven miles from Ipswich and five miles from Woodbridge. One hundred years ago it consisted of the church, the 14th century Hall, the Fox inn and a score of tiny houses, with less than 200 population.

St Mary's church stands at the heart of the village. The Domesday Book records the existence of a church here in 1086. Like most ancient churches it has grown and altered over the years. On the morning of 16th October 1987, when hurricane winds caused havoc and devastation in Suffolk, the east wall of the church was blown out. The stained glass window lay in fragments underneath the rubble. Miraculously, one undamaged piece of glass, the face of Christ, was recovered by a workman. This is now to be incorporated into the new plain glass window, which was put in when the wall was rebuilt after much hard work and fund raising efforts.

One of the highlights of the year was the Easter Fair held in Fen Meadow, Woodbridge. The show's tallest man would hold a guinea above his head challenging anyone 'who could take could have it'.

George Page of Newbourne could! He was seven ft seven ins tall, consequently he and his brother were given contracts touring the fairs and were known ever after as 'The Newbourne Giants'. They are buried in Newbourne churchyard.

The Fox inn dates back to the 16th century, most of the old beams coming from old sailing ships. The stagecoach used to stop there on the journey between Felixstowe and Waldringfield. Every Whit Wednesday 'Frolics' were held on the green in front of the inn, crowds came from miles around for barn dances, hornpipes and to see *Chieftain*, a stallion who was brought round the villages by his owner for 'services rendered' to the local farms. *Chieftain* used to walk down the passage in the inn which led to the bar for his quart of ale from a wooden bowl, then quietly back out!

The character of the village was changed considerably in 1936 by the Land Settlement Act. Smallholdings were provided by the government and the Carnegie Trust for unemployed miners from County Durham, some having been on the famous march from Jarrow to London in the same year. A house, greenhouse and a few acres of land were allocated to each tenant, produce being marketed and sold by central administration. On the outbreak of war it was decided to accept tenants who had farming or agricultural experience thus creating a cosmopolitan community. This scheme carried on until its closure in 1983, when the smallholdings were sold individually.

Newbourne Springs is now a conservation area. The Felixstowe Water Co used to pump up to 500,000 gallons of water a day from the springs, but this was discontinued because the nitrate levels were above those permitted by the EEC.

Newton Green 🐑

Just beyond Sudbury on the road to Ipswich one comes to Newton Green, the village on a golf course.

Until the early years of the 20th century, the cottages surrounded an outsize village green on which the parishioners grazed their horses and cattle. Then one day came ladies and gentlemen in tweeds and plus fours and Newton Green Golf Club was born. The club gave every villager a bag of coal each year as rent. Later it became two pounds of tea and now, prosaically, an amount of money is handed over to the Greens Trust which helps all village organisations. And every year, the club play the villagers in one of their long-standing fixtures.

As there were four Newtons in Suffolk, the appendage 'Green' was attached to Newton for postal convenience during the 1930s. Until about 1700 it was 'Newton Juxta Sudbury'. It was, however, a settlement long before the Norman Conquest.

All Saints' is a 14th century church but possibly built on an earlier Saxon site. It now stands in farmland but was once surrounded by wooden and thatched cottages. These were burnt down when the Black Death swept through the village, leaving only two manor houses – Butlers and Newton Hall. Since 1975 the nave and the tower have been owned by the Redundant Churches Fund and the congregation have only to maintain the chancel where services are held.

The Saracen's Head, a partly Tudor building, stands on the A134. Outside the pub is a large mounting stone where travellers are thought to have changed horses en route to the East Coast ports. During the reign of James II, one of the earliest public collections was organised by the landlord for the Huguenot refugees. There are several descendants of the Huguenots living in Newton Green today.

The village has never had a ruling family or a big house. One house has a Roman well which was, so legend says, a resting place for Boudicca's Iceni warriors on their way to sack Colchester. But the favourite Newton legend is of that medieval lady of the manor who chased the local tax-collector into the village dungheap.

North Cove ஜ௸

North Cove is a small village which lies off the main road between Beccles and Lowestoft. Many years ago it stood on an estuary and it gained its name to distinguish it from South Cove in Blything Hundred.

Although there is no manor of North Cove in the present day, there was a manor of Wathe's Hall which Henry II gave to Robert Watheby around the year 1200. The site of this ancient manor, surrounded by a partially filled moat and majestic oaks, can still be seen today. Now a farmhouse, Wades Hall, which was built in 1600, stands next to the manor's site. This is a listed building and the local schoolchildren enjoy visits there to see the original fireplaces, bread oven and ancient timbers. The present occupants, Mr and Mrs Daines, grew corn and let the marshland to local farmers for cattle grazing.

Nearby stands North Cove Hall which was originally an Elizabethan house. In 1760 it was completely restructured with red bricks which were burnt locally in the wood now called Ash Covert. In 1974 the present owners, Mr and Mrs Blower, made available an area of 46 acres for a nature reserve.

The church, St Botolph's, dates from the early 13th century and contains some recently restored wall murals from that period. Next to the church stands another listed building, the Three Horseshoes inn, which existed in the time of Charles II. It has hosted the local hunt, the Waveney Harriers, and provides welcome food and drink for passing motorists and holidaymakers as well as the locals. In 1980, when the village bypass was under construction, the medieval 'lost village' of Worlingham Parva was discovered opposite the inn. The remains of a church and graveyard were found and the bodies were reinterred locally.

The village runs down to the river Waveney where passing pleasure boats make their way to Beccles and Oulton Broad. These have replaced the wherrys which transported coal and corn, in bygone days, to and from the staithe. Fishing is a popular pastime along the river bank.

The villagers worked in various small industries locally, including market gardening, farming and weaving. Willow carrs produced wicker for baskets, alder carrs were grown for brushmaking and charcoal. In the past the village enjoyed the luxury of several shops, a pork butcher, fish and chips and two village stores. These have disappeared now and only one remains, North Cove Stores, supplying newspapers and groceries to the villagers.

Nowadays the villagers work in the local towns and city of Norwich. Some are employed in the North Sea oil and gas industries and are transported to and from the oil and gas platforms by helicopters which fly from a neighbouring field. A few still work on the land as generations have done before them.

Norton ✿

Norton is a large, scattered village approximately seven miles east of Bury St Edmunds, with its focal point being the crossroads where the busy A1088 Ipswich–Thetford road crosses the roads leading to Tostock and Great Ashfield.

The Domesday Book records that Nocturne/Norturna was King's land, kept by Godric; about 500 years later Henry VIII was to search – unsuccessfully – for gold at Norton, bringing miners from Cornwall to work in the Suffolk mine.

Since then the village seems to have had a fairly peaceful existence, although the Enclosure Act of 1814 must have given rise to anxiety for those villagers with grazing rights to the village heathland; these rights were removed and in lieu of them the villagers were given 'allotments', on which some of the houses in Heath Road were built.

Norton Hall is still one of the most important houses in the village, as is Manor Farm, with its stepped gables and 'solar extension' to the rear of the farm house. Little Haugh Hall stands in parkland, through which flows the river Blackbourn; it was formerly the home of Cox Macro, chaplain to George II.

Norton is fortunate in having an excellent playing field and village hall; there are shops, a garage, post office and two public houses. The school is thriving and there are several village organisations including the Women's Institute and the Twinning Association – Norton is twinned with a village in France.

As well as the church, there is a Baptist chapel built in 1843 and a thriving Salvation Army corps founded in the 1880s. St Andrew's church is known for its late 14th century stalls, with carved armrests and misericords, which include the martyrdom of St Edmund and St Andrew. At the rear of the church there is a shelf where the 'charity bread' used to be left for the poor of the village – there were several benefactors and annual charity payments are still made.

Although there are several farms still in the village, most people travel to work in Bury St Edmunds or the surrounding villages where there is more employment. Although the village is busy with heavy lorries passing through constantly, it is very different from when Norton was self-sufficient, with its own bakers, blacksmiths, fish and chip shop and, until fairly recently, a bus company.

Occold 🐑

In Domesday times Occold was known as Acholt – 'Ac' the Old English name for an oak tree and 'Holt' Old English and Old Norse for a wood or thicket. Its full, but unused, name was once Occold-cum-Bedingfield.

In the 1860s Occold appears to have been a thriving village containing a large number of businesses; three blacksmiths, three carpenter's shops, three greengrocers plus a post office, two wheelwrights and two public houses. One of the public houses, the Three Bottles, was a wayside inn for over 500 years and the landlord was bound by law to offer respite to weary travellers. It was closed a few years after the Second World War and is now a private dwelling.

Two churches were mentioned in the Domesday survey, of which only one remains. St Michael's is situated in the centre of the village and is of Norman origin. It was built mostly by voluntary labour, the locals working after their day's toil in the fields, having collected the majority of the stone from the rivers that ran on either side of the village. A nunnery once stood nearby and old coins have been found in the grounds where Church Farm now stands.

The centre of the village also contains a chapel which has been extended twice, and a school built in 1849. Both are used extensively and are very much a part of village life today.

At one time there were three Halls and a windmill, the area being mainly farming with the inhabitants working on the land. Only two Halls now remain, Occold Hall and Benningham Hall and although farming is still the main industry, because of modern farming methods there is not the employment within the village.

There is more history attached to Benningham Hall than any place in Occold. The present Hall was built sometime between 1700 and 1800, but an older house stood further back surrounded by a moat and drawbridge – a protection against robbers. In the 10th century the second church stood nearby, only a field bearing the name Chapel Field now remains although in the past coffins have been unearthed. Benningham Fayre was a great event hundreds of years ago and competitions were held such as ploughing matches.

People travelled for miles to attend these events and sell their wares. One such traveller was hanged from the Gallows Oak by the villagers after admitting to the murder of a maid at the Hall one Sunday morning.

An old legend states that at the time of the murder the master and mistress of the Hall were at church. The church bells rang of their own accord and the clergyman stopped the service believing something sinister had happened. The master arrived home to find the remains of the maid's body in the fire.

Now the shops have all gone, and only one public house remains, the Beaconsfield Arms built in the time of Disraeli. The villagers fought to keep their post office without success.

It may appear to some that Occold has become a dormitory village, but not so. The influx of people since the mid 1970s has brought new life and a community spirit second to none. From funds raised during and since the Queen's Jubilee a village hall has been built and a playing field provided for the village and its school. A village sign depicting the origins of Occold has been sited on a grassed area where once stood an old reading room which had fallen into decay. Footpaths once unused and impassable are being opened and conservation is a priority of the parish council.

Offton 🦢

The name is said to have been derived from the legendary King Offa, King of Mercia, who was responsible for the famous Offa's Dyke. Here in Offton (Offa's town) he had his castle situated on the highest point overlooking the valleys, ideal for scanning the countryside for approaching enemies. Although no remains of any fortress have ever been discovered, the mound and surrounding moat is still in evidence and is being lovingly preserved by the landowners.

St Mary's church in the centre of the village was also important enough for the Puritan William Dowsing to come and deface the religious decorations on the font. The church is mainly 14th century, but in parts quite new. The floor was re-done in 1887 in honour of Queen Victoria's jubilee. The tower can boast an eight bell peal, something that has been achieved by dedicated bell ringers over the years. The oldest bell dates from the early 1500s, the newest one was dedicated in 1983.

Farming has been the major source of income for the villagers for many years which is reflected in the close knit community. Once it was a thriving village with a wheelwright, a blacksmith, a post office and a school as well as a general stores. Now it has no shops at all, even the post office closed down in the 1980s after generations of the Green family had run it since 1914. The only remaining public place is the Limeburner's pub and even that is strictly speaking in Willisham.

It is a long, stretched village with old listed buildings mixed in with more modern ones. Castle Farm, Court Farm, Mount Pleasant Farm, Poplar Farm, Maskells Hall and Tollemache Hall have all been big farms in their day. Now they are all residential.

The village has and still does host a number of unforgettable characters. Malcolm Fiske was a great benefactor to the village. Although he was farming from Willisham Hall he had a great love for Offton as well as for his own village. And there was Harry Nicholls, the barber, who was so intent on catching the latest gossip that he was likely to nick your ear whilst cutting your hair. The children dreaded going to have a haircut.

And one character known to everyone is 'Daddy' Minns. This name was given to him by his friends in their pre-school days. He was always seen in a box cart which happened to have 'Daddies Sauce' written on it and this name just stuck to him for life. He was churchwarden for many years and used to ring the bells, managing three at a time when he had to.

All in all this quiet little village has many tales to tell and from its high viewpoints one can spy a good deal of rural life. Its greatest charm is its tranquillity and natural beauty, not yet spoilt by urban development.

Old Felixstowe 🐑

'Old Felixstowe', although now part of the large seaside resort and port of Felixstowe, still maintains its village character. White's 1844 directory describes Felixstowe as a 'delightfully situated village and bathing place on the sea coast'.

It is said that Felixstowe derives its name from Felix the Burgundian, who converted the East Anglians to Christianity, and became the first Bishop of Dunwich in AD 630. It is thought that he lived here. Also it has been suggested that Felixstowe did not receive its present name until a priory of black monks dedicated to St Felix was founded by Roger Bigod, Earl of Norfolk.

The population of Felixstowe in 1871 was 760. In 1891 the German Empress and her children visited the resort and increased its popularity as a 'spa'. This is borne out in the census figures of 1901 which showed a population of 2,720, and this has continued to rise.

At the centre of 'Old Felixstowe' is the parish church of St Peter and St Paul, dating back to the 12th century. In 1873 the chancel was rebuilt using bricks from a martello tower. Nearby is the community centre which is a well used modern building where many local organisations meet on a regular basis.

Scattered farms can be found surrounding Felixstowe, and although some people still work on the land many local residents are employed in the holiday industry, in the port, and many commute to Ipswich. A large number of people have chosen Felixstowe to live in after their retirement.

At the mouth of the river Deben, about a mile to the north of Felixstowe is the hamlet of Felixstowe Ferry. For many years a chain ferry ran from Bawdsey on the other side of the river Deben to Felixstowe Ferry. It is a small community that boasts a public house, and a sailing club. Fresh fish can be purchased from huts on the beach. The approach to Felixstowe Ferry can be hazardous at times as the road runs through the middle of the golf links. A club was established here in the 1880s and it is still as popular today with residents and visitors to the area.

Old Newton & Gipping ❧

A few yards from the parish church at Stowmarket lies the now empty Linton House, the Stowmarket residence of the founding family of Gipping, the Tyrells, who came to the area in the 15th century.

Gipping chapel and several farms are the only buildings which remain to bear witness to the great medieval estate which was sold off at the turn of the 20th century, after the Hall was demolished.

Legend – and William Shakespeare – tell of the part Sir James Tyrell played in the deaths of the little princes in the Tower and that the chapel, dedicated to St Nicholas, was erected in penitence for this deed, but numerous authors have a different tale. Built in the 1480s of flint and stone in the Perpendicular style, the Tyrell knot features frequently in the fine flush panelling and bears the words, 'pray for Sir James Tyrell and Dame Ann his wyf'.

In Gipping, the farmhouses called Chapel, Gate, Wood and Rookery are all still well loved family homes, while Gipping Lone has been restored to its former glory, having in the 20th century also served as a home for motherless boys, run by Rev Edward Falconer, who departed this life in 1948 and entered the record books as surviving to be the country's oldest working vicar at the age of 98.

Leaving the parish of Gipping, one travels the short distance to Old Newton, passing one of the oldest dissenting Methodist chapels in the county, before arriving at the parish church of St Mary and the 19th century village school. In recent times, both the church and school have been under the very real threat of closure, but they are now flourishing and have become, together with the post office stores in the main part of the village, the essence of life in Old Newton.

The modern village is sited a mile from the church and school, as the result of most properties being deserted following a plague. The 20th century has seen house building develop.

There are two pubs in the village. One is over the level crossing at Haughley Junction – the Railway Tavern, though from the village hall it is but a short step to the Shoulder of Mutton, a square Victorian building where many thoughts giving rise to various organisations in the village have germinated and taken root.

If one can remember to turn left out of its doors, a short walk will take one towards Stowmarket along the B1113, and from the rise of the land around Halfway House one can see distant church towers. On a Tuesday evening one can hear the bells of St Peter and St Mary ringing out across the valley just as they would have done in the Middle Ages, when in the time of Henry VI the first Tyrells were buried in the family vault in Stowmarket church.

Onehouse & Harleston 🐾

The villages of Onehouse and Harleston lie to the west of Stowmarket. Over 100 years ago the benefices of Onehouse and Harleston were united, with any social events taking place in the church room at Onehouse. The school was closed and purchased as a community centre. The two villages are served by one public house, the Shepherd and Dog.

Harleston green was originally a piece of swamp land; during the First World War Mr Terry of Harleston Hall introduced a drainage system which gave better grazing for the domestic animals. During this period also many new herbs were introduced and a doctor from Haughley regularly came and collected herbs for medicinal purposes.

Harleston church, St Augustine's, strictly speaking only consists of a nave and was probably built as a chapel to Harleston Hall. The church has a reed thatched roof, Early English windows, a turret with one bell and no electricity. The church was due for closure by the diocese, but the villagers raised monies for the repairs and services are regularly held by candlelight.

One of the most distinctive buildings on the eastern border of Onehouse is Stow Lodge, originally the workhouse, plans for which were drawn up and approved in 1779. It was erected in 1781 for the 14 parishes of the Stow Hundred. The cost was more than £12,000 and described in 1810 as having 'more the appearance of a gentleman's seat than a receptacle for paupers'. The external appearance is basically as it was then. The inmates had a humble Christian burial in shallow graves in the grounds now known as the 'Paupers Graveyard'.

It is reputed that in 1578 Elizabeth I visited Onehouse Hall, the home of Master James Rivett, a successful landowner. Through the village there is a grove of lime trees said to have been planted in her honour. On the death of Charles Pettiward in 1936 the estate, which covered six villages and most of Onehouse and Harleston, was sold in separate lots.

The first rector of Onehouse is recorded in 1312 but the origins of the church of St John the Baptist predate the Norman Conquest. The round tower of Anglo-Saxon origin – a rare sight in Suffolk – is original and may have been used as a watch tower. The nave is also original and the two bells are dated 1604. In 1673 the church served the old Saxon Hall nearby. The porch is reputed to have been added for the visit of Elizabeth I. Today the congregation uses the Prayer Books of both Elizabeths in their worship.

Orford & Sudbourne 🌿

The villages of Orford and Sudbourne are steeped in history. Both have suffered the onslaught of flooding and storm damage over the centuries and in 1987 Sudbourne lost its magnificent forest in the hurricane.

Orford is attractive from its quiet remoteness to the beauty of its buildings, wide streets and outstanding natural beauty of its river and quay. It is thought that many of the timbers remaining in the houses, inns and church originate from ships involved in the battle of Sole Bay and from shipbuilding that was carried on in the 1600s.

Early in the 1900s coal was delivered by barge to Orford Quay and was housed in the warehouse (now a fine chandlery, tea rooms and restaurant). Coal was also taken down the river by barge to Snape Quay where people could take carts to collect their own coal. In the 1920s there were many shops in the village including butchers, grocers, drapers, cabinetmaker, tailors, blacksmith, bicycle shop, harnessmaker, bakers, coal merchant, barbers, bootmaker and shoe repairer.

There are many legends and smugglers tales connected with the village. If you visit the Jolly Sailor inn you will see Chinese Muff Dogs encased there which were said to be smuggled in ladies muffs. Then there is the tale of the Orford Merman who was caught by local fishermen. He was taken to the custodian of the castle, Bartholomew de Glanville, who tried to get him to talk. He was later returned to the water guarded by three lines of nets. He dived under these and entertained the spectators for a while, then returned to the sea never to be seen again. This was recorded during the reign of King Henry II. In 1899, two men, while digging on the cricket pitch, saw a figure rise from the ground. A skeleton was found, thought to be a Miss Dimmock of Sudbourne Hall who had disappeared in a mysterious manner. In the 1930s a ghost wearing a clergyman's hat and robes and apparently reading, was seen floating along an upper corridor in the terrace of the now Orford Supply Stores in Pump Street, (a marvellous village shop with a tremendous range of goods and cheery service!)

The castle and the church are Orford's two most prominent buildings and were built in the reign of Henry II. St Bartholomew's has great associations with first performances of Britten's music and is still used today for concerts during the Aldeburgh Festival. The church is floodlit at night and commands a stately position overlooking Church Street.

Orford has a fine town hall which is used for many social events and meetings. It stands facing the Market Square as does the post office and the Butley Orford Oysterage, famous worldwide for its oysters and smoked salmon.

During the Second World War a low flying German bomber dropped bombs on the Market Square, destroying Chapman's shop, and on Ferry Road killing 13 people, including two boys home on leave. Sudbourne was evacuated for a battle school in the war. Every house was vacated and the tanks rolled in. Sudbourne stood locked and empty for six years. Even the birds disappeared and an eerie silence reigned.

Sudbourne once had a manor house, five shops, a post office, school and hospital. All of these have gone but there is now a growing community and recently a brand new village hall has been built in place of the old army hut.

Orford and Sudbourne have changed in recent years in that they have become the haunt of holidaymakers, artists, birdwatchers and yachtsmen, but fortunately have remained unspoilt. The *Lady Florence* boat cruises up river for its daily trip, fishermen go out for their catch, the RSPB warden goes over to Havergate Island and life continues in a peaceful way.

Otley 🐾

There were ancient settlements here – remains of Iron Age pottery have been found and a Roman road passes through. Today Otley is busy rather than picturesque. Make no mistake, it has its share of pretty cottages tucked away but its strength is in the people who live there – a mixture of young and old, newcomers and old timers.

There has been a school here since at least 1846, the 'modern' one being opened after harvest in 1912.

For a small place in these modern times Otley has a lot of industry. Apart from farming there is a refrigeration company, a coach company and a fencing manufacturer, not to mention the vineyards. There is also a successful agricultural and horticultural college which runs both professional and recreational courses. And for those with a thirst there is thankfully still a pub, plus a grocery store with post office.

Of course, compared with say the turn of the century this is probably not a lot. At that time, taking a stroll through Otley would have been a different matter with all its shops and tradesmen. For instance there was the collar and harnessmaker. With horses still being used on the farms this was a very busy place and at least three men worked there. The owner of the White Hart pub also kept horses plus three carriages – this was the taxi service. Otley's other pub had already closed down by this time although the windmill was still in existence.

St Mary's has always played an important role in the village life, the present building dating from the early 13th century. One very unusual feature of the church is a baptistry font, six ft long, two ft eight inches deep and always full – the water level maintaining itself naturally. This is not used and was only discovered in 1950 when the floor of the vestry was raised. Otley's Baptist chapel was built around 1800 and it is assumed that the font dates from before that time.

Otley's coat of arms is that of the Gosnold family whose name is linked with the early settlers of America, and Otley Hall, a handsome Grade I listed building, was at one time their family home. After a somewhat chequered history, 1911 saw the sale of Otley Hall back into aristocratic ownership and it was then that its remaining farm buildings were replaced with gardens and woodland to take on the look which it has today.

Now it is rumoured that a ghost wanders the grounds as, tragically, during the 1930s the Hall's new cook, just a young girl, drowned in the moat. Nobody every really knew whether it was an accident or not. The Hall is open to the public just three days a year and worth a visit. You may not see the ghost but hopefully you will see the beautiful black swans swimming on the moat.

Pakenham 🐚

Six miles north-east of Bury St Edmunds lies Pakenham. A rural village of about 800 inhabitants, it takes its name from Saxon settlers in the 7th century; their leader Pacca sailed up the Waveney (from Pakefield) and Blackbourne to make his home on the hill. The family name of Peck still exists in the village.

Pakenham forms a reversed 'L' shape round a fen; the short arm is a pleasant village street crossing a stream. Opposite the council estate is the entrance to Nether Hall, the 'Big House' in Pakenham. It was bought in 1874 by the Greene family, Members of Parliament, who practically rebuilt it. From the lake in the park flows the village stream, through the fen into the millpond. It is said that Sir Walter Greene quarrelled with Sir Compton Thornhill of the Lodge; when digging the lake he had the spoil built into a bank known as 'Spiteful Bank' between the houses, so that neither could see the other.

The church of St Mary stands on the hill at the apex of the 'L'; it is a cruciform flint building, partly dating back to its founder, Walter, about 1100. By the church stands the old vicarage, now named Mulberry House; overlooking the mulberry tree is the famous Whistler Window. Bricked up and rendered, doubtless because of the window tax, the blank wall tempted Rex Whistler in the 1940s to paint a realistic figure of an 18th century parish priest, with wig, gown and candle, writing his sermon. Rex Whistler was killed in action in 1944; in his memory the window was preserved by framing and glazing it.

Fen Road forms the long arm of the 'L'. On the hill near the church stands Newe House, new in 1622; it has a fine Jacobean facade with Dutch gables and mullioned and transomed windows. Further down the road are several cottages stemming from bygone industries in Pakenham. A group set at right angles to each other were former sheds for drying osiers; at The Whitings and Whitings Farm is the site of a chalk pit which once produced weekly hundreds of balls of whiting for whitewashing houses. The Wheelwrights Cottage is now a coalyard. At Pudding Hall nearby, now demolished, there was a thriving industry in making hurdles; these were in demand by both sheep farmers and steeplechasing courses, and were sent to Scotland and Ireland. Nearby is the Royal Oak, an old inn which served the fen until about 1970.

Further on at Grimstone End a brick-floored Roman kiln with a complex system of furnaces and flues, was found in 1955; later a Bronze Age barrow and pottery kiln were uncovered. Here there is a view of the windmill; built about 1820, with tarred brick tower and domed cap. It is in working order, with three pairs of stones. The water mill can also be seen, with its pond on a tributary of the Blackbourne; the Norman mill has been replaced twice, and the Suffolk Preservation Society restored it in the 1970s. It is open to the public in summer; milling takes place regularly, the flour being sold to visitors. These mills make Pakenham the only parish in England with one of each, in working order.

Also at Grimstone End is a Methodist graveyard, all that remains of the Ebenezer chapel. Still further down the fen, by the Ixworth bypass is the site of a large Roman settlement, partly excavated in the 1970s. Many artefacts are in the Ipswich Museum. Nearby Mickle Mere, often flooded in winter, is a haunt of wildfowl.

Much of Pakenham lies north of the Bury–Ixworth road. At Redcastle Farm a large Roman villa was found, with mosaic floors and roof tiles. On the Queach Farm, a ridge across two fields is known as the Roman Road, and seems to run from Icklingham to Grimstone End. At the Great Livermere boundary is Puttocks Hill; here King Charles I was said to fly his falcons – 'puttock' is an old word for a falcon – and his falconer is buried in Great Livermere churchyard.

Peasenhall with Sibton ✎

Peasenhall *with* Sibton, because though they are separate parishes, they function in many ways as one village, a delightful and rewarding place in which to live.

After the Norman Conquest, King William gave the manor of Sibton to Sir William Malet, and Peasenhall to the Bigod family. It was a nephew of Sir William who in 1150 founded the Abbey of the Blessed Virgin Mary at Sibton, the only Cistercian house in Suffolk. The church of St Peter was erected in the reign of William Rufus and has many later modifications and additions, the most striking being the beautiful early 16th century single hammer beam and arch braced collar roof. All that remains of the once great abbey are a few broken and crumbling walls which can be seen from the road running past the church.

Among the many fine monuments in the church are several to members of the Scrivener family, into whose possession the manor of Sibton came in 1610 when Ralph Scrivener erected a house for himself overlooking the village. The Scrivener family have played an important part in the village ever since, building schools and almshouses and only recently have Sibton children joined the Peasenhall children in their Hackney Road school, 100 years old in 1995. Sibton Abbey estate and neighbouring Sibton Park, owned by the Brooke family, have helped preserve the spacious 19th century character of the countryside.

Peasenhall's past is dominated by the famous drill works, where James Smyth & Sons manufactured the well-known agricultural drill, which was exported all over the world. James Josiah Smyth, grandson of the founder, built a hall as a reading room for his workers in the style of a Swiss chalet, as Switzerland was a favourite country of his. This unusual building startles first-time visitors with its unique architecture. The drill works ceased to manufacture in 1967 but on the site are now several new enterprises.

The heart of Peasenhall is the spacious Street, with its many mature trees, the watercourse down one side and a charming variety of buildings, many of them listed. The whole Street is a conservation area, which ensures the future of the red telephone kiosk and the Victorian letter box. One of the little shops has become a most welcome tea-room and there is still a post office that sells almost everything and a grocer whose famous hams have earned a Royal Warrant. The butcher's shop, bought some years ago by the late Rev Jack Thickitt and run by two of his sons, has customers who come from far and near to buy its home killed meat. The garage, which was once the old Angel public house where quoits were played in the yard, organises and runs coach services and does a brisk business; both the Swan in the Street and the White Horse at Sibton still welcome customers.

Standing in the Street looking east, the eye is charmed by the magnificent old timbered Woolhall, which since the 15th century has been known as 'The Newe Inn'. A few years ago it was sadly dilapidated but it has been bought by the Landmark Trust, beautifully restored and is now let to holiday visitors.

Look west, and there to the left of the crossroads stands Stuart House, once known as Providence House, the scene of the dreadful murder of poor little Rose Harsent. There can still be seen the attic window where Rose set her candle as a message to her lover; it was in the kitchen below that she was done to death. The crime remains a mystery to this day and books have been written speculating on the identity of the murderer and visitors come from far and wide to look at the house and visit Rose's grave, still tended, in the cemetery.

Beyond the village centres are the farms, keeping on the rural tradition, charming cottages and lovely old farmhouses, many listed and sympathetically restored. Although the post mill at the top of Mill Hill has been dismantled, the smock mill at its side still stands.

In 1969 the BBC chose Peasenhall to make a film demonstrating that village life was alive and well. In 1937 Mr William Aldred of Sibton was a leading character in a film called *This was England*. He was the last practitioner in the country of the art of the Saxon method of sowing, double-handed broadcasting. A charabanc was used to take villagers to the cinema and Mr Aldred watched himself in the first film he had ever seen.

Pettaugh 🐚

Pettaugh clusters mainly around the junction of the Roman road running north from Coddenham with the 'Debenam–Ipswich turnpike', which is crossed by the A1120 Stowmarket–Yoxford road. The population, approximately 130, is roughly the same now as that given in the Domesday Book.

A tall post mill stood at this junction and a few years ago the village elders could sit and have a leisurely chinwag on the village green. Now all this has disappeared under tarmac and a stream of traffic, much of it very heavy indeed, uses the busy crossroads.

Nearby is the church of St Catherine which at one time was served by the monks of Leiston Abbey. This was their westernmost destination and they would have made the journey from Leiston on foot.

Happily the village post office store remains and flourishes. At the turn of the century the Misses Cooper ran the shop. It is said that Miss Fanny would halve a sweet, and trickle sugar through her fingers to ensure that not a grain too much fell on the scales for the customer. 'And all the while she was a du-en it she would keep a-lookin' at ye out o' the corner o' her eye', said a villager.

Pettaugh Hall was owned by the Fastolf (Falstaff) family around 1524–1670. The attractive old Bull inn, opposite the stores, once had a successful meadow-quoits team. It is now a private house.

In former times, as in the present day, helping hands were extended between neighbours in times of hardship or sickness. Charitable offerings were not always fully appreciated, however. One lady found the house-holder out so left her gift in his kitchen. She was later thanked by the recipient who said 'I sniffed and I smelt and I thought "that suffen she ha left fa my airs".' He had dressed his chilblained ears with home-made potted rabbit meat.

A travelling hardware store, the ice cream man on his yellow motorcycle with portable icebox in the sidecar, five butchers and three bakers served the village not so long ago. Many people had their own chickens and pigs, and some had cows. Most would have grown their own vegetables and the countryside around provided rabbits, birds, mushrooms and hedgerow fruits. Alfie Payne came from Crowfield in his horse-drawn covered wagon to sell greengrocery and to buy animal feed from Cuttings Mill. The village once had its own smith, wheelwright and shoemaker. Today the traditional rural life of the village has gone, but the friendliness remains.

Pettistree 🌿

One of the nicest things about Pettistree is how rapidly, on leaving the Woodbridge/Wickham Market road, one finds oneself in a country village, for its harmonious blend of pretty thatched cottages and houses old and new are almost unseen and unsuspected from the main road with its constant flow of traffic – albeit less hectic than before the building of the bypass. Although some of the 200 or so residents live scattered around the outskirts, the heart of Pettistree lies in a wide area around the church and the Greyhound inn, the long rear wall of which intrudes right on to the churchyard. It is thought the inn was built before the church, so the builders were able to get their food and drink there.

Today the Greyhound is a welcoming place, heavily beamed and in winter warmed by huge log fires. It is said to have been haunted, but in more recent times rather by small happenings and unaccountable cold draughts that cause dogs' hackles to rise, than by any manifestations. Perhaps this is on account of the legend that the birth of a baby 'lays' a ghost, for in 1952 a baby was born at the Greyhound, thought to have been the first for 130 years, and apparently this should be sufficient to put paid to any ghostly wanderings.

The church of St Peter and St Paul is 15th century with more recent additions, having several richly carved bench-ends and a 16th century brass showing the effigies of Francis Bacon and his two wives. The east window was inserted in 1901 by an American lady in memory of her parents, who had early connections with Pettistree.

The churchyard is a particularly interesting one, peaceful and well-kept, and maintained with nature conservation very much in mind. Some sections are managed as a traditional hay meadow, cut once a year to encourage wild flowers and butterflies.

An amusing tale from the past tells how tramps on their way through Pettistree to shelter at the workhouse in Wickham Market, knowing they might not be admitted if they had money on them, would stop to bury it just beyond the churchyard, and then dig it up again on their way off later. The narrow lane where the money was usually buried is, of course, known as Rogues Lane.

Over the years many changes have inevitably taken place among the residents. Only 20 years ago almost all worked in the nearby Wickham Market area and on the surrounding farms, and most had lived in Pettistree all their lives. The horizon has naturally widened; now there are professional people here and those whose careers take them further afield, as well as the retired who enjoy Pettistree's friendliness and peace, and are usually all too ready to join in with village activities.

Playford

Playford is a small village four miles from Woodbridge and five miles from Ipswich. Either way you descend a hill, finding the village nestling in the wooded valley of the Finn, winding along to join the Deben at Martlesham Creek. A pack-horse bridge once spanned the river, long since gone. The river today is a mere stream, but until just over a hundred years ago it was navigable to the water mill and millstream, when villagers used tub-boats on it. Downstream from the mill is the mere, its depth unknown. One day some of the villagers tied three wagon ropes together in an effort to find out how deep it was, but the ropes never reached the bottom, so the problem was unsolved.

The church of St Mary stands high on a ridge. Passing through the lychgate, ascending the steps, the path leads to the porch with the magnificent tower, both built by Sir George Felbrigge who resided at

Playford Hall

Playford Hall in the 1300s. Two pre-Reformation bells hang in the tower, still sounding after 500 years. Outside the church stands a granite obelisk to the memory of Thomas Clarkson, 'friend of slaves', who with William Wilberforce founded the Society for the Abolition of the Slave Trade.

The Finn once flowed into the ten ft wide moat surrounding Playford Hall, now a fine example of Tudor grand style. Residents of the Hall in the late 1800s expected the villagers and their children to curtsey to them when meeting, but one strong willed lady who considered all people equal refused and cost her husband his job!

Across the fields stands Hill House, 400 years old, part of the Bristols estate until the 1950s. Arthur Biddell, High Constable and Land Agent, was tenant early in the 1800s and bred red polled stock a long time in advance to other Suffolk breeders.

Opposite the church lychgate stands Airy's Cottage, so named as it was bought by Sir George Biddell Airy in 1845. As Astronomer Royal at Greenwich from 1835 to 1881 (it is thought the Greenwich Meridian was his brainchild) he often stayed here.

A wooden gallery ran across the west end of the church until the early part of the 1800s to accommodate the 'singers' and a village musician. The story goes that this band called every Sunday at Sir George's house for the loan of a metal tea-tray 'to get the key-note', returning it to the kitchen dresser after service. Later a portable 'hurdy-gurdy' playing six hymn tunes was introduced; the mechanism jammed and repeated the Old Hundredth; unable to be silenced it was removed to the churchyard to play itself out.

In 1901 the population was 238, today it is about 225. The occupation of the villagers was on the land or at the Hall and cottages were built for them by Mr Biddell from materials from Woodbridge Barracks when sold in about 1815. After the Second World War, things changed, some cottages were pulled down and land sold for development. Modern housing brought business and professional people who preferred a quieter mode of living, commuting to Ipswich or British Telecom at Martlesham.

Polstead 🐦

Polstead – 'the place of pools' – takes its name from the large ponds at the bottom of the hill which leads to the centre of the village. It is a Saxon name but it is thought that there has been a settlement here for perhaps 2,000 years.

No one could call Polstead a compact village. Its houses, farms and woods are scattered over some 4,000 acres along the northern slope of the valley of the river Box. The main village is grouped round the village green at the top of Polstead Hill and here you can find the village hall, a large modern building, the school (now closed), an inn and several old houses, one of which was once the village forge.

On the far side of the ponds, standing high above the valley and looking over the fields to Stoke by Nayland, are the church and Polstead Hall, in what was once the manor deer park. The Hall is a handsome Georgian house with some much older parts. The 12th century church of St Mary has two features which make it unique among Suffolk churches – its stone spire and the arches in its chancel and nave made of very early bricks. Between the church and the Hall lie the remains of the Gospel Oak – reputedly 1,300 years old and 36 ft in girth when it finally collapsed in 1953. Traditionally, Bishop Cedd and his Saxon missionaries preached beneath this tree in the 7th century and an open air service is still held here on the first Sunday in August.

Although so near to the busy little wool towns of Hadleigh and Boxford, Polstead does not seem to have shared in their industry and wealth, and its annals over the centuries have little to record. Its main claim to fame was for its cherries, the Polstead Blacks – 'of a refined and exceptional flavour', and an annual Cherry Fair used to be held on the village green in mid-July.

In 1837, however, it had fame of an unwelcome kind thrust upon it as the place of the 'Murder in the Red Barn'. Maria Marten, the local mole-catcher's daughter and a girl of no great reputation, disappeared with her lover, William Corder, a local farmer's son. Three times Maria's step-mother dreamed that the girl had not eloped but was lying murdered beneath the floor of an isolated barn. This indeed proved to be so, and the dramatic circumstances of the discovery turned a sordid, common-place crime into a 'cause celebre', which aroused a frenzy of public curiosity and interest. Corder was hanged at Bury St Edmunds and Maria lies in Polstead churchyard, her gravestone almost chipped away by souvenir hunters, but the story of the Red Barn (which burned down long ago) persists in a melodrama which is acted to this day.

Polstead has inevitably grown and changed. It has sadly lost its school after 114 years, the mill ground its last corn in 1926, it has never had more than the sketchiest bus service, its old village shop closed and has been replaced by a thriving voluntary enterprise. It remains at heart an agricultural community and a very pleasant place in which to live.

Preston St Mary 🐏

A one street village, Preston St Mary stands 260 ft above sea level along a central clay ridge. From the ridge the arable, pasture and meadow lands of the farms spread out to the stream of the Brett in the west and a tributary of the Stour on the east.

There are signs of an earlier Saxon settlement in the foundations of the present church and in the fact there is part of a protective moat on its eastern boundary. A finely sculptured Norman font bears witness to a building on the site before 1485 when the church of St Mary the Virgin was constructed. For a time Preston also had a priory owned by Trinity Priory of Ipswich, from which Priory Farm derives its name.

A village inn existed opposite the church prior to 1670 when the main bar room and living quarters above were built, to which additions have been made. In 1744 the sixth bell had been cast and hung in the church by local forgemasters, and the inn and the next door cottage assumed the name the Six Bells.

Robert Reyce was born at Preston Hall in 1555, and was destined to become Suffolk's first and most distinguished historian. *The Breviary of Suffolk* was published in 1618. His book details every aspect of Suffolk life from its fertile soil, sweet meadows and clear rivers, to the wild and domestic animals, its climate and the dissents, political and ecclesiastic that shaped its economy. Robert Reyce also set up a charity to provide apprenticeships for Preston children. At the age of seven, for £5 a year they could be housed, fed and taught a trade. The charity still exists but the £5 hardly pays the price of a text book!

Gradually the mixed farmlands of Preston carrying Suffolk stud horses, large flocks of sheep, bullocks and milk cows, and corn changed and divided into smaller holdings. The smithy, the wheelwright and three of the shops including a drapery closed, only the post office stores remained until 1972. The last of Preston's four windmills was demolished in 1832, some of its parts sent to Debenham to restore the windmill there, and only the foundation masonry of the Mill House mill remains. The farmers expanded corn production during and after the Second World War but by 1960 sought alternative crops – orchards, blackcurrant fields, linum, evening primrose and pigs. Some of the old farm holdings, The Priory, Maisters, Mortimers, Swifts, and Rookwood also survive, as do some of the families who have lived in Preston for generations.

The three pairs of council houses built in the 1930s and the modern brick villas have blended with the restored daub and wattle cottages. The 1843 village school has become the centre for community activities. The 'incomers' have started new enterprises – a pottery, a graphic design service, and a modernised family inn, but most important there is a new generation of young people.

Ramsholt ⚓

In medieval times Ramsholt was probably a considerable settlement, being, after Bawdsey which was further inland from the estuary, the first on the north side of the river Deben. A ferry is recorded as early as 1502, and in the Middle Ages people crossed the river daily, thus making a link with the village on the other side, rather than the division which it is today.

Early in the 20th century vegetables were still being taken across the river by boat, and barges brought coal to the dock where it was collected by local merchants, while others picked up crops, particularly sugar beet. Coprolite, fossilised animal dung, which was formerly used as a fertiliser, was dug up in large quantities in the neighbourhood and this was collected. Today there are 200 moorings for private sailing boats.

About 1850 there was a lime kiln near the dock, and it appears in some records as a chicory maltings, so it may have served both purposes. It is said that there was a smuggler's cave in the vicinity, and it is likely that the beaches, cliffs and woods were frequented by smugglers. The Ramsholt Arms was originally a farmhouse, the pub being in the house at the top of the hill.

All Saints' church belonged to Butley Priory in the Middle Ages, and is now in the benefice of Alderton with Ramsholt and Bawdsey. It has a Norman tower, which many people believed to be oval, but within it is round, the appearance being due to the buttresses which were added at a later date.

Peyton Hall is listed in the Domesday Book as Peituna. It was then a royal manor, but the original mansion had disappeared by the late 16th century, although traces of a moat can still be seen to the south-east of the remaining building, which is probably early 19th century.

Before the Quilter family acquired the estate in the 1880s it consisted of open fields and sheep walks, but after that date woodlands were planted for game. The Adeane family bought the estate in 1959 and now the land is farmed by them, with Norman Simper and son renting approximately 1,000 acres.

Older inhabitants still refer to the track between the dock and church roads as Ramsholt Street, and here was the school, with 58 children in 1913, an alehouse and chapel, while there was a reading room at the end of one of the cottages below the church. In 1839 the population of Ramsholt was 192. Today it is estimated at 34.

Rattlesden 🐝

Rattlesden nestles in a tranquil river valley, midway between Stowmarket and Bury St Edmunds. It was once the port for Bury St Edmunds and the stones for the abbey were evidently brought up the river Ratt as far as Rattlesden and then transported by land. As late as the 13th century, barges of 'considerable size' made their way up the winding river from the Orwell. Today, the river is merely a stream and Rattlesden is one of those Suffolk villages that now enjoy a mixed population of locals and newcomers.

As the river was an important feature of the village centuries ago, so the main street is today and a central landmark here is the parish church of St Nicholas. This is a large 15th century church, noted for its restored double hammer beam roof and its sumptuous oak rood screen, erected in 1909.

Rattlesden is a scattered village with four main hamlets. Away to the south, High Town Green runs into Poy Street Green, while in the north, Clopton Green looks over the centre of the village towards the Top Road and the aptly named housing area of Windy Ridge.

The residents from all corners of the village are well-served as far as facilities are concerned. There is a good village shop opposite the church and further down the main street the local post office. There are two public houses in the village and, as well as the parish church, a Baptist chapel. The primary school serves a large area, from Felsham and Brettenham to Gedding and Rattlesden itself.

For years Rattlesden had good corn land and cow pasture helped with the strict rotation. Now sugar beet takes its turn and grassland gives way to much more barley and wheat. Some local farmers keep pigs – there is a large breeding unit in the village – and people from quite far afield come to buy their milk and cream from the vast Jersey farm at Punchards.

However, Rattlesden today is more renowned for its acres of wind-swept 'prairies' where many of the old hedgerows and woodlands have been ploughed in in the interests of large scale mechanized farming. Some of the remaining hedgerows can still be shown to be hundreds of years old and may even have been in existence when the Romans tramped the Peddar Way. Research has highlighted the possible course of this Roman road in the south-east corner of the parish.

Few visitors would pass through the village without stopping to inspect the whalebones next to the bridge. Apparently, many such whalebones were put up in villages in the 19th century, during a craze for odd ornaments, and some locals claim to be able to forecast the weather from them!

In 1972, Rattlesden hit the headlines when Christie's offered for auction a gilt bronze statuette, circa 1180, of St John the Evangelist, which had been found by a local man while out hoeing his sugar beet field. This three and a half inch find realized the astonishing sum of 36,000 guineas.

Redisham

Redisham Magna and Redisham Parva are anciently two independent parishes but for several hundred years the latter has been joined with the parish of Ringsfield. Redisham Magna is the village and Redisham Parva is Redisham Hall, with its large park and estate. The original Hall was destroyed by fire and the present one built as a replacement. The ruins of the small church of Redisham Parva are to be found in the park.

The parish church of St Peter, small but well cared for, is situated in the centre of the village, with fine Norman doorways. The one on the north side is blocked but that on the south side forms the main entrance to the church, with a fine old oak door. The pulpit dates back to the 17th century. The parish is linked with four other parishes in one benefice with a priest-in-charge, but likes to preserve its own identity.

The recent churchyard survey carried out by the Women's Institute revealed some interesting facts. The oldest gravestone is dated 1755, in which year the first records were kept. One stone of special interest marks the grave of an illegitimate baby of eleven months whom the father had denied. The mother, knowing that the father walked that way to work, had the following verse inscribed on the stone, to shame him:

'Remember me as you pass by
I am the child you did deny
Glad you were to hear the sound
Of the bell that tolled me to the ground.
If you were free of sin as I
You would not be afraid to die
As I am now so you will be
So be prepared to follow me.'

At one time the village boasted eight farms but, sadly, there are now only three. Sugar beet was one of the main crops and was taken to Brampton station, half a mile away, for loading. Milk was also taken there every morning for transport to dairies near Halesworth station, seven miles away. Brampton station then had its own station master living in the station house – alas, nowadays there is no staff at all. Most of the men at that time worked on farms, the railway or in factories in nearby Beccles.

Unfortunately, the village shop and public house no longer exist. The nearest are now two miles away. The public house used to be a meeting place for farm workers to get together at the end of the day to discuss matters of common interest. Despite many changes, the village is still a very friendly and pleasant place in which to live. It has a fine community spirit which shows itself specially in organising events or in a crisis.

Redlingfield 🐝

This small village lies some three miles south-east of Eye, having a population of under 200 inhabitants traditionally engaged in agriculture, although numbers are now greatly reduced since the advent of mechanisation on the farm.

There are several fine farmhouses, one of which, Redlingfield Hall Farm adjoins the church of St Andrew. This is a very modest building as Suffolk churches go, but it is built on the site of a former nunnery, which has a most interesting history. One of the barns on Redlingfield Hall Farm was once the refectory or dormitory of the nunnery. The archives reveal that this was a Benedictine priory of nuns founded in 1120 by Manasses, Count of Guisnes and Emma his wife, who was the daughter of William de Arras, Lord of Redlingfield. There was a prioress, 13 nuns, and three chaplains on foundation, the numbers fluctuating over the next 417 years between seven and ten. Always a poor house it was exempted from taxes in 1291 because of extreme poverty, its chief assets being corn and wool. The nuns gave a daily dole of bread, beef, herrings and pence to the aged poor at Lent and Easter costing £9 per year. The house became richer in the 14th century through grants of manors, land and church.

Episcopal visitation of 1427 revealed scandals. Isabel Hermyte the Prioress confessed that, among other faults, since 1425 she had not been to confession or mass, she had slept apart from the dormitory in a private room with the novice Joan Tates, and she had been alone with Thomas Langelong, bailiff, in private and suspicious circumstances, eg in a small hall with the windows closed. She resigned but the whole convent was blamed and made to fast on bread and beer on Fridays and Joan Tates had to head a solemn procession of the whole convent the next Sunday, with no veil, dressed in white flannel.

At the present time Redlingfield has no shop or post office and very little public transport. It once had a school and a pub, the latter having been closed down by the brewers due to poor trade and now a private residence.

Redlingfield has an excellent village sign, erected in 1977 to commemorate the Queen's Silver Jubilee and this stands on the village green together with the ancient stocks.

Rendlesham ❧

Rendlesham, referred to by the Venerable Bede as 'the hall of Rendil', is a small scattered community. It has no shop, school, inn or post office. For many years up until 1920 it consisted of the Rendlesham Hall estate, with the farms and cottages clustered in groups around the park, the hamlet of Friday Street being somewhat further away.

The church, dedicated to St Gregory the Great, occupies a commanding position overlooking the Deben valley. The building dates from the 14th and 15th centuries; the interior is well proportioned and attractively light, owing to the absence of stained glass windows. The east window is unusual in that the rather fanciful tracery is made of wood. The space west of the priest's stall was once occupied by a large box pew complete with fireplace for the comfort of the family from the Hall.

Rendlesham Hall was finally demolished after the Second World War. Though three gatehouses still remain, two are of special interest. Ivy Lodge near Tunstall is a sham ruin meant to look as though it was built in the 13th century but actually built about 1790. Woodbridge Lodge, built at the same time, has a central chimney disguised by three heavy flying buttresses. The central room is hexagonal.

Up until 1920 the family living in Rendlesham Hall owned most of the parish; around the extensive park were farmlands which merged into woodland and heath. Lord Rendlesham and his friends enjoyed shooting pheasants, partridges and hares. Point to point races were also organised.

Since the end of the Second World War Bentwaters air base has expanded to cover much of the land in the eastern part of the parish, the rest is farmed, producing sugar beet and barley, and of recent years varieties of soft fruit have been grown.

Rendlesham may now seem to be small and insignificant but it has a long history. There is strong evidence that Redwald, when he was king of the East Angles, had his palace close by the site of the present church. When he was converted to Christianity a church was erected in the vicinity which became quite an important centre of the 'new' religion. It is recorded, however, that after a time 'he had in this church one altar for the religion of Christ and another little altar for the sacrifices to devils'.

Since 1939 much interest has been aroused in the Sutton Hoo ship burial a few miles downstream on the bank of the river Deben; the general opinion now is that Redwald was accorded the honour, as befitting his rank, of this magnificent interment. If this was so, it is possible to imagine his funeral procession wending its way down the lane opposite the church to the banks of the Deben and from there by water to Redwald's last resting place.

Reydon ✤

Reydon was probably given its name by the Danes. The literal meaning is 'the upland on which the rye grows'. The manor of Reydon is mentioned in the Domesday Book, with a population of about 300. Two churches are recorded. St Margaret's has survived, and, although hard to date exactly, was the mother church to Southwold.

Not far from the church stands Reydon Hall, a fine Elizabethan mansion. Agnes Strickland was born at the Hall in 1796 and devoted herself to history and literature. She remained at Reydon Hall until moving to Southwold in 1865. She died nine years later and is buried in Southwold churchyard.

The history of primary education began with the establishment of the parochial school, a small brick and flint building near the church, erected in 1866 by public subscription. Now the older children are transported to schools at Beccles and Halesworth. A sad loss to village life and a move which was vigorously opposed by local residents. St Felix School, a private boarding school for girls, was built in 1902 on a site with fine views over the river Blyth to the sea.

On the same road and bordering Henham is Wolsey Bridge, built, it is said, by order of Cardinal Wolsey while he was staying at nearby Blythburgh. Whatever the origin of the name the bridge made a safe crossing for cattle on their way to Ipswich Market across the marshland. It is now a causeway.

Reydon hit the headlines in 1909. On the night of 26th October, in a terrific gale, a balloon with a French couple on board, blew 800 miles from Nancy in Lorraine across the North Sea, striking the cliffs at Easton

Bavents and eventually coming down near Reydon Grove. The lady passenger baled out at Potter's Bridge (the north-west boundary to the village) and, although injured, made her way to a house at Blackwater. The man was unharmed.

At one time there were two inns, the Bear at Reydon Corner, and the Quay. Both are now private houses. The Bear stands not far from Buss Creek, a narrow river dividing Reydon from Southwold. Years ago, Buss Creek had an outlet to the sea, enabling fishing busses to use the river. The Quay, built in 1737 did considerable trade in the days of the river Blyth and Buss Creek navigation, receiving cargoes of coal, chalk and lime. Farm produce and timber were taken away. Both inns were as close to the marsh as possible and were the haunts of smugglers.

Reydon Wood, not far from Reydon Hall and the church is an ancient site, once a mass of tangled undergrowth. This has been taken over by the Suffolk Trust, paths have been cleared and nature walks and camping sites are provided.

Since the Second World War there has been a considerable amount of infilling and several new estates have been built. The population has greatly increased (2,200 in the 1981 census). In 1987 a new parish of Reydon was created with the addition of Easton Bavents, with its problems of coastal erosion – thus Reydon is now bounded on the east by the sea.

The Rickinghalls 🐌

Rickinghall lies east of Bury St Edmunds, south-west of Diss. The two sections are known as Superior and Inferior, and follow the underground course of a stream which runs very erratically through the villages on higher and lower ground, with the division passing right through Hamlyn House, originally a mill in the mid 17th century, now a pub. The borders cross between properties all along the High Street, and houses side by side can be in either Superior or Inferior.

There are two churches, both St Mary's. The Upper Church incorporates a Knights Templar chapel and ancient stone wall seats on each side. It is now closed, though it was used during the Second World War as a school for London evacuees. The Lower Church dates from the 13th century and has a round tower.

At one time Superior had a guildhall, a Knights Templar preceptory on its borders, and more recently a chapel and mill, now all gone. Three mills, a maltings and a ladies school existed in Inferior.

Roman occupation is suggested by a colony of edible snails, and coins with other artefacts found in Garden House Lane and elsewhere.

Listed timber-framed buildings exist throughout the villages, some thatched, and the whole is within a conservation area. The main street runs the length of the villages, and has houses running all along it, with some new housing development interspersed among the older properties.

Three small new estates named Wheatfields, Pennyfields, and Church Meadows have nearly doubled the total population. Traffic in the Street is very heavy and there are hopes for a much needed bypass soon. The village once boasted the largest common in Suffolk.

Among other noteworthy buildings is the school (1854), and an Elizabethan dwelling which was brought in sections from Stowmarket, and there is a moated farmhouse where members of the Tyrell family lived; one of whom during the 16th century was beheaded for the murder of the Princes in the Tower.

The village had several pubs but now only three remain, the oldest being 16th century. The others are now converted into homes. Once there was the Dyer School, a village library, forge, wheelwright, boot-makers, hurdle makers, printers, undertakers, hardware store, draper, basket maker, butchers and bakers. Now there is a post office, bank, newsagents, grocers, butchers, an electrical shop, garage workshop, a craft shop, and three antiques shops, as well as a shoemaker's and a farm craft centre in Superior.

During the last century famous inhabitants included the brothers Hamlyn who wrote books for schools, and more recently, Basil Brown, a well respected archaeologist and resident (died 1977) who traced the Saxon ship burial site at Sutton Hoo, among his other local discoveries.

Many of the present inhabitants are retired people, but working occupations vary considerably, with a few commuting to London. Farms are still very much in evidence. In spite of much new building which has taken place, the village retains its character, because many of the original village families remain.

Ringsfield 🐦

The parish church of All Saints is situated some two and a half miles south-west of Beccles in a little wooded valley. Each year the churchyard comes alive with snowdrops and aconites, followed closely by primroses and daffodils. Local people welcome these first signs of spring bringing hope of warmer days ahead.

Little can now be found of the church's early history. Work on the church tower was started in 1450 but some earlier wills leaving money for repairs suggest that the church existed well before that. It was extensively restored and extended in 1883 under the supervision of the well known architect, William Butterfield, and was rethatched in 1953.

In the spring of 1949 two robins nested in the lectern and brought up a family there. The 'Ringsfield Robin' has been remembered in the carving on the fine new lectern and in the porch gates and has been incorporated in the village sign soon to be erected on the village green. The previous lectern with the nest intact may still be seen in the church. The church has been flooded on several occasions when the adjacent stream has overflowed – most recently in September 1968 when assistance from the fire brigade was needed to pump out.

Across the stream and the adjacent bridlepath lie the fruit fields maintained by a local family where, in the halycon days of summer, one can 'pick your own' delicious strawberries, raspberries, gooseberries etc and 'dig your own' potatoes.

Less than a mile along the bridlepath is Ringsfield Hall, which in 1972 became a Christian country centre run by a small community mostly for groups from churches and schools.

Recent development has been concentrated around Ringsfield Corner, about one mile south of the church, which has become the focal point of the village and where the post office and general store continues to be a valuable asset for surrounding villages as well as this one. Nearby is the village hall opened officially in January 1983 and which has already won several awards in the 'Hall of the Year' contest run by a local newspaper. A new village green has been laid and, with the village hall and the existing playing fields, will become the hub of village activity in the future.

A little way along School Road from Ringsfield Corner is Ringsfield Free church, a red brick building built in 1909 to replace the previous wooden building erected about 1850 to provide a place of worship for dissenters, who had until then been meeting in private houses. Further along School Road is the school, originally built around 1860 and since enlarged and partly rebuilt.

Despite recent changes and additions, Ringsfield has retained its rural charm and is a very desirable and pleasant village in which to live.

Risby ❧

Risby is a delightful village four miles north-west of the town of Bury St Edmunds. Mentioned in the Domesday Book it has ancient links with the past. In early days the village was owned by the abbey in Bury St Edmunds. The flint walled church, with its round Saxon tower, is dedicated to St Giles. The beautiful 15th century rood screen was restored in 1966 by the generosity of the Pilgrim Trust, which has brought out the medieval colouring and gilding. On the south wall can be seen early 13th century wall paintings.

The village sign stands proudly on the green, depicting a once thriving fruit and farming influence. Farming is still very much part of the village, though sadly most of the fruit trees have now gone. Sugar beet, carrots, wheat and barley are the main crops, pigs and sheep are still reared, and wine is made at the local vineyard, Highwaysmen.

The original village hall was given to the village by Sir John Wood, the last of the squires from the neighbouring village of Hengrave. Adjoining this hall is the village community centre, offering the amenities of a town within the peace of village life.

The attractive flint walls, not just of the church, but around many parts of the village, including the original school, give one a glimpse of a bygone age. Many of the elderly remember stone picking in the fields to build the A45 which runs parallel with the village. Much of the ground is stony but the village has some wonderful gardens and a thriving garden club.

Risby also has its own inn, the White Horse, and also the Crown and Castle, both renowned for good food and friendly atmosphere. Nearby is the 400 year old thatched barn, an antiques centre of great renown which also contains a coffee shop with groceries, furniture restoration centre, garden centre and post office. The village coal merchant is still on the green, and his family carries on a tradition of nearly 100 years.

Rougham 🐝

Rougham has 26 miles of road, and is a series of small hamlets. It was a 'plague' village. Once centred on the church, all the original houses were burned down and they were replaced by houses in the various hamlets viz:– the Green, High Rougham, Kingshall Street, Blackthorpe etc.

There has been a settlement in the village since Roman times as evidenced by the excavation of the tumulus at Eastlowe Hill, in the 19th century. The church of St Mary has a south porch dating from the 13th century. Years ago, there were two pubs in the village, the Royal Oak and the Bennett Arms – (the latter keeping the name of one of the residents of Rougham Hall); now the Royal Oak is closed, as are the shops which included a bakery and a sweet shop. The post office and general store is still functioning but as this is in Kingshall Street, most people shop in the supermarkets of Bury St Edmunds.

Rougham achieved a certain notoriety during the Second World War because a USAAF bomber base was situated here. Clark Gable, Glenn Miller, Bing Crosby, Dinah Shore and Bob Hope were some of the 'big' names who appeared there. The Americans left their roads etc which the local council and private developers then built houses along – the Downs, Newthorpe and Mouse Lane. The hangars became an industrial estate.

Rougham Hall is now a ruin, having been bombed in the Second World War. Before the war, there was an annual flower show held in the grounds, the highlight being admission to the 'pleasure grounds' – the garden surrounding the Hall itself. This was much enjoyed by the ordinary folk of Rougham.

On the road leading from Kingshall Street towards Bradfield St George there remains a mystery. A house has appeared here – and disappeared. The last person to see this apparition was a daughter of the last rector to live in the old rectory – now the Chantry. Another rectory was built adjacent to the church before the Second World War, circa 1935.

Rumburgh 🦌

Rumburgh is situated four miles from Halesworth between Wissett and St Margarets and close to an area known as 'The Saints'. The name Rumburgh is said to mean a village which is surrounded by a ditch, bank, or hedge and which can only be reached by a 'broad-bridge' or a 'fallen log' and there is still a rectangular moat around part of Abbey Farm House.

A Benedictine priory was founded here just before the Norman Conquest and the church (dedicated to St Michael and St Felix) was built on the extreme northern boundary of the parish. The priory was closed by orders of Cardinal Wolsey in 1528 and its lands and manorial rights changed hands briskly throughout the succeeding centuries. The first vicar was appointed to the church in 1550 and this is all that remains of the priory. The west tower of the church with its weatherboarded top and tiled pitched roof gives an interesting appearance and inside the church there is a graceful wooden rood screen unusually complete. The tower dates back to the 13th century and the porch is a 15th century addition.

There is also a flourishing Methodist chapel which was built in 1836 but the school which was built in the 1850s was closed after some 100 years and children now mainly go to schools in Bungay and Halesworth.

In March 1758 certain landowners gave land, which was conveyed by deed of feoffement to the Rumburgh Town Estate. Hence the trustees of the Town Estate became known as the Rumburgh Feoffees. The rents from this land were to be yearly used for the advantage of Rumburgh as decided by the trustees. One of the founder members of the trustees was William Aldrich who is an ancestor of TV personality and broadcaster David Frost, and seven members of this family are buried in Rumburgh church. In these days the Feoffees make donations to any worthy cause in the village or any individual in need of financial assistance and it is a body of people from all walks of life.

Rumburgh's prosperity lay chiefly in the Middle Ages and this is evidenced by the building of medieval farmhouses, many of which remain today. A cottage in Rumburgh Street is said to be the smallest in East Suffolk and it is thought it may have been the pay office for the wool industry in the area.

The Rumburgh Buck, a very popular village pub, was once part of the Church estate. Whilst in the hands of the Church it was administered by the Parochial Church Council. It is said that back in the days of the priory the Buck was used as a place where the monks' guests would stay. This fine old building has been kept in the main in its original design and still has a flagstone floor. At one time the following poem was displayed on the wall:–

'The Buck stood free with branching horn,
Eight hundred years ere we were born,
He finds good food, and rest, and drink,
For man, and friends of man, we think.
So traveller – rest, refresh, and pay,
Then cheerily speed you on your way.'

Rushmere St Andrew 🌿

Rushmere St Andrew is situated two and a half miles east of Ipswich. The church dedicated to St Andrew gives the parish its name. Rebuilt in 1861, a church has been on the same site as far back as Saxon times. Further extensions have been carried out in 1968 to accommodate a growing parish. There are many interesting features, including near the door a tiny hole through the wall, with some faint scratches around it. This is the remains of an ancient sundial. A straw would be pushed through the hole and its shadow, falling on the marks, would show the time of day.

At the junction of Lamberts Lane and The Street, the Limes Pond is one of the two duck ponds in the village. Originally, the duck pond was not fenced off, as it is today. Local residents can remember the cows having a drink at the pond on their way to and from being milked. This pond (together with Chestnut Pond) is a focal point in the village, and provides great joy for old and young alike.

In the centre of the parish there are 168 acres of common land, known as Rushmere Heath. In the mid 19th century conflicts broke out between the lord of the manor, the Marquis of Bristol, and the commoners. Nat Ablitt (1784–1865) played an important part in the defence of commoners' rights, and on his cottage (now demolished) he fixed a tablet testifying to the everlasting rights of the Rushmere Commoners. This tablet is now on the front of the Baptist chapel, built in 1859. As recently as 1958, Rushmere Heath was purchased by the commoners. Ownership is now vested in four trustees, and a committee looks after the day to day administration. The heath saw its last execution in April 1763 when Richard Ringe was hanged at the gallows and his accomplice Margery Beddingfield was strangled and burned for the murder of her husband, John Beddingfield of Sternfield.

The western boundary between Rushmere and the encroaching suburbs of Ipswich is along the strangely named 'Humber Doucy Lane'. During the Napoleonic Wars a camp was set up on the heath for the French prisoners of war. Many of the men enjoyed the 'sweet shade' of the lane, and their 'Ombre Douce' has through the years gradually changed to Humber Doucy. Before the post-war building boom altered the village greatly, a farmhouse stood on Humber Doucy Lane almost opposite a lane called Seven Cottages Lane, with a pool and a gate. On the gatepost was a cross, painted red. The story is that a young soldier in the First World War, home on leave, could not face returning to the inferno of the trenches. He painted the cross, then drowned himself in the pond.

Trees are an enduring feature of the Rushmere landscape and the lime trees that tower over The Street are of particular interest as they were planted by Christopher Milton, brother of the poet John Milton, who was deputy recorder in Ipswich in 1674.

At one time Rushmere St Andrew boasted a blacksmith and a shoemaker, and in recent years a wheelwright. These crafts have now disappeared from the village. Over 100 years ago, John Cobbold planted a hop-garden in one of the more fertile areas of the parish and built a 14 room beer house. The building was pulled down in the 1960s. Close to the hop-garden John Pell and Sons produced the white 'Rushmere Bricks', and it is said that some of these were exported to America.

Rushmere St Andrew today is a residential village, with many of its inhabitants employed in Ipswich, Felixstowe and the surrounding towns. Small modern housing developments have become a feature of the area over the last 25 years or so, nevertheless Rushmere, surrounded by beautiful countryside, maintains its tranquillity amidst the hustle and bustle of 20th century life.

Chestnut Pond, Rushmere St. Andrew

Sapiston 🐦

Historically, Sapiston seems to be far less interesting than many of its neighbours, yet the village is pleasant in its rural solitude with nothing to tell a stranger where the adjacent village of Honington ends and Sapiston begins – only a tributary of the Little Ouse which winds its way to a water mill. Sadly, the mill is not now in use, but a splendid farmhouse, still known as 'The Grange' in honour of an old time manor situated close by, can be found. In this part of Sapiston lies the now redundant church of St Andrew, which was built by the Normans and today is of interest even after the lapse of 800 years.

During the 19th century the school that was erected for the children of the parish by the Duke of Grafton in 1841 was demolished, as were so many of the picturesque thatched cottages. No longer does the village have its hurdle maker, shoemaker, grocer, draper or its house of refreshment. One of the few reminders of the Victorian era is the original wall-mounted cast iron postbox, bearing the VR cipher. The mail is still delivered to the doors of the 60 or so houses and cottages making up this scattered village, following the same route as it did many years ago from Bury St Edmunds via Ixworth.

Village life now revolves around the village hall, a building formerly used as a chapel by the American Air Force at RAF Honington. In 1946 the American Forces transferred the building to its present site as a gift to mark their appreciation of the friendship given to them by the local people during the Second World War.

If you walk round the village you are never far from the noise of the Royal Air Force Tornados from Honington air base that fly overhead, but they never seem to disturb the pheasants and rabbits in the fields and hedgerows, nor do they detract from the enjoyment of this pleasant corner of Suffolk.

Semer 🐦

Semer is a small village nestling in the beautiful green valley of the river Brett which takes its name from the small lake or mere just south of the church. The village is spread with the village hall at its centre.

The oldest part of the village is found in Ash Street, spelt Asce Street in the Domesday Book of 1086. At that time there was a mill there. Unfortunately that has gone but there is also a delightful hump-backed bridge here.

The church of All Saints is a Decorated structure of flint and stone dressing. It has an embattled western tower containing three bells. The rectory was burnt down in 1953. Semer now shares a rector with the parishes of Watfield Nedging and Naughton, but all villages work very hard to ensure the continuance of their own parish church.

On the road to Hadleigh is Union Hill where once the Cosford Union workhouse stood. This house of industry was a model of its kind. The inmates were employed spinning yarn and it became more productive and beneficial than any other in the county. On wash days the women were allowed an additional five pints of strong beer. The old women were allowed tea and snuff. It was rumoured that whole families outside were supported by food stolen from the house. In 1859 a chapel was built and in 1870 an isolation block was added. The hospital is the only remaining building and is now a private residence. However, the small-paned iron windows from the workhouse are to be found in various houses around the village.

The village has, however, changed dramatically in the last hundred years. The population of poor farm workers has almost gone due to the advance in farm management and their replacements are professional commuters who have improved and enlarged the houses. Semer missed out on getting its new housing estate and now that the law prevents new building in the country, it is unlikely to get one. Due to this and other factors, the number of inhabitants has dwindled and so have the village services. Gone is the garage, the shop, the post office and all that remains is a skeleton of services. It is lovely to see Semer unspoilt, but there is a price to pay.

Shadingfield 🐝

The parish church of St John the Baptist has stood between the two hills by the Hundred river for more than 800 years, long before the A145 brought the traffic rushing past.

In medieval times this was a village of small farms and cottages scattered round a common called Shaddenfelde Green, where in 1257 a grant for a fair was given. An important packway from London to Norwich and Yarmouth via Beccles passed by way of the Elizabethan Hall to the Bow inn. Along this road Cromwell's men marched to London. They met opposition at the inn and in a farmyard, and two were buried in the churchyard as recorded in the church registers, which date from 1539.

The Cudden family lived in the Hall which was later destroyed by fire. Their tombstones pave the chancel end, and their coat of arms is incorporated in the east window of the church. The greatest treasure, now in safe keeping at Norwich, is the altar cloth with its original box and document made by Elizabeth Cuddon and given to the church on Christmas Day, 1632. It was rediscovered in the Hall garden wall.

Great changes took place in Georgian times. An old chart for stage-coach drivers shows a course across the common over a causeway. When the new turnpike was built it followed this route. The common was enclosed and sold by the Commissioners for the Crown. Small farms were added to the larger ones. Farmhouses were given new frontages and grander names. Thus South Farm became Turnpike Farm and Place Farm became Park Farm. The new Hall, now faithfully restored, was built by Thomas Scott who owned several farms which are now part of Sotterley estate.

Now, new farming practices have changed the map again, obliterating many small meadows, hedges, ponds, ditches and paths, and many of the wild flowers. Agriculture is geared to the Common Market and to the needs of the sugar beet and deep freeze factories. We no longer see the fine Suffolk Punch horses or the corn stacks in the fields. There is only one small dairy herd left. The general stores and post office are closed, and there is no blacksmith at the forge. Most men and women commute to work, few men now working on the land. Fortunately, the Fox inn, once renowned for its tug-of-war and quoit teams, is still doing business.

Social life centres round the church rooms. The 'Abbey', as it is called, was given to the church by Mr Alfred Woods in 1898, and is licensed for Anglican services. At the turn of the century there was a leaning towards mission type services led by the Misses Anna and Eugenie Sadd. This is not surprising as a number of men served with the Lowestoft fishing fleet. Some, having completed the harvest on the land, walked to Lowestoft by way of the fishermen's footpaths, and joined in the herring harvest or sailed on the westward voyage through the Caledonian Canal to catch mackerel. When they came home, the Abbey resounded to the singing of songs of the sea, and the favourite hymns at the Services of Song.

Shelland 🌾

Shelland is a small village situated in an undulating landscape. It lies three miles to the north-west of Stowmarket.

In 1461, the lord of the manor of Shelland at Rockylls Hall was a Henry Bourchier, who was Earl of Essex. A descendant of his, also Henry, died in 1539 after a fall from his horse. His daughter Anne became wife of Sir William Parr and their daughter Katherine became one of the wives of Henry VIII. In 1885, most of the village was owned by the Tyrell family of Gipping.

The village of Shelland has witnessed fluctuating populations, varying from twelve citizens and two plough-pulling oxen in 1066 to 109 people in 1841 and thence dwindling in size to the present day figure of 48 inhabitants.

Shelland church is one of only four in the country which are dedicated to King Charles the Martyr. It is noted for its famous barrel organ which is played most Sundays and was built in 1810. It was restored in 1940 for £120 and more recently for £2,500! There are three barrels each with twelve tunes and 250 hymns can be sung. From 1885 to 1935, the organ was played by a Mr Armstrong. He was succeeded by his son who was organist until 1965, since when the present organist has continued the task.

In 1966, electricity was installed in the church, but the oil lamps were retained and electrified to maintain the traditional look. Other features of the church include the box pews, wig stand, a triple decker pulpit and an unusual colour scheme. The favourite explanation for the bright colours is that they represent the jewels in the gates of the celestial city. However, it could be true that the wainwright who painted the walls was just using his leftover pots of paint!

There is a large green at Shelland with a few houses scattered along the boundary. There was a school there about 200 years ago and there was a blacksmith's shop but now there are no amenities and villagers rely on neighbouring villages or the towns of Stowmarket, Bury St Edmunds or Ipswich for education, recreation and shopping.

Shimpling 🐚

Equidistant from Bury St Edmunds and Sudbury, the village of Shimpling straggles for two miles through what is called The Street to where the church, St George's, is tucked away in a hollow by the Chad brook and approached down an avenue of impressive lime trees. The church is noted for an excellent example of Victorian stained glass and a Norman font. The Faint House is a unique small stone building in the churchyard where ladies could retire when the overtight lacings of their stays caused them to swoon during the service.

A mile away lies the Old Rectory, a moated part-Tudor house which is reputed to have originally been a rest house for monks from Bury St Edmunds.

Between Shimpling and The Street lies the Chadacre estate. The present Hall was built by Thomas Hallifax, a banker, in 1834. He took a great interest in the village of Shimpling and was responsible for building many of the farm cottages. In 1841 he built the village school which was extended in 1871 by his sister, Ellen, and is the oldest primary school in Suffolk. Pupils at that time numbered 135. Sadly the school was closed in 1989 with only 32 children on the register. A Trust Fund was set up by the Hallifax family in 1863 to provide pupils with pinafores and such aids to their education as were not provided by the authorities. The Trust is still in existence today to help the village children with their education.

The Hallifax family died out and in 1919 the first Lord Iveagh, the story has it, was so horrified at the ignorance of his farm workers when he found a lad stuffing manure into a wound on a horse's flank as his idea of a cure, that he purchased Chadacre with 580 acres and endowed it as an independent agricultural institute, the only one of its kind. It was intended to educate East Anglian farmworkers and cottagers' sons free, and farmers' sons at a fee.

The institute served its purpose well and Chadacre-trained boys were always in great demand. But with changing times and methods it had to close in 1989. The Hall has now reverted to private ownership and the chapel has been demolished.

The parish of Shimpling has always been very much a farming community and the houses and cottages reflect this in their style and types of architecture going back over the years. Comparatively few new houses have been built and those that have blend in unobtrusively. There are the ruins of a windmill and a coal shed built in 1861 by the Hallifaxes to house coal for the needy of the parish.

The village pond has disappeared but as late as the 1930s villagers were taking their water from the pond and the three pumps and several wells in the village which produced a poor and scanty water supply and much illness and disease.

Over the years the post office and shop have closed. The school moved away and only the Bush, a thriving and popular public house remains as a focal point. A large proportion of the residents commute to work elsewhere and with the farmers busy on their land the village gives the passer-by the impression of old world timeless tranquillity.

Shipmeadow

A cosy little village nestling three miles east of Bungay and west of Beccles on the river Waveney, bordering Norfolk. It has 794 acres of mixed soil. In the 1800s there were 265 inhabitants, now there are about 90.

In 1765 it was decided to build a House of Industry (workhouse) for the Wangford Hundred Incorporation. A huge 'H' block of a building meant to hold 450 people, standing on 44 acres of land, was erected at a cost of £8,500. A pest house was also considered essential. The inmates all had tasks from the age of five upwards. A taskmaster would arrange casual work with local farmers, especially at seed time and harvest time. It is now being converted into very desirable homes with a wonderful view over the Waveney valley.

In 1871 there was a post office, carpenter, shopkeeper, butcher and pig dealer and farmers. Only the farmers and the carpenter, who is still a Mr Howlett, have survived. The church of St Bartholomew (now redundant and sold) stands on an eminence overlooking the vale, a stone and flint building with chancel, nave and short tower with one bell.

The Community of All Hallows began in 1854 as Shipmeadow Penitentiary for Fallen Women. The young women, known as 'penitents', were dressed in lilac print with white caps. They spent most of the day in household chores, gardening, cord and twine making and needlework, all performed in complete silence. In 1855 it was decided the house was unsuitable for health reasons as it stood on low marsh land and a death had occurred due to this. Ditchingham near Bungay was the chosen place and the move made in 1859, where today it is well known for its school and hospital. The house in Shipmeadow is now a farmhouse where

Sisters from All Hallows occasionally visit, always with a small gift.

Today as you approach from the west, at the bottom of the hill opposite Nunnery Farm stands a new motel. This was built on the site of the old blacksmith's shop, built in the early 1900s.

Shotley & Erwarton 🖎

Shotley is situated at the tip of the peninsula and has the river Orwell on one side and the river Stour on the other. Shotley was one of several hamlets which made up the district and was mentioned in the Domesday survey of 1086. Also mentioned in this survey was a church which had a very large tower, visible from the sea. The tower is recorded as having fallen in 1674, but was rebuilt and again fell in 1823, when sadly it was not rebuilt.

There is a rhyme which goes;

Shotley church – without a steeple
Drunken parson – wicked people.

Though there is no evidence to support the rumour of the 'drunken parson', it has been said that the parapet on the church porch roof was just the right height to conceal a barrel of rum during smuggling days, maybe this is the origin of the rumour. It is also said that because the water tasted so much better than the water in Harwich, over the river Stour, people used to come over to Shotley and take the water back and sell it at a halfpenny a bucket – perhaps they collected it from the church porch roof!

Shotley's biggest claim to fame is probably *HMS Ganges*, known throughout the length and breadth of Britain by the seamen who trained there. In 1899 it was a ship that lay just off Shotley Gate, then a hospital was built on shore, followed in 1903 by the building of the main shore establishment. The main feature was the mast, 142 ft high, which is now a protected monument. In the naval days a junior rating could very often be spotted sitting atop the mast, reading a book – presumably it was the only place in the establishment he couldn't be 'got at'. The establishment is now used as a police training centre, but the mast is 'out of bounds' to the police officers.

Erwarton is a small hamlet lying between Shotley and Harkstead on the river Stour, with more than its share of history and legend. A visit to the church will tell you of the connection with Anne Boleyn. Anne's aunt was married to a Calthorpe who lived at Erwarton Hall and Anne visited her as a child, and after she became Queen of England. The story goes that on her death Anne's heart was brought to Erwarton church as she had requested. A tall story you may think, but in 1836 whilst repairs were being carried out, a lead casket was found in the south wall. This contained a little black dust. The casket was resealed and placed in a vault in the Lady chapel, which is now beneath the organ site. This was witnessed by Joseph Amner, who had heard the story handed down from his grandfather. Joseph died in 1874 having been sacristan of Erwarton church for 50 years.

Erwarton once supported a post office, shop and a public house, but at present there is only the Queen's Head, which has been tastefully extended and now boasts a restaurant.

On the river Stour at the Ness are the remains of the old quay where the barges belonging to the Wrinch family, who still farm locally, were loaded. The hold was lined with bundles of straw then filled with stuver, which was a type of hay made from clover; overhanging the top of the barge were bundles of straw. These loads, plus loads of fodder beet, were taken to London to feed the horses, and the barges returned loaded with stable manure or household garbage.

Shottisham ☙

Official sources describe the landscape setting of Shottisham as having an unique quality, which together with its historical development have recently warranted designation as a conservation area. The compact cluster of cottages around The Knoll, and dominated by the church, is linked to the mill buildings in the west by scattered properties and recent development along The Street.

It is probable that Shottisham's water mill is on the same site as the one mentioned in the Domesday Book as being in the manor of Wood Hall; the present building, now converted to residential use, makes a striking visual impact at the approach to the village. The mill was working until the 1950s, the associated coal-merchant's business being continued for some more years.

The Domesday Book also mentions a church at Shottisham, and the present 14th century St Margaret's still stands, in a commanding position, towering over the centre of the village and visible for miles.

Just below the church is the Sorrel Horse inn, parts dating from the 16th and 17th centuries, and still with a thatched roof. Tales persist of involvement with smugglers, and an underground passage between the pub and the church, but to date there is no evidence. With a Customs and Excise officer now living in the village, its use, if ever, has presumably been interrupted!

Records show that the population was at its peak during the 19th century, with 372 inhabitants in 1851, slowly declining to 147 on the present electoral roll. Over a hundred years ago life would have been rugged and demanding, with the inhabitants rising to meet each problem from their own meagre resources. About a mile from the village is a large field called Poors' Common, which provided bracken, used as litter for pigs, and twigs from small trees and gorse for bread ovens, materials much valued by those with commoners' rights. These rights have unfortunately been lost, and the pigs, perhaps fortunately, no longer feature in back gardens. The memory of men struggling home carrying loads on their backs still remain.

Whilst there is a village shop and post office and deliveries of bread, meat, fish and hardware, the resident tailor, butcher, wheelwright, blacksmith, harnessmaker and shoemaker who were in business at some time during the last 150 years have all disappeared. The milkman and his wife who deliver so conscientiously, also provide a marvellous link with families through many villages, and messages can travel almost as fast as BT links!

All around the village is a countryside where farming, mostly arable, and forestry dominate, rich in wildlife and criss-crossed with paths and tracks leading to the river Deben, Sutton Hoo and Rendlesham Forest. Those with eagle eyes may discover evidence of earlier human occupation – flint arrowheads and pieces of pottery of all ages since the Roman occupation. And going back to prehistoric times, the light sandy soil still yields the occasional fossilized shark's tooth or shell.

Snape 🐚

Snape was originally known as Snapes, meaning 'boggy place' and probably the first settlement was down by the river. In the 12th and 13th centuries there was a large increase in the population, and the main centre of occupation moved to the drier and higher ground around the common.

At the beginning of the 19th century a corn and coal business operated at Snape Bridge, but due to illness the owner sold up to Newson Garrett and in 1854 he began malting at Snape. The story goes that as there was a need for expansion, Newson marked out the front of the maltings with his walking stick, but he did not walk in a straight line and the slight bend at the front of the building is still noticeable. With new techniques in malting being introduced the buildings were not easy to adapt and ceased to operate in 1965.

Today Snape, situated six miles from the coast at Aldeburgh and four miles from the market town of Saxmundham, is known internationally for its famous Maltings concert hall, the acoustics of which are considered to be among the finest in Europe. The Aldeburgh Festival Committee took over the buildings and converted them into the opera house and concert hall. In 1969 they were severely damaged by fire, but were speedily rebuilt under the inspiration of Benjamin Britten and Peter Pears. Sitting on the edge of the salt marshes, the beauty of the Maltings complex attracts thousands of music lovers and visitors every year.

Benjamin Britten once owned the Old Mill in the centre of the village and lived there for a short while. It was here in the tranquillity of Snape, that he wrote the opera *Peter Grimes*. His connections with Snape are represented on the village sign which was erected in 1987 by the Snape and Farnham branch of the Royal British Legion.

An Anglo-Saxon ship was discovered in 1862 by Aldeburgh historian Septimus Davidson. Since 1985 an annual excavation of the site has revealed a second boat and burial ground, providing valuable information about life in Anglo-Saxon Britain. The acid sandy soil has preserved bodies and artefacts almost perfectly.

Snape Bridge was a fine old humpback bridge built in 1802. In 1959 it was replaced by a wider bridge. The old bricks were saved and used to build the bus shelter which now stands on the common, the original 'hump' now forming the top of the shelter.

There are many fascinating, gruesome and sometimes romantic tales of smuggling and Snape also has played its small part in helping the 'free traders'. Overlooking the marshes is the Crown inn. From a dormer window an 'all clear' signal would be given to the smugglers allowing them to bring their illicit cargo up the river, and over the common. Sometimes they would 'borrow' horses and carts from the local farmers – repaying them by leaving a very acceptable cask of spirits or case of tea in a corner of the barn.

Playing a very important role in the village today is the primary school, which was built in 1905 in memory of Mr Newson Garrett. It is a happy thriving school, having survived threatened closure in recent years.

Somersham

Somersham has a mixed and interesting history. It is thought that the origin of the village dates back to a Saxon settlement perhaps as early as the 5th century.

Approaching Somersham from Ipswich the road travels beside the brook which flows through the village to the river Gipping. Until recently when there were heavy storms it flooded and could isolate the village, as it has obviously done through the ages. The high path along the brook is called the 'carnser' (an old Saxon word for high path).

The village straddles the main street except for recent housing developments. Church Lane leads past St Mary's church which is Saxon in origin and mentioned in the Domesday Book. The church is mainly 14th century with a very ancient arch in the porch which is said to be one of the oldest in the county.

By 1964 the planners had given their approval to an expansion plan for Somersham. So began the commuter age for this little village. Where once there were green fields, houses and bungalows appeared and in about twelve months the population doubled and the task of creating a new rural community began. The village is far enough away from the town of Ipswich still to be thought of as 'country' and people enjoy escaping to it from the hustle and bustle of the towns. Now, with the recent electrification of the inter-city rail line, London seems nearer still!

Most of the old and attractive houses in the village border the main street and are now listed. Somersham village sign reminds visitors that once horses were brought to the flourishing forge from the surrounding villages and farms. Today, the actual site of the old blacksmith's forge is marked by an anvil in the garden of Forge Bungalow. There were many small farms and most of the population worked on the land around the village. Today there are only two, divided by the village street.

The Duke of Marlborough has probably always been an inn because it is sited on a crossroads. Various tales of haunting add to its interest! Around the inn are some of the oldest houses stil remaining in the village. The house opposite, once a shop and blacksmith's, still has a 'pudding stone' built into the wall to stop carts hitting the main structure. It is now the Studio where students are attracted from home and abroad for courses in pottery, embroidery and art. Another cottage industry nearby manufactures an air freshener.

Somerton 🐝

This tiny hamlet of about 60 inhabitants is mentioned in the Domesday Book and is situated high up on the edge of the Glem valley. The main part of the hamlet is approached by a long hill from Somerton Hall close by the Glem, or from Hartest on the B1066, again by a hill and a long winding lane.

The small flint and stone church of St Margaret stands at the highest point overlooking the beautiful undulating countryside where Hawkedon and Glemsford churches, barns and cottages add to the panorama. There are chancel windows in memory of the Hale family who bequeathed the four almshouses on the hill from Lower to Upper Somerton, endowed in 1912 by the trustees of Miss Finetta Hale, now sadly rather neglected and used by young homeless people.

The Old Hare and Hounds pub in Lower Somerton became a private home after the Second World War but until and during the war it had been the favourite meeting place for a drink and chat by the local farmers and workers and was the place to go for orange juice and cod liver oil for babies!

Prisoners of war were billeted at the Old Rectory. The Italians provided an interesting episode in the quiet hamlet, they worked well but loved singing and many was the time when the loaded carts went by accompanied by lovely Italian lyrics. An old gramophone and records provided music and, although not according to the rules, they loved giving the occasional 'musical evening'. They certainly did not consider themselves as enemies and neither did the people of Somerton. Some displaced persons from countries such as Latvia were the last group to occupy the rectory. They were quiet and pleasant and were good at making baskets from the willow in the hedgerow. Many beautiful baskets and cradles are still in use, memories of the strange vagaries of war.

Attractive farmhouses of the 17th century, such as Somerton Hall, Church Farm, Brittons Farm, Manor Farm now are intensively farmed. Large machines mean bigger fields so rather less hedges and wild life areas but at the present time, with 'set-aside', some meadows and fields of wild flowers can be seen again. The fields of poppies during the autumn of 1990 were a welcome sight. More trees are being planted. Because of the need for less labour on the farms, Somerton like many other rural areas has cottages lived in by people of other walks of life.

Claude Rogers, a well known artist who lived at the Old Rectory with his artist wife Elsie Few, loved painting scenes of the Burning of the Stubble, a phenomenon which was both exhilarating and frightening to watch but thankfully now is to be banned. Claude with his artist's brush recorded these scenes for posterity.

South Elmham 🐝

South Elmham is a group of North Suffolk villages known locally as 'Saints Country', which includes Homersfield and Flixton as well as the South Elmham villages of All Saints-cum-St Nicholas, St Cross, St James, St Margaret, St Michael, and St Peter.

There is evidence of early habitation in the area with a Bronze Age cremation urn and a magnificent Saxon drinking glass being found at Flixton, a Romano-British kiln and pottery sherds at Homersfield.

The area is mainly agricultural as it has been for centuries. Industry has crept in with gravel workings at Homersfield and Flixton, which also has a poultry packer and a mushroom farm – together employing several hundred people.

All Saints-cum-St Nicholas was two separate villages until about 1620 when St Nicholas' church fell down and was never rebuilt. A stone cross now marks its site. The ancient little church of All Saints catered for both parishes for the next three centuries. In 1978 it was made redundant owing to its remote location. It is now well looked after by the Redundant Churches Fund.

St Cross is a pretty little village with its ancient church of St George of varying styles. In this parish is the site of the 'Old Minster', for which South Elmham is best known. Dating back to the 14th century, its origin is still something of a mystery. It is now the focus of a Farm Walk starting at South Elmham Hall.

St James is the village that tradition says 'hedged the cuckoo' in to keep its song to itself. Its church occupies the highest site in Suffolk and is an ancient structure with a Norman devil's door. A village of scattered farms – Park Farm is said to be the location of a medieval deer park of the early bishops of Norwich.

St Margaret is a small village rambling along each side of its village green. The church is an attractive little building mainly Perpendicular in style. The village stocks are kept in the porch.

St Michael is another small village – of open landscape where its church dating back to Norman times stands on the common. It is the only village in Suffolk where all eleven men who served their country in the Great War returned home.

St Peter is the smallest of the parishes, with a Norman doorway to the church. The jewel of St Peter is its ancient Hall, parts of which are said to date from 1250. It was the family home of the Tasburghs before they went to Flixton. A small room at the top of the stairs is said to be haunted by a nun.

Homersfield is a picturesque village with its old houses, some thatched, grouped around its village green, overlooked by St Mary's church, an ancient Norman structure. Since the new bridge over the river Waveney was built about 1970, avoiding the centre of the village, Homersfield has lived a peaceful existence. The old bridge, the first reinforced concrete iron bridge in Britain, is now redundant except for pedestrians, but remains a feature of the village. It was built about 1870 by the Adair family whose armorial bearings are displayed on its side and who years ago had the right of toll on passing and repassing.

Flixton, like Homersfield, borders the river Waveney. Although no evidence exists the village is believed to be named after St Flik, the first East Anglian bishop. The village sign, erected in 1921 by Sir Robert Shafto Adair, shows the bishop in his regalia.

It is a village of much woodland. Standing on a hill, the church here is mainly Victorian although the site dates back to about AD 700. After various stages of decay, the ancient building was replaced in the 19th century at the expense of the Adair family. Its lozenge-shaped tower is unusual, being one of only two of this type in England.

The famous Captain Boycott (from whom the word 'boycott' comes) died at Priests House in 1897 while he was estate agent for the Adair family.

During the Second World War, Flixton became the home of the renowned 'Bungay Buckeroos', who flew on bombing raids to Germany from the airfield here – they were the 446th Bombardment Group of the American Eighth Army Air Force. Most of the land of the old airfield has now been returned to agriculture.

Once several public houses served these parishes. Now only the Black Swan at Homersfield and the Buck at Flixton remain dispensing hospitality to the neighbourhood. The last to close was the White Horse at St James early in 1990. The Norfolk & Suffolk Aviation Museum is sited by the Buck inn. Well signposted, it attracts many visitors during the summer months.

The Lighthouse at Southwold

Southwold ✒

Southwold, a comparatively small town lying in the centre of the Suffolk Heritage Coast, still retains a village atmosphere so much appreciated by many visitors.

In 1989 Southwold enthusiastically celebrated the quincentenary of the granting of its charter by Henry VII in 1489. Records of the year's celebrations supplied by all the local organisations, including the WI's 'Scrapbook of the Town', were sealed in a chest, which was then dedicated and buried under the choir stalls of St Edmund's church.

The distinctive feature of the nine greens came about as a result of the fire in 1659, which destroyed so much of the town. Over the years since, the somewhat haphazard rebuilding of the town in different architectural styles and the greens have given the place a charm of its own. Apart from St Edmund's church, the lighthouse, built in 1892, is another dominating and well known feature of the skyline.

Much of the town's history is preserved in the museum, the Sailors Reading Room and the RNLI Museum. The six guns prominent on Gun Hill are 18 pounder culverins cast in Elizabethan times and presented to the town in George II's reign. The Casino (1800) also on Gun Hill was built as a reading room, but of recent years has been used by the Coastguard.

To the south of the town are the common and marshes, donated in perpetuity to the people of Southwold by William Godyll in 1509. In addition to walking, the area is used for golf, tennis, cricket, rugby and soccer. Birdwatching is a popular pastime for inhabitants and visitors alike. Beyond the marshes lies the river Blyth whose harbour is used by fishermen and pleasure craft. The few fishing boats are all that is left of a once prosperous industry.

Past history of the sea is epitomised by the smugglers' window still to be seen at the Lord Nelson inn, and sections of brickwork thought to be part of a passageway from the cliffs to the inn have been found. Also here it has been said the ghost of a man in a frock coat has been seen to walk into the cliff. This is only one of the many ghostly stories.

At the north end of the sea front is the pier, now, because of storm damage, much shorter than it was when the Belle steamers used to call on their way from London up the east coast. Also here opposite the pier are the putting green and boating lakes.

Adnams Brewery is important to Southwold and its horse-drawn drays are a popular sight. St Felix' school on the outskirts provides jobs for a number of inhabitants.

Being a seaside holiday place there are, besides the two main hotels, various private hotels and boarding house establishments. In addition there is a generous supply of eating places besides all the public houses. In 1990 Southwold was awarded the Blue Flag for its clean beaches.

Sproughton ✎

What are people's reactions if you say you live in Sproughton? Do they vaguely know of the 'treacle mines' – the sugar beet factory which was built on Devils Wood during 1925. Or maybe they have heard of Sproughton Dockyard, where one could go for a pleasant afternoon boating. Other people might have experienced traffic difficulties along the narrow High and Lower Streets. The residents are thankful for the western bypass which was built in 1984/5. Or perhaps the 16th century Wild Man or the more recently converted Beagle have been a meeting place for friends. The Wild Man legend is that many years ago there was a ruffian roaming about the district. The villagers eventually caught him on the site of the inn which now bears his name.

Sproughton has been in existence for many centuries although it was not mentioned in the Domesday Book. During excavations many Neolithic/Bronze Age artefacts have been found showing that there were local encampments.

The picturesque mill house of the 1600s and the 18th century mill, which was last used for milling in 1947, has attracted many artists. In 1793 the river was converted into a navigable canal from Ipswich to Stowmarket. Barges ceased to ply the river in the 1930s.

Opposite the mill is the church of All Saints which has stood there since the 1200s. During the years it has been altered and extended, especially in the Victorian era. The 16th century rectory stands nearby.

Sproughton Hall is 17th century and the tithe barn is approximately of the same date. In 1978 Mrs N. Hughes Reckitt gave the barn to the village. Restoration work has been carried out and the place is now used for sports and other activities.

The almshouses in Lower Street were originally built by Elizabeth Bull of Boss Hall in 1634 and were rebuilt by Margaret Cooper in 1876 and modernised in 1976. Next to these is the 'Cage'. It is reputed that the last person to be confined escaped by breaking through the roof.

The village sign which is on the green depicts the mill and the legendary Wild Man. This was given by the WI in 1983 and was one of the last signs that Harry Carter of Swaffham carved.

In 1855 Sir Fitzroy Kelly of the Chantry built Chantry Row and over the middle arch is his crest and motto which reads 'Turris Fortis Mihi Deus' (God is a strong tower to me).

Abbey Oaks, a mock Tudor building, was erected in 1911 for Lord Woodbridge – who was then Arthur Churchman whose family were tobacconists. About the same time he had Marylands built for a children's home.

The now demolished 19th century Monks Gate was taken over by the government for French prisoners in the Napoleonic Wars. There was a rumour that there was a tunnel from this house to the church. Quite a number of locals had been frightened when they passed by old Monks Gate at midnight. It was said that a lady in white could be seen at a window holding a lighted candle and then she would walk from the house up Popes Pit opposite.

Stanton 🐦

Stanton was mentioned in the Domesday Book, but the Romans were here before that; the Peddars Way turns a corner at Stanton Chare, and nearby are the remains of a Roman villa. A walk along the main street past some attractive 16th century houses leads to a footpath known as the Grundle which is a miniature tree-lined gorge, a favourite place for walks.

Stanton is unusual in having two medieval churches, All Saints' and St John the Baptist. Both were in use within living memory but now St John's is roofless. But this does not stop villagers from holding a service there once a year.

The village is full of children's chatter; there are two schools, both new, a primary school and a middle school which serves the surrounding villages. Its name, Blackbourne, recalls the name of the medieval hundred.

Our American friends occupy some houses near High Wood. This American territory was leased to the USA during the Second World War in exchange for a shipload of tobacco.

About a mile outside the village is a small industrial estate which contains about 40 small businesses such as engineering and printing and a mushroom farm which provides local employment. Stanton is a lively active village with a population of about 2,000. It is well stocked with shops, a general store, a butcher, hardware shop, newsagent, hairdresser and a bakery which recently celebrated its centenary with the same family.

Stoke Ash 🌿

The village lies on either side of the Roman road, now the A140. The 'road' has always been the reason for the existence of Stoke Ash.

Newcomers looking for the post office are amazed to be directed to 'Stoke City' as Stoke Ash is a small place with only 230 inhabitants. So why a City? It is at the south end of the village on the east side of the road, a charming collection of timber-framed houses, some thatched and some brick.

This was in fact, the Roman citadel and many Roman artefacts have been found. The citadel must have been a convenient staging post near the ford and not far from the camp at Coddenham. The numbering of the houses adds to the present day illusion of a City. For centuries, the City houses were part of the Thornham estate, and these are numbered anti-clockwise through the villages round Thornham Magna, those in Stoke Ash being 137–158. In the old days, the centre of village life was the pump in the City near the old workhouse, the post office and shop, the pork butcher, the slaughter house, and the herring smoking plant. The fish were collected from Lowestoft and sold locally from the cart. Now only the post office and shop remain as the centre of village life.

Between 1930 and 1980, there have been three council house developments between the village hall and the church. Here is modern Stoke Ash, and between the village hall and the City private house infilling has taken place.

The middle section of the village, until the 1930s, consisted of farm-land with scattered cottages, farmhouses, the church of All Saints and the school. There was also the carpenter's shop, the cobbler, the cycle repairer and the blacksmith. The blacksmith's shop continues and, until recently, was a meeting place for farmers bringing their implements for repair. It has survived precariously on the busy A140 but is now frequented by gardeners having their shears sharpened and buying garden paving stones.

There is still a cycle repairer. The original one, Mr Lockwood, is remembered annually with gratitude. His affection for his old school prompted him to make a bequest from which every child, on leaving school, receives a book.

Colsey Wood House was at one time a very large H-shaped building with a moat and fish ponds. It was a Benedictine convent until the Dissolution when the nuns were said to have thrown a golden statue into the moat. Further legend has it that a tunnel connects it to Wood Hall.

214

Wood Hall Manor is first recorded in 1206. It is a moated house, the moat dating from the late 1300s and the present house from 1600.

The final hamlet is at the north end of the village. The turnpike, with its toll gate was sited here, but now the A140 has been straightened it has become a backwater. The chapel was built here in 1846 seating 600 and still serves many parishes. In the mid 1800s it had a famous preacher. One Sunday, when a woman arrived late for the service, he stopped speaking and rebuked her roundly for being late. She stood at the door and waved her pattens in the air and said, 'You would have been late, too, if you'd walked seven miles in the mud on these!'

Stoke-by-Nayland ✿

Stoke is a beautiful village of Constable Country with a large number of listed buildings, many of whose modestly plastered exteriors hide timber-framing going back sometimes as far as the 14th century. Three out-standing buildings, the Guildhall, the Maltings and the Black Horse inn, have had their timbers exposed in relatively recent years.

The village is still, to a considerable extent, an estate village, that of Tendring Hall, and during the 15th century it was a seat of Sir John Howard, who became the first Duke of Norfolk. He completed the work begun by his grandfather of rebuilding the church of St Mary, which today is a magnificent example of a church of the Perpendicular period. For the past 200 years or more the estate has been in the possession of the Rowley family, whose present day representative, Sir Joshua Rowley, is the Lord Lieutenant of Suffolk.

In the 1500s, at the height of its prosperity, the Guildhall would have been a very busy place as there were four guilds in all, and it would have been an impressive sight when they processed from the Guildhall through the lychgate to the north door of the church. A sad end to this pomp and glory came when the wool trade diminished and the Guildhall for a time became a workhouse. Nowadays the Guildhall forms three separate dwellings and one family has the pleasure of sleeping in the beautiful reception room with its lovely fireplace.

The poor were housed in two sets of almshouses. Those bequeathed by Lady Anne Windsor stand on the high bank, The Downs, as you reach the top of the hill from Nayland. Pretty, black and white tiny dwellings, they are still administered by trustees. The second set overlook the churchyard but these are no longer almshouses and belong to Babergh District Council.

As in a number of Suffolk villages there was a campen close, where for centuries a primitive form of football (camping or camp ball) was played – the name meaning 'struggle' as in Hitler's Mein Kampf. The game seems to have been one of unarmed combat and many injuries and even, in some villages, deaths were recorded.

The Black Horse, the Angel and the Crown public houses are all old buildings worthy of a visit for their catering and attract great numbers to the village and therefore provide jobs for the villagers. Stoke also has a large middle school and a newly extended primary school.

To the east of Stoke, about two miles on the Stoke/Higham road, you reach Thorington Street. Here you will find Thorington Hall, an Elizabethan house belonging to the National Trust and now the home of a well known author. Also in Thorington Street lives Mr John Death, Master Thatcher, whose family have been thatchers for at least a hundred years. Nearby at Weylands Farm, Roger and Cherry Clark have their wonderful Suffolk Punches and their land is still ploughed by these handsome creatures. At the bottom of Thorington Street, if you turn right into the lane, you will see Thorington Mill which is now being restored.

Stonham Aspal

In 1962 remains of a Roman bath house were uncovered on the outskirts of the village, proving the Romans had a settlement here. Remains had already been found previously in various parts of the village.

Stonham was mentioned in the Domesday Book (1086) and appeared to be measured in three parts, probably later becoming the three parishes of Stonham Aspal, Earl Stonham and Stonham Parva.

Robert de Aspal was rector of the village in 1294 living with his family at Broughton Hall and they gave their name to the village. The altar tomb in the church of a knight is supposed to be his. It is thought his family began the building of the church although it has been added to and altered many times since. The wooden top to the tower was built to house ten bells. Theodore Eccleston, an ardent campanologist who lived in Crowfield in 1742, had the five bells of the church taken down. Three and a half tons of metal was added to them and they were recast as ten bells. The original stone tower was not large enough to house all these bells. The Ten Bells has been taken appropriately for the name of the village pub situated opposite the church.

Broughton Hall is still surrounded by a moat and has an Act of Parliament clock still working. This was bought when time pieces were taxed in 1797 so villagers could see the time.

John Metcalf, a rector of the village who died in 1612, was a great benefactor to the village. In his will he left a large chest, and amongst various legacies was instruction to found a grammar school for boys of Stonham Aspal and neighbouring Pettaugh. The chest now resides in the church vestry and held church and village documents until recently. The Metcalf Grammar School began in 1667 and existed until 1872, when a Metcalf Educational Trust was formed. It still helps with the education of children in the village. The present village school began in 1845.

An interesting find in 1980 was a hoard of coins dated 1547–1625 at a derelict cottage. They were judged to be treasure trove, probably someone's life savings. As the value of the coins was quite high for that period however, and the cottage a humble dwelling, villagers much prefer the idea that they were gained illegally, possibly by highwaymen, and hidden there.

Originally, Stonham Aspal residents were occupied mainly in agriculture and allied trades such as blacksmith, carpenter, carrier, whitening maker, grocer and baker. New houses have been built and buildings changed, such as the Methodist church built in 1868 but sold in 1965 and converted to a house. On the site of the sawmill the village hall was built in 1933 and is still used regularly for village functions.

Now most village residents work mainly out of the village. Employment within the village is still found with agriculture, a furniture manufacturer,a jigsaw puzzle factory, a fruit farm with a commercial centre housing shops, a restaurant with conference facilities, a garden centre and a golf range. Unfortunately there is no longer a post office, but still a pub and a butcher's with a grocery section. Village sports facilities include tennis courts and a thriving football club.

Stowupland ◌

Stowupland Hall, built c1810, is situated to the north of Stowmarket. It has a strange ghost story attached to it, remembered by a former resident.

'My father lived in Stowupland Hall during the 1920s/1930s. In those days there was a large dining room, fireplace and two windows. When you sat by the fire in the winter time, at 8.00 pm precisely every evening you could hear a tapping noise come through the skirting board. It came from one of the windows right round to the fireplace. We thought it was mice. But no matter how many mice we caught from under the floorboards, the tapping continued.

'In 1945, Stowupland Hall was sold and the new owner told me that he had heard the tapping noise from the window to the fireplace too. When he died the Hall was taken over again and alterations made to the inside of the house.

'Near the front door there was a wide entrance hall that went straight through the house, and on one side of that hall, in the wall, there was a place which, when tapped, you could tell was hollow behind. When carrying out these alterations the new owner asked the builder to knock a piece of plaster off to see what this hollow space might reveal. There they found the remains of a child, a baby, that had been walled up for many years.

'As soon as they found the skeleton and the hollow place was made into an alcove, no further incidence of tapping was recorded in the dining room.

'The following may be an explanation and is a quote from Charles Freeman's diary, 30th September 1825. 'My wife was put to bed at noon of a stillborn male child'. There is no mention of a burial ceremony. As stillborn babies were unable to be christened they could not be buried in the churchyard. So could the remains found in the wall be of this poor baby?'

Stradbroke 🐑

'Statebroc' or 'Stetebroc' in the Domesday Book, the derivation of Stradbroke's name has been a matter of conjecture. There certainly was a brook, which is there to this day, and the village sign depicting 12th century Bishop Robert Grosseteste helping the 'poor wandering Suffolk poet' James Chambers, buried in the churchyard across the brook, is a constant reminder of its antiquity and continuity.

The 14th century All Saints' church is at the centre of the village and almost opposite the timbered black-and-white 15th century Town House given by Michael Wentworth, lord of the manor, in 1587. The Town House has been home to shops, a school, a poor house and even a fire engine, and modern times see it containing a hardware shop and a hairdresser as well as private residences. The church owes its high tower to 15th century William de la Pole, Earl of Suffolk, and shows a bright star at Christmas welcoming travellers not only to church and chapel or home, but also to the three inns in the village which all serve meals.

Stradbroke continues the tradition illustrated in its sign of mixing old and new, grand and ordinary, in its mixture of people and houses. There are 1,000 inhabitants living in a variety of houses, modern brick or ancient thatch, semi-detached or manor houses, all combining together into a unity.

Self-sufficient when snow blocks the way to Diss or Eye or Framlingham, the village boasts shops to supply every need. In the past it also had a chemist and once it produced gloves and hats. Versatile John Catchpole, who kept the Ivy House, not only made wine and had his name on the bottles but was hosier to Queen Alexandra. There are families whose names have been known in one form or other for generations and those who've come in recent years. Some work in the local shops and businesses, the post office, the bank, farms, offices, hospitals, schools and companies nearby and some commute to London.

There is a large retired population, many of whom work hard in the various clubs and societies held in the purpose-built village hall opened by the 'Aussie' Earl of Stradbroke in 1984. Out of one such group, the WEA, *Stradbroke Notes*, a collection of historical facts about the village, has been published, containing detailed documentation, and is available from the rectory or the post office.

Stratford St Mary 🌿

Stratford St Mary is the southernmost village in Suffolk, situated on the Essex border. Bounded by two hills, Gun Hill and Stratford Hill, the village lies in the valley of the river Stour, which runs through it. A possible site for a Roman encampment and temple, it finds fame in that Queen Boudicca certainly rode through it.

Although it was mentioned in the Domesday Book very little is known about the village before the 14th century. Parts of St Mary's date from 1200, but according to local wills the building of the present church really began about 1455 when the generosity of the Mors family made it possible for the western part of the north aisle to be completed. Most interest in the church is in the letters which are found round the exterior walls. Only one other church, in Germany, is thought to possess such inscriptions.

Stratford St Mary is in the heart of what is known as Constable Country and the subject of several paintings by the great artist, John Constable (1776–1837). Perhaps the most well-known is *The Young Waltonians*, a painting of the lock and river Stour which can be identified very clearly today. The mill was used to produce macaroni, but was also an oil mill, producing linseed oil from flax. A drawing by Constable entitled *A House in Water Lane* can also be identified since the house in the drawing is Ravenys, still standing and lived in today.

It is soon noticed that through the village are no less than four public houses, a reminder of the times when the main London road went through Stratford St Mary. During the late 18th and early 19th centuries trade with London flourished, and every schoolchild knows that turkeys and geese were herded through the village on their way to market. Gooseacre, a meadow next to The Corner House was known to be a resting place.

From 1800–1850 the population of the village was about 650, but during 1960–1970 it was only about 350, increasing noticeably present-day to approximately 750. The later figure is explained by the new development of houses built from 1970 onwards.

Certainly, Stratford St Mary is thriving, with many activities and organisations. There is a primary school, which serves several villages, as well as two shops, two garages and several businesses. The pumping station, on the bank of the river, has an important purpose, supplying water as far as the Abberton reservoir south of Colchester.

Sturmer 🌿

Sturmer is a small ribbon village in a finger of Essex which indents into the Suffolk borders near Haverhill. At first sight it may not excite the attention, but a closer inspection uncovers a long history.

On the Haverhill side there is a mound or tumulus, but its origin or purpose is still open to speculation. The church, close by, dates from Norman times and the graves record families who have lived in the village for generations.

Rubbing shoulders with the church is Sturmer Hall, a well proportioned house built on the site of a much older dwelling. Abbotts Hall is at the other end of the village, and the other properties range from small thatched or slate roofed cottages and timber-framed farmhouses, to council houses and modern houses built for commuters to Cambridge or London.

Beside the Red Lion public house was Dillistones Nursery. Here the Sturmer Pippin apple was propagated, but it grew better in New Zealand, where it was taken by a member of the family. The Dillistones were more renowned for the quality and variety of the violets they grew. Each evening bunches would be made up, and sent by train to London, where next morning they would accompany the breakfast trays served to lady guests in the best hotels.

Until the advent of easier transport the village was self sufficient. Osiers were grown on the meads and young people and the unemployed could earn money stripping them ready for the basket maker. There was a sweet maker, a sausage maker, greengrocer and fish merchant, a carpenter/coffin maker, a blacksmith, a postman, a grave digger, and a woman who 'laid out' the dead, to name but a few.

Electricity replaced oil in 1937 and a sewerage system was put through the village in the mid 1970s to replace septic tanks and a system quaintly referred to as 'bucket and chuck it' where all waste had to be buried every two or three days. There are even a few street lamps to lighten the darkness.

Stutton ✒

Stutton, never to be confused with Sutton or Stuston, both very different, is one of Suffolk's long, thin villages, hiding its undoubted charms away from the main road, and revealing its delights to the walker rather than the motorist.

The earliest settlement was probably below the church, where the Holbrook bay of the river Stour provided a source of food and water, and where the gently rising ground up to the church would have given shelter and warning of marauders. By Domesday, it boasted six manors, Stutton Hall, Crepping Hall, Crowe Hall, Alton Hall, Argents and the Rectory, and the settlements around these can still be defined and seen to be amalgamated into the village as we know it today. Rather sadly, there has been no one family associated with any one of these manors for any length of time, although Stutton Hall has had links at intervals with the Tollemache family since the 18th century.

At one time, in the 1790s, Queech Farm was famous under Mr King

Cottages at Stutton Village

for its Suffolk Punch horses, and in the middle of the 19th century there was an attempt made to bore for coal below Crepping Hall – how success there would have transformed the area! The river Stour which forms the southern boundary was once the main route to and from London, and all the big houses fronting the river still have traces of the loading stages used by the Thames barges which carried hay and local produce to London and returned with manure from the London horses, manure which carried diseases and was responsible for many epidemics.

In the 19th century, Rev Thomas Mills was rector and village benefactor for 60 years. Chaplain to four monarchs, he enlarged and re-ordered the church, founded the village school, and started many of the 26 clubs and societies which still flourish today.

Over the last few years a corner of the parish has disappeared under the waters of Alton Water reservoir, a feature which has brought an influx of water sports enthusiasts plus walkers of the many footpaths – a mixed blessing, with corresponding increases in traffic and litter. No longer is Stutton the agricultural community it remained for 800 years, but neither is it yet a dormitory suburb, and it possesses a great community spirit which makes anyone who has moved in reluctant to leave.

Sweffling 🦡

Sweffling lies on the east bank of the river Alde. The village is scattered, with a main Street. St Mary's church looks over the village, and is set high on glacial gravel. St Mary's most important treasure is a 14th century leather wine-bottle cover, about eleven inches high and with

221

richly tooled decorations. It is kept in Christchurch Mansion, Ipswich. Sweffling covers 1,120 acres and has a population of 159.

There were three small manors in Sweffling, Dernford being the largest. Dernford Hall is the oldest house in the village, dating back to Tudor times. The original Elizabethan manor house was destroyed by fire in the 19th century.

The village has always been inhabited by working people. The majority of men in the mid 19th century were agricultural labourers, with a small group of farmers and blacksmiths. Sweffling had several drillmakers working for the Smyth brothers of Peasenhall. One brother, Jonathan, lived in Sweffling and was buried in St Mary's church in 1868.

Early in the 19th century Sweffling had a general store and two sweet shops. Fish and chips were served from an old railway carriage until it burned down. Milk, butter and eggs were bought from the farms. There were three mills in the village where corn was ground into flour. Pork was delivered by the village pork butcher, who went on foot, basket on arm.

Today there are no shops, the villagers go to nearby Framlingham or Saxmundham. School was held in the vestry in St Mary's church, until the National school was opened in Rendham in 1841 (now the village hall). New school premises were later built, but with the decline in village population this also closed and presently children are bussed to Saxmundham and Leiston.

The village has a thriving public house which was built in 1810 by the Kerr family, who owned many local pubs and brewed their own beer. In the 1840s records show that several coroner's inquests were held in the White Horse.

A big annual money-raising event is the Sweffling Street Fair, the proceeds going to both church and village hall upkeep. On the day, the Street is closed and the stalls set up along the roadside. Each year there is a different fancy dress theme.

The cricket club and tennis club have recently created a tennis court and cricket ground, with a pavilion for both clubs to share. In recent years the bowls club has moved to a new green in the village.

Syleham 🐝

The small but scattered village of Syleham lies in the lovely Waveney valley. It is made up approximately of 1,607 acres of land and eight acres of water. It may be that Syleham derives its name from an Anglo-Saxon word 'sylu' meaning 'a miry place', which is a good description of that part of the village bordering the Waveney where the marshy water meadows are – and where the luminous marsh gases, called 'Will-o'-the-Wisp' or known locally as Syleham Lamps, frequently led travellers astray in the old days.

The church is well worth a visit. It is very old with its Anglo-Saxon tower and stands alone, connected with the rising ground to the south by a raised causeway. Somewhere near the causeway leading down to the church stood the Cross and here in 1174 Hugh Bigod surrendered his castles of Bungay and Framlingham to Henry II after leading a rebellion against the King. In the spring the daffodils and snowdrops bid a warm welcome. Modern references to this church speak of a dedication to St Mary, but there is evidence that it was once dedicated to St Margaret and that is what the people of Syleham prefer.

Monks Hall belonged to the monks of Thetford and at that time it consisted of 240 acres with a mill and a church. It now belongs to Colonel Leader, who bought the Hall in 1936. It is a fine timber-framed house mainly dating back to the 16th century and has over recent years been lovingly restored. The Leader family has always played an important part in the community.

The manor house of Syleham Comitis was held for many years by the Earls of Suffolk, Wingfields and de la Poles. The present house dates back to the very early 16th century, but it is mostly an 18th century house now.

It was on the banks of the Waveney that the old water mill stood which was in existence when the Domesday survey was compiled. Visitors to Syleham can still enjoy a walk by the river. Alas the old mill disappeared centuries ago, but in White's Suffolk directory of 1844 reference is made to 'an extensive water corn mill which was converted into a linen and cotton manufactury about five years ago'. Locally grown flax produced drabbet and other cloths. More recently girls used to cycle from many areas of Norfolk and Suffolk to work in what was known as Syleham Mills. Richard Emms, who owned this mill for many years, lived nearby in Syleham House, overlooking the river. The firm was finally taken over by F. W. Harmer of Norwich and it went from producing jackets, trousers and jodhpurs to jeans. It was at the beginning of 1990 that it closed down with the loss of many jobs.

There is also a windmill, one of only six examples remaining in East Suffolk, known as a post mill, which was brought over from Wingfield on rollers across the fields. It was working until recent years and the last miller, Mr Bryant had two women working for him who did the hard work of stonegrinding the flour. Unhappily the old mill was more or less destroyed in the hurricane of 1987 and lies in ruins.

Like many small villages, the school, public houses and post office are all closed. The two pubs, the Black Horse and the White Horse, are both now private houses. The small school closed just before the Second World War, most of the children going to nearby Wingfield. It is now the village hall, which is shared by Wingfield and was extended in 1988.

Tattingstone 🌿

'One and two halves to Tattingstone' was the rather macabre joke in 1967 when two suitcases containing a dismembered body were discovered in the gateway to a field skirting the road to Bentley. For several months the unsolved murder focused attention on the village which is situated on the edge of the Shotley peninsula, six miles from Ipswich on the A137 to Manningtree.

Pieces of Romano/British pottery suggest that there has long been settlement here and certainly by the 6th century the Saxons had given it the name of Tatituna. By the time of the Domesday survey the village was made up of three Anglo-Saxon manors and even today the village is clustered in three areas.

Until the early 20th century, Tattingstone was very much a traditional manorial village with most of the land held by one family. The early 18th century brought radical change when those who had made money in trade were able to indulge in property speculation, like Thomas White of Gloucester who bought the run-down estate and promptly ordered the building of a fine new 'palace'. His son, also Thomas, set about landscaping his parkland and planting many of the magnificent trees which have survived disease, hurricanes and the Anglian Water Authority. It was this Thomas who was responsible for the addition of a folly.

The much larger red brick house which dominates the centre of the village was the Samford House of Industry built in 1764 to give a home to and provide work in the weaving business for the poor of the surrounding villages. Among those who found refuge there in the latter half of the 1700s was Anne Candler who during her 25 years stay regularly contributed poems for publication in the *Ipswich Journal*. The workhouse had an isolation hospital to which, in former days, locals suffering from diphtheria or scarlet fever were brought for nursing. It also had its own cemetery outside the main grounds. Today, this area, where grave markers can still be seen, is preserved as a wildlife sanctuary. The walls surrounding the old building came down and in 1948, it became St Mary's Hospital specialising in geriatric care. Plans for the hospital's closure leave a question mark hanging over the future of one of the village's most important landmarks.

St Mary's church is unusual in that the entrance is via the north door from the main road through the village. The south doorway looks out on to the green – now used as a recreational area for tennis, football and cricket. At the far end is a bridlepath, probably once a main road, which runs from Pond Hall up to the Heath and the A137.

The Waterloo was opened originally in 1815 to serve as an alehouse for the estate workers and is still carrying a six-day licence. Its adjoining shop which houses the community post office is the only one now left.

Another sign of the times was the closing of the Methodist chapel which once served surrounding villages. Fortunately, this fine example of early Victorian building has been skilfully converted into four dwellings. There has been some new building in the village but not enough to change the character of the place.

The biggest change in recent time was wrought by Anglian Water Authority with their construction of the Alton Water reservoir. Initially this meant the destruction of woodland copses and fine specimen trees as well as cottages and farmhouses. The ancient moated Tattingstone Hall was among the casualties. It was feared that the White Horse area would be cut off from the main part of the village by the flooding but the erection of the spectacular Lemon's Hill bridge solved that. The road that passes the White Horse now ends at the water's edge, making it hard to realise that it was once an important main road and the White Horse, with its adjoining smithy, a very busy coaching inn.

Thurston ✒️

Thurston is a village that, since the Second World War, has grown and is still growing. It lies four and a half miles to the east of the expanding market town of Bury St Edmunds. A directory dated 1844 quotes the population as 599, the present population would probably be somewhere around 3,000. A new estate being built is now joining what were virtually two separate halves of the village.

The church, St Peter's, was rebuilt in 1860 after the tower collapsed one night. The story is that the lad passing at the time was afraid to say anything in case he was blamed for the collapse. The stained glass windows in the church are mainly Victorian although there are fragments left of the medieval glass from the previous 14th century church. One modern window in the south aisle is a replacement made necessary after an American Flying Fortress crashed with a full bomb load, fortunately only blowing out the one window.

Thurston station has been kept open, after threat of closure during the Beeching era, although now only a 'halt'. The busy goods shed, signalbox and staff have all gone. There are of course accidents where there is a busy railway and one recorded in November 1863 is of a 43 year old woman who was killed instantly after falling over the banisters at the station. It was assumed that she was attempting to slide down these same banisters. We used to attempt this as children, but at 43!

There are three public houses in the village, all of them have been there for some considerable time. One is recorded in the 1844 directory and the other two in a directory for 1892. It was certainly easier to drive home in those earlier days if you were 'over the limit'. One publican regularly loaded a gentleman from an adjoining village into his trap, giving the pony a slap, knowing the gentleman would be transported safely home by the pony.

The village hall, known as the Cavendish Hall, was given to Thurston in 1912 in memory of William Tyrrell Cavendish who was one of the unfortunate passengers to go down with the *Titanic*. There is now a new community centre, opened in 1991.

The old granary buildings have been restored and have become a small unit business centre, and the station staff houses also house a business. Shops include a post office and general stores, bakers, butchers and hairdresser.

Trimley St Martin
& Trimley St Mary 🌿

The twin villages of Trimley St Martin and Trimley St Mary are situated between the Orwell and the Deben rivers within the Felixstowe peninsula. One of their notable features is that the two churches are in the one churchyard. The local tale of two quarrelsome sisters building the two churches to vie with each other has no basis in fact.

Trimley's most famous son was Thomas Cavendish, who lived at Grimston Hall. He was an Elizabethan adventurer, born 1560 and lost at sea in 1592. He was the second Englishman to circumnavigate the world, bringing home much booty. The village sign of Trimley St Martin depicts Cavendish, and the Mariners pub in St Mary's has a painting outside showing his three ships. Also on the village sign is an inscription attributed to Cavendish, 'My God, said Thomas Cavendish, whatever may befall, I'll ever love dear Trimley and the oaks of Grimston Hall'! The old French cannon standing at the corner of Gunn Lane was probably brought back by sailors.

At one time the inhabitants of Trimley were known as 'Treacle Miners', perhaps connected with the digging out of coprolite, the forerunner of fertilizer. In 1914/18 in Trimley and district there was the last recorded outbreak of bubonic plague, when five people died in Trimley.

Today's inhabitants of what is almost a small town in population are employed at Felixstowe dock, British Telecom at Martlesham and industry in Ipswich. Farming is still carried on but with much reduced numbers. The villages' two halls are well used and sporting activities such as bowls, football, tennis and squash are all enjoyed. There are two public houses, the Mariners in St Mary and the Hand in Hand in St Martin.

Troston 🌿

The village of Troston lies seven miles north-east of Bury St Edmunds, close to Breckland and bordering the RAF base at Honington. The parish of 1,779 acres is triangular in shape with the apex at Rymer, formerly Ringmere. Here ten parishes meet, originally given access to the water.

The population of 780 includes service families housed about a mile from the village centre.

Earliest evidence of habitation is the tumuli situated on former heathland. These are believed by archaeologists to date from the Bronze Age 2000–1500 BC. Troston Mount, the largest of the three remaining mounds, stands adjacent to Broadmere, earlier called Bradmere, and it may have been used before the Norman Conquest as the meeting place of the Court of the Bradmere Hundred, an old administrative district.

Until the enclosures of the 19th century, nearly half the parish consisted of heathland, supporting sheep rearing. Gradually it came under the plough, and finally disappeared in the Second World War – a sad loss to the village.

The present church of St Mary was begun about 1200, and the chancel shows the Early English style of architecture. Wall paintings in the nave of St George and the dragon, St Christopher, and a Doom picture are of particular interest. In 1983 Troston welcomed its present woman priest.

At the Reformation the manor of Troston passed from the Abbey of St Edmunds to the Bacon family, whose descendants were related to Francis Bacon. They built Troston Hall in the early 17th century.

In the following century the Lofft family inherited the estate. Robert Lofft was a great benefactor to Troston, which by this time was a larger, Victorian, self-sufficient village, with a mill, a brickworks, two blacksmiths, a wheelwright, five shoemakers, a butcher, a baker, a tailor, a general store, a Methodist chapel and two public houses. Lofft restored the church, built a school and a school house, and eight three-storey cottages for his workers. He refronted Troston Hall and other houses with bricks made in Troston. Many of them were stamped with his own design and can be seen today. During his lifetime he bought any land that was for sale, until he owned almost the entire village. However, his ventures left him bankrupt, and he had to leave the Hall to live in one of his worker's cottages. After his death in 1900 the estate was put in the hands of trustees, and it was sold as a whole in 1919, but in 1923 it was split up and sold in lots. By then the population had decreased and most of the amenities of the former century had disappeared.

Today Troston is a typical agricultural dormitory village. There are two farms; one of 1,178 acres is owned by the German industrialist, Helmut Claas, and the other by John Browning, lord of the manor. Fourteen buildings are listed. The Methodist chapel has been converted into a post office and store, and there is a garage where the wheelwright's once stood. Business ventures in woodcrafts, dried flower products and hairdressing are now well established. The school, which closed in 1945, has become the village hall, where organisations catering for all ages meet.

Due to service and business life, part of the population is continually changing, but some people have put down roots. Troston is a quiet village, except when the jets roar overhead.

Tuddenham St Martin 🎑

Tuddenham St Martin is a small village four miles north-east of Ipswich, with 309 on the electoral roll. Small groups of houses have been built in the last 50 years, but in The Street the cottages which once housed families of up to ten children are now home to young couples from the town, who, sadly, often feel the need to move when the second baby is born. These terraced cottages have no garages, so car parking is a problem for residents in the narrow village street. Otherwise the street must look much the same as it did 100 years ago.

The hill is crowned by the church, St Martin's, which dates from Norman times, perhaps even Saxon times, and there is still a Norman doorway in the north wall. Inside the church the stone font dates from 1443, and there is a beautifully carved medieval pulpit. The pews are mostly 15th century, with animal carvings and poppy heads on the pew ends.

At the turn of the century brick making was a very important industry, the clay being dug at the top of the village, washed in a pit behind Oak House, and sent through a large pipe which ran behind the cottages in The Street to the brickyard which was near the present Brickfield House.

There was a forge in the centre of the village, and up on the hill stood the windmill, long since gone, but in more recent times there was a mill where the houses in The Granaries now stand. It supported about 20 families and produced animal feeds and malt. Bushells of malt and hops were available for home brewing, to be used by farmers at harvest time. Mr Douglas Green, the last owner, closed the mill in 1982.

There were several shops in the village – one at the Old Post Cottage, a bakery, also a butcher's shop, and next to that the abattoir, which operated on Tuesday – Ipswich market day – and had above it a reading room. More recently there was a village shop and post office in the centre of the village, but that also closed and is still greatly missed.

Down by the river Fynn is the Fountain, dating from the 14th century. In the early days it is said to have provided refreshment for the drovers taking their stock to market in Ipswich, and for this purpose opened at 5.30 am on market day. In 1905 it was taken over by the Parker family, who were also builders' merchants, and it was in this family until recently.

There are eight farms in the parish, but they employ far fewer people than in years gone by. The traditional crops of sugar beet, wheat, winter barley and feed beans now have added to them oil seed rape, linseed, runner beans, asparagus, chicory and even Christmas trees. One farm has embraced 'set aside', combined with conservation work. There is a flourishing Pick-Your-Own site on the outskirts of the village, offering raspberries, loganberries, blackcurrants and blackberries in season.

Tuddenham St Mary 🦋

Tuddenham St Mary, dating back to at least AD 854, derives its Anglo-Saxon name from the phrase 'Tudda's Home' and has charm, character and history.

In the 1801 census there were 268 inhabitants but this has now grown to approximately 400, including some personnel from the nearby American airbases at Mildenhall and Lakenheath.

The village enjoys the benefit of a number of charities, one of which is the Cockerton Trust, founded by John Cockerton in 1723 to provide a free school for poor boys and girls of Tuddenham. A new school was built in 1962 and now accepts pupils from surrounding villages who are transported here by bus.

A mill was known to exist here in Saxon times and is mentioned in the Domesday Book. The present building dates from the 18th century and has been renovated and converted into a superior restaurant featuring the water wheel and exposed beams. The river Linnett, a tributary of the river Lark, leads to the mill and was used to carry grain and flint in barges during the 19th century.

Many of the buildings, including the old bakery, the smithy and the original Methodist chapel, were constructed of flints. The chapel was demolished during the Second World War by a bomb which exploded in the street nearby. It was rebuilt in 1951 and both it and the 14th century parish church remain open for worship. One of the five bells in the

Tuddenham Mill

church is inscribed 'Thomas Draper made me 1591' and registers date from 1563.

A ghost, of the headless variety, lightly clad and riding a horse, is said to be seen galloping over the meadows by the river at Temple Bridge. According to legend, Temple Bridge was a notorious highwayman's hold-up point on the old coaching route that passed through the village.

Today Tuddenham is still surrounded almost entirely by farmland, much of it trust land, but a variety of other businesses operate from within the village. It retains one of the three original pubs, a post office/ general store and many clubs and sporting activities which help to preserve the community spirit unique to a village environment.

Ufford 𝔤𝔢

Ufford's history can be traced back to Anglo-Saxon times with certainty, and probably beyond. At the heart of this quiet, old village is the church with its wealth of woodwork and font cover, dating from the second half of the 15th century, said to be the most beautiful in the world. The cover is telescopic, rising to a height of 18 ft in tiers of canopied niches, topped by a carved pelican. The rectory, built during the same period, is one of the few medieval priest's houses left in Suffolk. Outside the church, the 18th century stocks and whipping post are still in good condition – perhaps they were not used very much!

Other old buildings include the almshouses near the church, a pictures-que pair built by Bishop Wood in the second half of the 17th century; they had lain empty since 1986 but now have been beautifully moderni-sed. The Dower House, also close to the church, was built about 1715, and Ufford Green, frequently mentioned in old deeds, was largely absorbed in its grounds. The two inns both date from the 17th century, the Crown on the highroad taking its name from Restoration days when it was built, and the White Lyon is older still. Finally, worth mentioning, are the Sickhouses which were built to provide isolation for villagers during the plague.

Ufford is the birthplace of the famous Suffolk Punch, which is depicted on the village sign. The original, Crisp's horse 404 of Ufford, was foaled in 1768 and from him are descended virtually all Suffolk horses to the present day. Mr Thomas Crisp of Ufford advertised his stallion in 1773, 'to get good stock for coach or road' at a fee of five shillings. No name was given to the horse but he was described as a five year old bright chestnut, standing a full 15½ hands. Mr Crisp's route was to the Greyhound at Kirton, the Lion at Martlesham, the Queen's Head at Woodbridge, the Bell at Saxmundham, and the Crown inn at Framling-ham.

The buildings have all been modernised in one way or another over the years, and so has the way of life. Only 100 years ago this was dominated by the estate system, the Squire up at the 'Big House', namely Ufford Place, and the villagers in the cottages in the surrounding lanes.

It would seem that not only the buildings have changed but also the weather. There was one special event eagerly awaited each year – the Ice Carnival. The river from Melton to Ufford used to flood frequently and always froze as the winters were colder. During the Carnival cars were parked so that the headlights lit the ice, all the trees were decorated with coloured ribbons and paper and there was dancing and ice-hockey.

And now, the Big House is no more. Modern houses have mushroomed over part of the estate, and recently a golf course has been constructed over much of the rest. Community spirit and concern for the welfare of neighbours is still evident, although of a different kind from a century ago.

Walberswick 🐟

Imagine a fishing centre of some importance; 13 barques are trading with Iceland and the Faroe Islands, whilst 22 fishing boats are setting out from the harbour. This was Walberswick in 1450. As it prospered, so a great new church was built where prayers could be said for those at sea.

Gradually the coastline changed, due to a combination of erosion and the southerly drift of shingle along the coast, which created a bar at the mouth of the harbour. Fishing and trading suffered, and when all church lands and revenues were seized by the King in 1538, and a severe fire followed soon after, the prosperity of Walberswick declined dramatically, leaving the town very poor and depopulated. So, in 1585, the great bell of the church had to be sold, and 100 years later a smaller church was built within the old. This is still in use today. The ruins of the former church give an indication of its size.

Over the centuries, storms and floods have devastated this part of the Suffolk coast, causing the loss of hundreds of ships and much damage to property. The most recent severe flood, in 1953, breached the sea wall in several places; many fishing boats were carried away, including the ferry boat. A ferry has existed between Walberswick and Southwold for hundreds of years, although its operation has changed since its commencement, from rowing to chain ferry, to steam ferry, and back again to rowing.

In 1986, the village sign, depicting a sailing ship, was stolen from the outskirts of the village and never recovered, but an exact copy now stands proudly on the village green. Here too can be found the old school, now The Parish Lantern; and what was once a Congregational chapel is now the Heritage Centre, providing information on all aspects of the district. Other interesting buildings are the Mercer's Hall, an old timber-framed house brought piecemeal from Lavenham in the 1920s; Valley Farm, with its king post roof truss, dating from at least the 17th century; and the old fish warehouses near the ferry, some built on stilts.

During the 20th century, the village has lost many of its amenities: the railway ceased operation before the Second World War, the school finally closed in 1976, and petrol is no longer obtainable, but there is still a general store and post office. Today Walberswick has over 400 residents. There is only one professional fisherman living in the village, but visitors bring their families to take part in the annual crabbing competition in aid of charity, and to go yachting and fishing for pleasure.

Waldringfield

The Waldringfield of today is a small piece of Suffolk rural delight. The village has an area of 904 acres of land and notably 190 acres of tidal river, salt marsh and foreshore. The core of the village settles comfortably into its pleasing farming aspects. The population growth has been modest, 228 in 1871, 281 in 1971, and around 380 in 1990. Thus the new building has generally grown into the village without jarring one's sensibilities.

The estuary of the Deben is generally acknowledged as one of the most beautiful in eastern England and the stretch which lies in Waldringfield as one of its loveliest parts.

In the spring of 1921 eleven enthusiastic sailors and lovers of the river met in a beach hut on the foreshore and from this humble beginning grew Waldringfield Sailing Club. The present membership stands at 650. Matching the Sailing Club's membership is that of Waldringfield Heath Golf Club which opened as a nine hole course in 1983. In a few years it has developed into a full 18 hole course with a most welcoming clubhouse.

Probably the oldest sporting club, however, is the Cricket Club which has been playing to a high standard since around 1900. Its playing field epitomises the traditional concept of the rural setting of the game.

This is very much a living village. However, its life from 1860 to 1907 was very different. As one wanders around Waldringfield one will come across many pits and hollows of various sizes. The coprolite industry thrived alongside the Deben during the latter half of the 19th century. The workmen digging in these pits to extract the coprolite were known as 'The Owd Cooprolitors' or 'The Men in Red', for their clothes were as red as the crag in which they slaved. Sometimes as much as a thousand tons was dug from fields near the Maybush inn and taken by barge to be ground and turned into super-phosphates by Fisons and Packards of Ipswich. Larger deposits found overseas and the development of artificial fertilisers brought the industry to an end in 1893.

'The Men in Grey' arrived in 1872 when Mr George Mason decided that there was more than enough of the raw materials of mud and chalk locally available to make Waldringfield Cement Works a viable proposition. Twelve kilns were at the heart of the operation and when they were fired all windows and doors were closed to try to keep out the foul fumes although the visual effects were impressive from afar. Hardly less environmentally damaging were the noise and dust caused when the great crushing mill was operating, whose 30cwt iron balls reduced cement clinker to powder. Tranquillity returned when the outdated process was moved to a modern plant at Claydon in 1907.

One is not long in Waldringfield before the dynastic name of Waller is mentioned. Their family of clerics, landowners, engineers and so on has been a force in the village for well over a century. The Rev T. H. Waller became rector of All Saints in 1862. His great grandson continues to serve the church today as did his father and grandfather before him.

Walsham-le-Willows 🌿

Walsham-le-Willows, a designated conservation area, is a picturesque 'street' village with a stream flowing throughout its length.

Puritans are believed to have removed the missing carved angels from the hammer beams in the beautiful, mainly 15th century church of St Mary. Suspended in the nave is a rare example of a 'Virgin's Crant', a tiny circular memorial dated November 1685 to Mary Boyce who died 'of a fatal wound from Cupid's Shaft'. This memorial was customarily garlanded with a profusion of white ribbons on the anniversary of her death and was an emblem of her reward in Heaven for her virginity.

Many of the older buildings in Walsham are near the church. The 15th century priory, now the rectory, formerly belonged to the abbey of Ixworth. The village museum exhibits during the summer months in the old scullery. Though very small, the museum gives a true flavour of past times in Walsham. Tiled Cottage, dating from the late 14th century, is believed to be the oldest remaining dwelling.

Two old public houses remain – the Six Bells (16th century) and the Blue Boar. In the late 17th and 18th century the latter held the annual Petty Sessions for the Hiring and Retaining of Servants. The custom, originating from Acts of Parliament, declared that ploughmen and other farm workers should be hired for a full year, not just day by day. By the middle of the 18th century, it embraced servants of all kinds. The weatherboarded houses opposite were once a workhouse.

Although times were hard, there were occasions in the year when people were able to enjoy themselves. One such event was the Ancient Order of Forresters' Annual Gala, held on what is now the sports field. Unfortunately things went tragically wrong on Monday 3rd July 1911. A fair was in attendance and an argument broke out about change given on the steam horses. Walsham men tried to wreck the horses and the fair people shot at them with rifles from the target stall. Serious shooting started when the locals fetched their own rifles from home. A passer-by in a pony and trap, the publican from the Anchor at Blo' Norton, received a fatal bullet wound. Seven other men received bullet wounds, while several more people received other injuries. It is reputed to rain in Walsham each year on the anniversary of the riot.

During alterations to the Priory the doubled-up skeleton of a 15 or 16 year old girl was found buried in a basement kitchen. One or two other bodies have been found in unexpected places and, with such a long history, it is hardly surprising that several ghosts are reputed to haunt the village and its surroundings. For example, on a bitterly cold New Year's Eve, a witch gathering sticks by the Badwell Road was knocked down by a coach and horses which failed to stop. Before she died she cursed the coachman. It is said that every New Year's Eve the coach travels the same road and continues through Walsham to Stanton. All who see it are supposed to drop down dead, or to die shortly afterwards.

Wangford cum Henham 🐚

In 1844 it was noted that Wangford was a large village on the river Wang, from which it got its name, situated four miles north-west of Southwold and on the Ipswich to Yarmouth road. Its parish was in two townships, Wangford and Henham, the latter being the manor of the area and the seat of the Earl of Stradbroke. Henham Hall was demolished in 1953.

The church of St Peter and St Paul is Perpendicular in style. The church originally had a wooden tower with a spire, over the north-east end of the nave, but in 1865 this was taken down and a new tower with five bells was begun. This tower, which still exists, was finished in 1870 and for some reason was placed at the eastern end of the church instead of the more orthodox western end. Against the churchyard is the site of an ancient arcade, a relic of a priory for the Cluniac monks. The present church was built on the site of the priory.

There are several old houses in the village. The vicarage is early 18th century with 19th century alterations and today has been split into three dwellings. Well Cottage has 1622 on the wall, but this has been disputed and 1755 is thought to be a more likely date. There are still two pubs, the Poacher, once an 18th century coaching inn and the Plough which dates back to late 17th century. There were several more pubs but these are now private houses.

In 1844 there were three blacksmiths, five boot and shoe makers, two farmers, two tailors, three publicans, a vet, a baker, a plumber/glazier/ painter, two beerhouses, two butchers, two grocer/drapers, a wheelwright, a timber merchant, a saddler, a corn miller, and a day and boarding school. Today there is just one good store/post office, plus a well used Barn Shop which grows and sells its own vegetables and much more besides.

At one time there were two mills, one was burnt down in 1928 and only the base of the other remains. There were also two chapels, but these are no longer in existence.

The main A12 road used to run through the centre of the village, but now there is a bypass and the village is much quieter. The village has a council estate and a new private estate, but is still compact. Many of the houses are holiday homes.

Wantisden ❧

This tiny village between Tunstall and Butley, which in the last half century has become completely overshadowed by Bentwaters air base, can be easily overlooked.

The small Norman church of St John with its tower made of hard corraline crag, dug from local pits, stands immediately beside the perimeter fence. Inside are some interesting features: the massive ancient font made entirely of small blocks of stone, the old plain benches, the ends pierced for rush light tapers and the carved Norman chancel arch flanked on either side by hagioscopes, or holy squints, through which members of the congregation could see the Elevation of the Host at Mass. There is an air of peace and tranquillity within this building in spite of its noisy neighbour.

Much of the acreage of the parish has been absorbed into the air base, but one large farm remains, and a scattering of cottages; the population is less than 50. This large farm has become noted for the efficiency of its irrigation and the excellence of its crops, a great contrast to the 450 acres cultivated in 1946 when it was calculated that the rabbit population was 9,000. It is also famous for the advanced conservation work in the river valleys and the Staverton Park area at the southern end of the parish; the reservoirs have been naturalised and attract a large number of birds, fallow deer wander over the area and recently red deer have been installed in a fenced deer park. Staverton Park is the remains of an ancient forest, a tangle of pollarded oaks and hollies, and was once hunted over by visiting royalty. On the edge of this area near the boundary with Eyke is a picnic place from which signposted walks lead over attractive countryside of heath and woodland.

About a mile to the south of the church is Wantisden Hall, a medieval manor house rebuilt in the 16th century by the Wingfield family. Wantisden was never a compact cluster of houses around the church; it was always scattered cottages in fertile pockets of soil all over the adjoining heath, linked to the central point of the church by a maze of tracks, some sheltered by ancient hedges of thorn and maple, others open, sandy tracks. Changes in farming from the intensive arable of the early Middle Ages to the prosperous sheep farming in the 15th century were hastened by changes in the weather. In dry periods the sandy heath soil was swiftly eroded by fierce spring winds, the population moved to fertile valleys nearby and the village became depopulated. There were many additional causes for the migration from this heathland settlement, but none of them was the Black Death; there is no record that it ever affected this parish.

Wenhaston with Mells 🐴

A well used footpath passes near a Bronze Age burial ring at the top of Star Hill. Here we find 'Peggy's Stile' – Peggy is said by some to have been a donkey, by others to have been a witchlike old woman. Whoever, or whatever, she has some ancient significance (perhaps as the guardian of the burial ring) for within living memory, naughty children have been threatened with, 'Peggy will get you'!

Roman potsherds, brooches, nails, glass, and heating tiles have been found here after fields have been ploughed, and near Blyford a six inch statue of Venus came to light.

Willelmus Treluskant farmed here in the 16th century and his great grandson, John Tradescant, is said to be 'the first English gardener'.

Saxon stones are embedded in the walls of St Peter's and a church was certainly there in 1086. The treasured Doom painting on a wood panel is to be seen within. This is reputedly the work of a 15th century monk from Blythburgh Priory. He obviously had some knowledge of female anatomy despite his calling, and a number of his subjects for the Day of Judgement show signs of medieval rickets.

There were alehouses in the village in former times, of course, (Rev Ambler was in trouble for visiting them in 1644). The present Compasses inn (then called the Anchor) was there in 1745. The Star inn dates from the 18th century.

Young men in the village often started work as poorly paid farm workers, especially in the summer months. A number went to sea in addition, in the herring drifters from Lowestoft, which offered better prospects. Some sailed to Ireland, following the herring shoals, and there bought donkeys which came back to local ports with them. They rode the poor beasts to their homes to be sold and grazed on the commons.

The five commons in the village served many useful purposes. Privileges included grazing, and collecting gorse stalks to fire the old brick ovens for bread-making. The grandfather of a present villager had a smoke house on his farm where he produced delicious bloaters made from local herrings smoked over oak dust.

There have, of course, been local artists and craftsmen. In 1928, Harry Becker died in the village having spent the last 30 or so years of his life here. His work is largely unknown, but an exhibition in 1988 showed his etchings depicting the drudgery and heavy rhythm of agricultural work before machinery eased the lot of the farmworker. He knew, too, the intimate relationship of man and beast in those hard times.

Westerfield ⚜

Through the ages the threat of war and the need to defend our shores has brought a dramatic, though temporary, increase in the population of many a tiny village and of none more so than Westerfield on the outskirts of Ipswich. To combat the threat of invasion by Napoleon Bonaparte some 10,000 troops were assembled and reviewed upon the green; a large area of open land in the centre of the village.

A memorial in the parish church commemorates a Major J. R. Whitefoord who, having successfully survived the Napoleonic Wars, was accidentally shot by a friend while out shooting. Another wall plaque in the church is dedicated to Henry Munro Cautley FSA, ARIBA, one of Westerfield's best known citizens. The son of a former rector, his books on Norfolk and Suffolk churches and also on Royal Arms in churches are standard works of reference. He will be known locally for having designed St Augustine's church, Ipswich and the Bartlett Convalescent Home, Felixstowe.

The church of St Mary Magdalene has one of the best examples in the county of Suffolk of a single hammer beam roof. Where the wallposts meet the ends of the hammer beams are angels with outstretched wings and also kings and queens carrying shields displaying emblems of the Passion. Where original, they are fine examples of the medieval woodcarvers' skill.

The village has now lost its rural flavour, the manor house no longer being the centre of farming activity, although housing developments in the 1970s and 1980s have been tasteful and mainly infilling. It has become a very desirable place to live for business people commuting to Ipswich, and further afield, hence a considerable drop in the numbers of young children who, in the past, would have attended the village school.

Westhorpe ⚜

Westhorpe is a small village situated in the heart of rural Suffolk, eight miles from Stowmarket and 15 miles from Bury St Edmunds. It is a small community of about 130 people. A compact village, it consists of one street containing most of the dwellings surrounded by farmland, in all a total of about four square miles. There are several houses of great charm in the village and thatched cottages sit comfortably beside modern houses and bungalows.

The Old Crown public house closed many years ago and is now a private dwelling. The village post office and general store, which was housed in a picturesque thatched cottage, has also been closed for some time.

Few villages can claim the distinction of being at one time the home of a queen. Mary Tudor, sister of Henry VIII, made her home at Westhorpe Hall following her marriage to Charles Brandon, Duke of Suffolk. Mary

237

was Queen of France for just a short period as her husband Louis was middle-aged and ailing and soon died, leaving her free to marry her first love. After her death it is said that her heart was buried at Westhorpe church and her body later interred at Bury St Edmunds. Unfortunately the Hall was demolished in the middle of the 18th century along with all its treasures. All that remains are the coat of arms placed in the brickwork of the new Hall and a lovely Tudor bridge over the moat. The Hall is now used as a residential home for the elderly.

The parish church of St Margaret is a finely proportioned 14th century structure, probably the least restored church in Suffolk. St Margaret's is still used for worship and is large enough to accommodate some 500 people, built at a time when the population of the village was over a thousand. With today's small population the running of this historic and beautiful old church is carried by a decreasing number of parishioners, a problem that affects many Suffolk villages. The rectory dating back to the 14th century is a beautiful thatched house nestling next to the church surrounded by mature trees and immaculate gardens and is the home of Sir John Plumb FBA, the renowned historian.

There are four wonders of Westhorpe, three of them growing at Lodge Farm. One is an oak tree with a 'key-hole' in it, another is an ash tree which always grows with square twigs. The third is a rare bush known as the Wild Barberry (*Berberis vulgaris*), made even more scarce by the destruction of all the bushes that used to grow in Shaker's Lane, Bury St Edmunds, when the A45 was constructed. The Barberry Moth feeds exclusively on this plant and was in danger of becoming extinct but swift action by the Suffolk Trust for Nature Conservation has prevented it. They arranged for a captive colony to be released on the bushes in Westhorpe until there are enough to breed and survive. Westhorpe's fourth wonder is contained in a field off Ladywell Lane. It is an example of medieval strip farming and while it is not known exactly how old the strips are, the tithe map of the parish, belonging to the lord of the manor, show the exact position of the present ones and where all the others used to be. These strips are of tremendous historical importance and should be preserved at all costs.

There are several farms in the village, the largest being farmed by E. J. Barker & Sons. During each year from farmers within the village some 3,000 to 4,000 pigs are fattened, the present system a world away from the old boys with two pails of swill.

Westleton 🐚

The Romans knew the parish and left a road still in use. Saxons farmed here and then a Norseman, Vestildhi, settled in a small valley here. Later, Vestildhi's Tun was recorded in the Domesday Book as Westlede's Tun. Now Westleton is amongst one of the largest parishes in area in the Suffolk coastal district. It embraces almost the last of the old sandlings

Westleton Duckpond

heath, reaches to the coast and includes the famous Minsmere Bird Reserve, amidst National Trust, common, forestry and agricultural land.

Central to the village is a large triangular green sloping to an attractive pond, locally known as the Green Ditch. In the vicinity are 18 lime trees, each one planted to commemorate the villagers who gave their lives in the First World War. A small boy whose short life was made happier by feeding the many ducks is also remembered by a stone collecting box. Standing majestically at the apex of the green is the village sign incorporating a sail beam of the old post mill, a mill stone lies at the base – a reminder of past dependence on two mills.

Cottages, mainly early 19th century in origin cluster along The Street and around two smaller greens. The Victorian school house is built of flint as is the old school, which once had over 100 pupils but is now the village hall. In 1868 the imposing brick Primitive Methodist chapel was built and for 100 years had a vigorous life. In its early days some of the congregation could not read. Ironically, today the chapel is an Aladdin's cave of second-hand and old books – a paradise for 'bookworms' from far and wide.

St Peter's church was built by the monks of Sibton Abbey in 1340. In Decorated style, the south side still has original windows with 'Y' tracery. The massive tower with eight bells collapsed in a hurricane in 1776. A smaller wooden tower replaced it, but this crashed when a bomb fell in the Second World War. The church is immaculately thatched by the village thatcher and his son, carrying on a family tradition.

Weston 🌿

Weston has a population of about 160 but is rarely shown on modern road maps, although marked on older ones when its population was only slightly smaller. The village lies about two miles south of Beccles astride the A145 road.

The main employment is agricultural though many work in Beccles. Part of the former is a notable success story. In 1969 a farmer's wife started growing flowers for drying and arranging on a cottage industry scale. One of the first in the market, 'Winter Flora' now employs 100 people in the busy period from August leading up to Christmas and supplies to over 1,000 retail customers worldwide, thus providing valuable employment to Weston and neighbouring villages.

St Peter's church, just east of the A145, dates from Saxon times and is mentioned in the Domesday Book. The church used to contain a celebrated shrine of the Virgin Mary but no trace of this remains. Next to the church for the last 30 years has been an increasingly popular event in early June – an old-fashioned traditional Rectory Garden Fete with all its evergreen attractions.

Across the A145 from the church is the southern end of an Elizabethan Hall – the northern wing was burnt down in the 18th century. The Hall has a circular window upstairs on the east side through which Queen Elizabeth I is said to have fired an arrow and killed a deer. There is also said to be a ghost. Local tradition has it that from the Hall there was a passageway to the High House south of the church where it seems the bulk of the village cottages was located. The High House was a dower house and was also used as a signal-station for the smugglers route up the Hundred river into the cellars of the ancient Duke of Marlborough inn (locally known as the 'Mulberry'). Sadly the old inn closed in the 1960s, was pulled down and replaced by a modern house.

Weston windmill has similarly gone. The mill was started by William Newson in 1837, who became the miller, and was completed by Samuel Nunn of Wenhaston who at the same time was building the well-known post-mill at Saxstead to the same design. Struck by lightning, it was destroyed by fire in 1896.

Wetherden 🌿

Wetherden lies four miles north-west of the market town of Stowmarket, close by the A45. The name means 'wether valley' and with the proximity of the 'wool towns and villages' it would seem reasonable to believe that in times gone by the mainstay of the village was its flocks. People alive today can remember the shepherd living in a shed on wheels, a sort of primitive caravan, towed by a horse from fold to fold. During the depressed years of the late 1920s and early 1930s flocks were sold off and of recent times arable farming has largely taken over, though slowly sheep are being reintroduced.

Although few people are now employed on the land, because of its proximity to Stowmarket there is little unemployment in the village. Indeed, one of the largest employers in the area, John Rannoch, is situated at Haughley Park, just outside the village and many men and women find employment there.

Wetherden today is a mixture of the very old and very new. Some delightful old cottages remain, especially around the church. One is said to contain a room where Mass was celebrated secretly after it was pronounced illegal. The church of St Mary, standing in a tree-encircled churchyard, is of flint in the Decorated and Perpendicular styles. It has a beautiful hammer beam roof with some carved angels that escaped destruction by Dowsing at the time of the Commonwealth.

Sadly, the village school was closed in 1986, but having been endowed by William Crawford of Haughley Park in the 19th century, the trustees have allowed the school to remain unsold for the present so that it may still be used for educational purposes. The village shop-cum-post office is still very much a 'going concern'.

Wetheringsett cum Brockford 🐑

Wetheringsett cum Brockford lies in the Hundred of Hartismere. The A140 runs along much of its western boundary, and it is approximately 14 miles from Ipswich and 29 miles from Norwich.

It has always been primarily an agricultural village consisting of widely scattered small settlements, and its physical aspects have necessarily been dictated by the needs of farming, but never can its appearance have changed so suddenly or so drastically as it did in the mid 19th and 20th centuries and again in the last few years.

In 1843 the recently appointed rector of Wetheringsett, the Rev Robert Moore, then aged 31, built himself a new rectory, the present Wetheringsett Manor Hotel. White's Directory says that it cost £4,000, and as an indication of the value of money in those days, the same source says that the East Suffolk and Ipswich Hospital, to house 50 in-patients, had been built in 1835–6 at a cost of about £2,500.

In the early 1900s there were two working windmills in Wetheringsett. One, pulled down by the 1920s, was on the road now known as Station Road, which leads from the church to Wetherup Street. The other mill was on the road leading from Wetherup Street, past the turning to Debenham, and near to the White Horse public house. This mill was bought by Frederick Aldred in about 1860.

The stones which did the grinding were enormous, four and a half to five ft in diameter and a foot thick. The bottom or bed stone was fixed, the top one was driven round as the sails worked the machinery, the corn was fed in through a hole in the top stone. The mill worked day and night when the wind was right, and needed constant attention, as the stones could be badly damaged if allowed to run out of grist. The miller and his assistant took it in turns to watch the mill. A stand by engine was used when there was no wind.

The mill worked continuously until the mid 1930s when it could no longer compete with the products of the power-driven roller mills in Ipswich and around. For a few more years the mill was used to grind corn from the family farm but it gradually deteriorated and finally plans were made to pull it down.

Wickham Market 🌿

People smile and greet each other in the lanes, roads and shops of Wickham Market. Is this perhaps a definition of a 'village'? With a population of about 2,300 it is larger than many other villages; there are about 20 shops acting as a centre for surrounding communities.

A native settlement or 'vicus' was established at the first good ford across the river Deben to trade with the Roman centre on the other side of the river. This name gradually changed to 'Wickham' in the Domesday Book, and a silver chalice in the church dated 1567 is inscribed 'Wiccom'.

The main coaching route from Ipswich to Lowestoft and Yarmouth crossed the river Deben by a bridge at the old ford and the village took full advantage of the passing trade. There used to be nine inns, including the famous White Hart on The Hill (now offices and flats) whereas now there are only two. There has not been a market in Wickham for about 300 years, but the square by the church at the top of the hill is still known as the Market Hill and still keeps its medieval appearance, apart from the parked cars and the public toilets. The main road through the village also retains its attractive character.

The 14th century church of All Saints is built on what, for Suffolk, is quite a hill. It has an octagonal tower surmounted by a tall, leaded spire, the whole rising to about 140 ft. This can be seen from afar; the bells also can be heard a long way off.

The unusual village sign draws attention to occupations in the past. There is depicted a steam engine which signifies a small but important iron works in the village in the 19th century which specialised in milling machinery; oziers are indicated because these were cultivated on the banks of the Deben and were used to make fences and baskets; the rather grim looking building is meant to be the water mill which actually is an attractive spread of buildings seen from the bridge and dates from the 17th century.

Wickhambrook 🦋

The village of Wickhambrook has seen many changes through the centuries, not the least of them happening today. The name is derived from the Old English meaning dwelling or manor by the stream. The village did indeed start as three manor houses, Badmondisfield, Geynes and Clopton, each of which is fairly near to the stream which runs through the village. The stream or brook runs in a slight valley and is fed from springs on the higher ground in the village. It eventually joins the river Glem and then the Stour, thus flowing into the sea at Manningtree.

Whilst travelling through the village, one quickly becomes aware that it is composed of a series of greens or hamlets, thus although the village is up to five miles wide in places its population is only 1,020 persons. Each of the eleven greens has an unusual name – Ladys, Genesis, Attleton, Ashfield, Moor, Nunnery, Clopton, Meeting, Farley, Baxters, Coltsfoot – and the local history society is busy delving into their origins.

Buildings range in size and age from the three manor houses through large, medium and small houses to cottages, some of mud and others of flint. There has been some new building of houses and bungalows and there is a small development of sheltered housing and also some houses for young couples.

As the village is situated ten miles from anywhere, during the 1920s there was very little employment. It was then that Justin Brooke, a great character, bought Clopton Hall and subsequently a number of smaller farms. He opened up many opportunities for the local people to become involved in fruit farming, the dairy business and other occupations. Unfortunately this fruit complex is no longer in being and most of the land has been put down to cereals, rape and sugarbeet production.

At one time there were three windmills but none are standing now. On the site of the Great Mill is a home bakery which delivers hot bread along with greengroceries and groceries three times a week. This is a living village – consequently there is still a school, shop, post office and garage, and indeed Wickhambrook is fortunate to have its own fire service. It also has one and a half pubs: the Greyhound and the Plumbers Arms, which is half in Wickhambrook and half in Denston.

Wilby 🦋

Wilby is a small hamlet in what used to be known as High Suffolk. The B1118 snakes through the village about midway between Eye and Framlingham. An observant driver might be forgiven for passing through Wilby without being conscious of the fact. It boasts no great houses, an empty pub-sign tells of a long-forsaken public house and there is not even a village shop to attract a motorist's attention. Cow pastures and hedged meadows gave way to cornfields in the 19th century and more latterly fields have been drained, hedgerows rooted up and ditches filled in order to accommodate combine harvesters and the like which, it seems, are necessary aids to modern farming. Wilby may appear an unremarkable village but landscape and bricks and mortar do not tell the whole story.

The Coronation Hall comes to life on a Saturday night when live bands attract ballroom dance enthusiasts from far and wide. People from all over Suffolk know of Wilby's existence because of its lively and happy weekly dances. St Mary's church (15th century) not only houses beautifully carved pews and two old wall paintings but the tower boasts one of the best sounding rings of eight bells in the county. The steps to the belfry are surely some of the steepest and narrowest ever. What makes Wilby such a special place is its people, so warm and friendly.

Wingfield 🐝

The village of Wingfield lies in the northern part of Suffolk not far from the Norfolk border. It covers 2,442 acres, but the houses are widely scattered and the population is now small, approximately 300 – in 1844 the population was nearly 700.

In the 14th and 15th centuries, Wingfield was the seat of one of the most powerful families in England and the imposing remains of its old castle are reminders of the days of the de la Poles, Earls and Dukes of Suffolk.

The church, St Andrew's, with its fine monuments and stately chancel, is one of the most beautiful in this part of Suffolk and fortunately has suffered little at the hands of destroyers or restorers. It was built in 1362 as the collegiate church of Sir John de Wingfield's Foundation. Wingfield College, lying to the south and now behind a Georgian facade, built at the same time, was until 1534 a college of priests and a centre of education for the district. Nowadays it is alive again with arts and music programmes each year.

There are several ancient houses in the parish of Wingfield. The Old Hall on the borders of Stradbroke and Wingfield at Pixey Green, is said to be one of the oldest, dating back to the 14th century. Goulders Farm, in the village, may well have been a guildhall in the 15th century and the White House on Top Road is one of only ten examples of the rare raised-aisle type in the country. (In the 1930s the elderly owner of The White House was served with a demolition order, which he ignored – he was sent to prison for a month but the house was spared).

A curious mausoleum was built on the green by an Absalom Feavearyear who, after a dispute with the vicar over the question of tithes, swore that he would never enter the church – either in life or death. He carved elaborate tombstones for himself, his son and daughter-in-law, Thirza. When the time came, he was buried beneath his tombstone in the small house he had prepared. It stands there still. His son and daughter-in-law are buried in the churchyard.

In 1535 a John Trower left a charity to the village in the form of a farm – Town Farm. The charity was to be used for the poor of Wingfield and restoration of the church. In the 1950s the farm was sold to the Feavearyear family and the proceeds invested. The charity is still distributing money each Christmas.

Wissett 🐝

Man has made his presence felt in Wissett for thousands of years. Neolithic man left his flint tools, and pieces of tile from Roman houses have been found. The Saxons built a church, parts of which are most certainly incorporated into the present one, St Andrew's, which also has notable Norman features.

The 15th and 16th centuries saw the building of many farmhouses and barns with massive oak beams which would have come from trees felled in the vicinity. The parish must have been heavily wooded in those days.

Later centuries have all seen some new building and alterations. Several old houses have had a brick casing put round the old structure, and those such as Wissett Hall have been much enlarged. A new vicarage was built for £700 in 1843, and sold by the Church in 1925. Some farms had new brick buildings in the mid 19th century. More recently council houses were built. They have now been mostly sold and a few new houses and bungalows have been built, but there has been no new estate development.

Wissett is a small rural community of some 200 adults. The little village street, with its church, pub and post office stores, lies in a valley alongside 'the beck', as the little tributary of the river Blyth is called.

The valley is flanked by gently sloping farmland growing arable crops and apples. A small vineyard has been planted at Valley Farm, and

The Grange, Wissett (by kind permission of Clive Graham)

Wissett wine will, hopefully, soon be available. The cows that were so common a mere 25 years ago have disappeared. Changing patterns of farming have meant that several of the old farmhouses are now privately owned.

Bleach Farm, surrounded by a moat, owes its name to the hemp industry. Old maps and field names show that most farms had a small area devoted to hemp at that time, and also retting (rotting) pits in which hemp stems were steeped in water to rot the fleshy part from the fibres used for weaving. The resulting sludge had to be cleaned from the pits every seven to eight years, and may have been the origin of the local expression 'The Wissett Treacle Mines'. Early in the 19th century Robert Aldred, who owned a hemp factory in nearby Halesworth, lived at Whitehouse Farm. The hempen cloth was used for clothes such as shirts and for huckaback and bed linen.

Woolpit 🐑

This village of some 1,600 inhabitants lies in the district of Mid Suffolk between Bury St Edmunds and Stowmarket. There seems to have been a thriving settlement since the 1st Century AD. Evidence of Roman occupation has been found and details of the settlement appear in the Domesday Book.

The 12th century flint church of St Mary dominates the village centre. It is famous for its magnificent porch of which it was said long ago that it 'may vie in elegance with any in the county'. Divided from the aisles by an arcade of fine arches, the nave has a splendid hammerbeam roof on which are carved figures of angels with outspread wings and representatives of the saints.

Many medieval wills mention the chapel of Our Lady of Woolpit, the whereabouts of which are not known, although there is a half-moated site nearby which is known as Lady's Well. This was a place of pilgrimage for many in the Middle Ages. The water from the spring has been analysed and found to be different from that of other wells in the vicinity. It was reputed to have healing qualities – particularly for the eyes. In medieval times it was a stopping place for pilgrims on their way to Walsingham. The area is scheduled as an ancient monument and is now being cleared and replanted under the auspices of the local history group.

The legendary Green Children were first documented by William Newburgh in c1400. The story concerns a brother and sister with green complexions who mysteriously appeared in a harvest field. The villagers took them to Sir Richard de Calne as no one could understand their language. Although they indicated that they were hungry, they would eat nothing, until some green beans appeared. The younger of the two, a boy, was always tired and lethargic and died but the girl grew accustomed to all foods and lost her green colour. She was baptised and lived with Sir Richard until her marriage, reputedly to a man from Kings Lynn.

There are many references to clay pits and brick earth in the 1500s and from that time on, the brick making industry developed until the Woolpit Brick Company was a major employer from the 1850s. It remained a thriving business until the 1930s.

Woolverstone ✎

This small village, officially a hamlet with surrounding scattered dwellings, is situated on the estuary of the river Orwell where it has existed since the Bronze Age and before. Legend has it that a Viking marauder named Wulf sacrificed a local maiden on a huge monolithic stone; hence Wulf's stone – Woolverstone.

The Woolverstone family held the manor from 1419–1580; then, after various changes of ownership, the property was bought by William Berners in 1773, when it cost him all of £14,000. He not only built the Hall (in 1776), but he and his successors virtually recreated the village and reigned supreme right up until 1937. Even today, some older inhabitants still look back nostalgically to the days of the Squire, and more especially to his annual 'largesse'. He provided workmen's cottages with ample gardens well spaced out along the main road (the B1456), houses for the schoolmaster and the head gamekeeper, and a large holiday home for impoverished clergy. Most of these buildings have a common design theme and architectural details which help give character to the village.

The second most important house in the village, St Peter's Home (now called Woolverstone House), was built by the celebrated architect Sir Edwin Lutyens, and run by an order of nuns for 'fallen women'. It has its own chapel and bell tower, and in recent years has been used as a boarding house for Woolverstone Hall School. An unusual and picturesque dairy, two lodges, a laundry and the village school were also provided, plus some Widows' Homes, decorated with the Berners monkeys. The Berners family adopted this distinctive emblem, it is said, when a fire broke out and the alarm was raised by their pet monkey who thus saved valuable lives and property.

The Squire was the universal provider. Everyone worked for him in some capacity, and he in turn instigated many of the village's social functions – Harvest Homes, children's parties and outings and the annual Flower Show, so it was something of a culture shock when he departed, having sold his beautiful Palladian mansion and the entire estate – all 5,799 acres of it – to Oxford University Chest in 1937.

In 1956 the whole estate was split up and sold, giving many of the villagers the opportunity to buy their own homes. Some properties have different uses; the old rectory is now a home for the elderly and the old kitchen garden has been developed into a thriving plant nursery.

Wordwell 🐑

The tiny Breckland village of Wordwell lies on the B1106 north of Culford. There are several natural springs welling out of the chalk below, whose waters collect into a small stream which flows through West Stow. The stream goes under the river Lark. This man-made conjunction is unique and is still evident today.

The earliest known inhabitant was a man called Thurketel who left Wordwell to the abbey at Bury in AD 958. There is a description of Wordwell in the Domesday Book of 1086.

The parish church of All Saints was built by the Normans and remained unchanged through the centuries until Victorian times when it was restored by Rev Benyon. In the early 1960s a shallow pit was discovered containing human bones in the field to the west of the churchyard. It is possible that this was a plague pit dating from the 14th century.

Wordwell church is distinguished by the presence of ancient stone carving on a tympanum over the north door which is similar to Celtic carvings. There is much conjecture regarding the meaning of the primitive carvings, which are mysterious in their profound simplicity. Two figures can be seen – one of a man with hands upraised and another with a ring or globe.

The land at Wordwell is light and, being in the Breckland, was suitable to sheep farming. Mr J. D. Sayer, who bought the estate in the 1930s, kept many Suffolk sheep. He is also remembered for his interest in the Norfolk sheep; he tried over the years to keep the breed intact but after his death the breed died out. The Suffolk sheep so plentiful today was bred by crossing a Norfolk ewe with a Southdown ram.

Today, Wordwell lies on the edge of Forestry Commission land and is in an environmentally sensitive area. The population is the smallest it has ever been. It is linked with the parishes of Culford and West Stow. The old medieval village is no longer evident though it is known that there were about 20 crofts to the east of the road. There are several footpaths which converge near the church. A portion of the Icknield Way is only a few miles to the north.

Worlingham 🐑

Worlingham is an expanding village situated on the Norfolk/Suffolk border, one mile east of Beccles. Farmland and marshes lead to the river Waveney to the north. Very little of the old village is left, it is made up of small estates of new houses. The old manor house now stands empty, and Worlingham Hall is the home of the present Lord Colville of Culross. Previous owners of the hall included the Sparrow family. One of the daughters of the Sparrow family married the Earl of Gosford, and she donated the original school in 1845. Unfortunately this thatched school was demolished in 1980 to make way for a new bypass for Beccles. Skeletons were uncovered during this work, which were re-interred in the churchyard with a headstone to mark the grave.

A new Church of England school was built in 1969 for around 100 pupils, and when the education system became comprehensive a middle school was built to accommodate the village and surrounding area, taking 400 children.

Miss Haddenham, the headmistress of the original village school, lived in the village all her life. She would tell of a monastery on the marshes and how, when she was a girl, her father had seen the ghost of a monk in Marsh Lane – some say it has been seen in more recent times!

The historic church of All Saints dates back to the 13th century. Originally the two parishes of Worlingham Magna and Parva had separate churches dedicated to St Mary the Virgin and St Peter, but these two dedications were incorporated in All Saints in the 15th century.

Worlington 🦢

This small community lies one mile south-west of Mildenhall in the north-west corner of Suffolk. Its border on the north is the river Lark which after its slow departure from the parish enters Cambridgeshire and the fens. One feels much of the river's speed has rubbed off onto the 'Worlies' over the years. Things do not change much in these parts. To the south and west is breckland running to the chalklands of Newmarket heath.

Seen clearly from the centre of the village and situated on the river bank is the 16th century Elizabethan mansion Wamil Hall, ravaged many times by fire. It is reputed haunted by Lady Rainbow although the stairs she walks disappeared in the most recent fire in 1961. She is also said to frequent nearby Elm Copse and a local horse rider maintains her mount always shys at this spot.

From the Cambridgeshire border for over one mile right through the parish runs the beautiful old green Roman road called Badlingham Lane. It is infrequently used now apart from a few horse riders, but annually on the third Thursday in September a group of pilgrims foot their way through the length on their way to Walsingham bearing a wooden cross. How long has this been happening?

Emerging from the lane one comes to the Royal Worlington and Newmarket Golf Club. Royal patronage was given by King Edward VIII when Prince of Wales, and his feathers are incorporated in the club flag. Cambridge University has long been associated with the club and in pre motor car days the undergraduates used to throw their clubs out of the moving Cambridge train onto the fifth tee, then walk back along the track from Mildenhall station and commence play from that point.

The cricket club also plays its part in the village sporting scene. They play on the superb village green where the ladies provide the famous 'Worli' teas. The first recorded match in Worlington was on Thursday 7th July 1814 and the prize was a 'pair of gloves'.

Worlingworth ✑

As you leave the wide open spaces of Tannington and enter Worlingworth, you may see on your right a string of racehorses exercising along the gallops of Worlingworth Hall, or later in the day, see them grazing peacefully on the grassland. The road narrows at Worlingworth Hall and winds between hedges and gardens towards the church. The cottages and houses are all homes now, but at one time there was a school, a forge and a wheelwright's, and also a magnificent line of cypresses.

Tucked behind the old forge is the oldest building of Worlingworth – St Mary's church. It was built from the 12th century, and the names of rectors are recorded without break from 1321. The church has a lofty double hammerbeam roof and each beam-end has the figure of an angel holding a shield. The church has been rescued from decay since the war, and the angels had their wings restored to them in 1962. At the same time the most startling treasure of the church was renovated – the font cover. It reaches to the height of 30 ft or so, and is intricately carved and decorated in gold, green and deep pink. Near the top is a palindrome in Greek which reads 'Wash my sin and not my body only.'

The road continues through the trees until it reaches the council houses and some fields. Shop Street begins here at the junction with Swan Lane. The Swan is thatched and little changed in decor since the war. In 1927 sparks from a steam-propelled wagon set fire to the thatch of a barn between the pub and the lane. It was on this occasion that the fire engine pump, dating from 1760, was last used. It was worked by hand using water from the pond and is said to have been capable of producing a continuous jet of water as high as 75 ft. The pump is now kept in the church.

Shop Street continues westward to Mill Corner past some beautiful old houses and farms that have had their hair-raising adventures with the deathwatch beetle. Mill Corner used to have two working mills. One is no more, but one other still has the brick structure and some of the floors and workings. The family who lived at The Mills have been there for over 60 years. The Greenard brothers used to have a coal merchants' business after the mill ceased working, but this was discontinued when the Mid-Suffolk Light Railway closed in 1952.

The whole of Fingal Street and Water Lane are much less populated than they were in days gone by, and most of the remaining houses are farmhouses. In spite of much new building around Shop Street, and many newcomers to the village, Worlingworth is still fundamentally a farming community. Everyone in the village is aware of the farming year, and their lives are dominatd by the seasons of country life.

Wrentham 🐝

Wrentham is situated on the A12 between Blythburgh and Lowestoft. In the Domesday survey mention is made of there being two churches. Presuming one to be on the site of the present church, there is no record as to where the other stood. The site of Wrentham Hall is known; it was on land now known as Blackmoor Farm and a few trees are left along the avenue leading up to it.

The present church of St Nicholas was built in the late 15th century and at this time most, if not all, the village was centred around it. This remained so for several years until the new London to Yarmouth turnpike was built in 1786, after which the village centre moved away from the church to its present position. Some alterations have taken place over the years but very little has changed the appearance of the village.

In 1647 Rev John Phillip was one of twelve people who forged a new church based on the congregational way of worshipping. Another of these twelve was a Francis Brewster of Pyes Hall, brother to the lord of the manor. Before Rev John Phillip went to New England at least two families, Thomas Paine with his wife Elizabeth and six children and John Thurston and family, sailed from Ipswich in 1637 on the *Mary Anne* and settled in Salem. The Thurstons were among the founders of Wrentham, Massachussetts and descendants from this family still exist in America.

Wyverstone 🐝

In 1936, according to 'Yeoman' of *The East Anglian Daily Times*, Wyverstone was 'rather off the beaten track', with leafy lanes, green fields, wide grass verges and a church with a massive tower rearing above the trees in the churchyard.

Today the verges are not so wide, the plough has removed the meadows, the trees hide the church tower and huge farm vehicles pass by, but, despite this, with no large housing estates, the character of the village is largely unchanged. It has always been small and scattered with seldom more than 300 inhabitants. This may seem a little uninteresting, but, like many villages, it has secrets to disclose.

Wyverstone, the name meaning Wigferp's homestead, was known in Saxon times and a church existed at the Domesday survey. After the Norman Conquest, one of three manors was held by Richard Hovell. A later member of the family, Robert Hovell, in 1231, obtained the privilege of an annual three day fair and Tuesday market day, but this has long since gone. The Hovell family lived on, fighting with Henry V at Agincourt, until in the 19th century, Dr Charles H. J. Hovell MRCS went to New Zealand with rank of Colonel to fight in the Maori Wars and remained there.

John Steggall was a colourful character in the 19th century, who became known as the Suffolk Gipsy. He was born in 1787, the youngest son of Charles Steggall, who was then a curate at Needham Market, but later rector at Wyverstone for 25 years. The family tomb can be seen in the south-west corner of the graveyard.

Yaxley

Yaxley manor appears in records in 1066. Both the Yaxley and Bedingfield families lived in Bull's Hall, both originally Catholic families. The Hall was actually transferred to William Bull in 1328 from Edward III. It is now lived in by John and Moira Buxton – interestingly the first Buxton trustees received it back in 1808. In 1833 the Buxton family moved but it was seldom a family home; instead it was tenanted.

Not only did the neighbouring village of Mellis have 94 children attending day school in 1912 but also Yaxley had its own school with 49 pupils. Now the village children attend a combined Yaxley and Mellis school.

Sir Frederick Ashton, the choreographer, buried in Yaxley in the late 1980s, is one of the village's most noteworthy inhabitants.

Badingham Church

Index

255